THE BIG DISRUPTION

THE BIG DISRUPTION

A Totally Fictional But Essentially

True Silicon Valley Story

~ **Jessica Powell** ~

A NOVEL

Medium Editions

THE BIG DISRUPTION by Jessica Powell © 2018 Medium

Cover design by Medium Editions
Production management by Stonesong Digital

ebook ISBN: 978-1-7320679-5-0

paperback ISBN: 978-1-7320679-6-7

THE BIG DISRUPTION originally appeared on Medium.

Postscript text originally published Oct 2, 2018, https://medium.com/s/
the-big-disruption/why-i-left-my-big-fancy-tech-job-and-wrote-a-book-b64c40484774

To my mother, who first taught me to write, and Luke,
who inherited the job in adulthood.

"Extinction is the rule. Survival is the exception."

—Carl Sagan

Praise for Jessica Powell's THE BIG DISRUPTION

"A zany satire . . . her diagnosis of Silicon Valley's cultural stagnancy is so spot on that it's barely contestable."

—Farhad Manjoo, *The New York Times*

"[Powell] wields Bonfire of the Vanities levels of absurdity and social observation to chronicle this particular northern Californian strain of masters of the universe"

—Lauren Smiley, *The Guardian*

"Jessica Powell is everything you want in a writer about power and money and lunacy in modern day Silicon Valley. She is an insider who has come outside, an insightful chronicler of the ridonkulous foibles of the digital overlords and a deft teller of tales. She was in the room and has managed to gleefully open its doors and let us see the antic circus inside. Such a view has never been more important as tech's damage becomes more and more clear."

—Kara Swisher, Founder and editor-at-large of Recode and New York Times contributing opinion writer

"The best books typically prompt us to laugh or think or learn something about the world that we might not have otherwise known. You will do all these things while reading this book, and more. This is a wild, incisive, and incredibly necessary look at the way that Silicon Valley works, and a wonderfully good read as well. The Big Disruption is a book that explains and defines this moment—the kind of book many of us have been waiting for."

—Tope Folarin, Caine Prize winner and author, A Particular Kind of Black Man

"From years of dealing with Jessica Powell during her time at Google, I knew she was witty. But I am sitting at a Starbucks laughing out loud like an idiot at her very smart new book *The Big Disruption*, a brilliant and funny satire of the male, engineer-driven culture of Silicon Valley where the leaders are cryptic and obtuse to reality."

—Walt Mossberg, tech journalism pioneer, former *Wall Street Journal* columnist and co-founder of Recode

PROLOGUE

The only animal left standing was a one-eyed sea lion named Fred.

The northwest wall of the Palo Alto Sea Park shark tank broke at four a.m. on a hot August night, releasing 780,000 gallons of water and fourteen angry sharks. They rode the wave in one sharp-toothed tsunami, penetrating the dolphin tank with open mouths, chasing the dolphins into new parts of the park.

Down came the manatee tank, the penguin's pen, and the piglet squid viewing room. The flamingo hut and the snake house withstood the pressure but flooded with water, the animals' terrestrial enclosures suddenly transformed into muddy aquariums. Noah's ark was now subject to a Darwinian reorganization in which for a few breathless seconds, snakes became exotic fish, tails dropping vertically like flutes bobbing in the water until they finally sank to the floor. Nearby, the flamingos honked in terror, their pink necks popping up above the waves like unfastened hooks, tangling in each other until they dropped below the surface.

As the water from the tanks expanded to the edges of the park, the depths once housing the sea's greatest creatures were now reduced to mere puddles. Fish were left flapping against the asphalt; the beluga whale flattened seahorses and starfish as it barreled its way through the park in search of arctic water. No longer traveling forward with carnivorous glee, the sharks came to a stop near the snack bar and began rolling about on their dolphin-stuffed bellies, emitting wimpy cries that would have delighted fish lower on the totem pole were they too not gasping in their newly parched environment. Within minutes, self-pity transformed to anger, and in their final moments, the sharks turned on each other in a cannibalistic bloodbath.

It all happened so quickly that by the time the rescue crews arrived, there was little left to salvage. The crew moved swiftly from one section of the park to the next, their faces increasingly grim. The manta rays spread flat like leathery carpets, the snakes roping above them in a bloated tangle. Colorful fish lay on their sides, mouths gaping, scales shifting like crystals in the slowly rising sun.

Word quickly spread of the catastrophe, and television news helicopters soon circled above. Everyone was looking for Belbo, Palo Alto's beloved walrus and official mascot. The rescue crew finally discovered the aquarium's prized pinniped underneath one of the felled walls, her death exacted by a slab of heavy concrete.

As the leader of the rescue crew turned to declare the end of their efforts, a loud croak bellowed from the northwest corner of the park. The crew ran toward the sound, which now repeated, like a foghorn, over and over. It was coming from the marine-themed jungle gym, one of the few structures that had survived the flood, thanks to its distance from the shark and dolphin tanks. As the crew approached, they saw a gray mass swaying atop the slide, partially blocking the sun. The rescuers shielded their eyes for a better view, and soon its form grew clearer. It was a one-eyed sea lion with a patch on its left eye.

At the sight of the rescue team, the sea lion barked again and clapped its hands. It balanced a ball on its nose, then put its weight on its front flippers and lifted its tail up behind its head. Without thinking, the rescue crew laughed and clapped.

Then the sea lion jumped onto its belly and sailed down the slide, landing on its stomach, flappers out to its side and a smile on its face. The crew rushed to hug the sea lion, to applaud its survival skills and hail the new mascot of Palo Alto. The animal clapped its hands again and croaked three times, and across Silicon Valley, the sea lion's bark dried the tears of the children watching the live news broadcasts. The sea lion showed them hope amid this sea of destruction.

One of the newscasters named it Fred.

A few months later, when the ground had finally dried and the bitter memories of the lost aquarium had faded for all but lawyers and insurance companies, the lot was purchased by a young internet company called Anahata. The founder of the company demanded that Fred be included as part of the property deal.

Fred was given his own wading pool next to the founder's office but spent most of his time waddling about the company's halls, pooping in the cubicles and barking at employees he didn't like, forcing Anahata's engineers to purchase sound-reduction headphones so they could work undisturbed. Fred did as he pleased and, in doing so, impressed everyone with his stubborn refusal to change his ways.

When Fred died of old age a few years later, all the employees gathered to pay their respects. During the dedication of a commemorative aquarium in the company's main building, the founder of Anahata, a man named Bobby Bonilo, told his employees that it was Fred who had taught him how to run his company. Fred, he said, had proven that it was fine to have one eye and waddle if you were better than anyone else at doing those things.

No one understood the metaphor, but all the employees committed it to memory as important career advice.

The commemorative aquarium was soon filled with brightly colored fish and crustaceans, as well as a giant squid the founder flew back from a remote island in the Pacific. The squid wowed the crowd with its undulating arms, which extended almost the full length of the tank, and its chomping mouth, which tore apart most of the fish the moment they were dropped in the water.

Nearly a decade on, the squid is nearly the size of a school bus and the aquarium's only remaining inhabitant. It floats in the central building of Anahata, today the world's largest and most powerful technology company.

ARSYEN

To interview at Anahata was a privilege. And the next, nearly inevitable step—to be rejected from Anahata—was a great honor. Just making it into the company's lobby already indicated that one was superior to 99.39 percent of the world's population. To be accepted, of course, required passing an even higher bar.

One by one, the gobsmacked Rejects filed past the Hopefuls sitting in the lobby, as unsure of their steps as they now were of their qualifications. They turned back to catch a final glimpse of Anahata's collection of gleaming white buildings, and smiled then, just briefly, knowing that despite their failure—a failure from which they might never recover—at least they were among the few to have glimpsed the world hidden behind the company's doors.

Arsyen Aimo surveyed his surroundings. It couldn't have been a friendlier place: wide green sofas, a gigantic refrigerator full of fresh juices, and a flight simulator to help pass the time in the unlikely event of a delay.

Sitting on the very edge of the first couch was a young man, hair uncombed, T-shirt wrinkled, emitting a faint odor of sweat. Crumbs of breakfast cereal cast a pebbled road across his chest. A thin folder jittered in his hand, its transparency revealing a document whose tidy bullet points and blurbs belied the man's unkempt appearance. His knees bounced lightly up and down, and he rocked as he sat, lips moving silently as though he were counting to himself.

On the second couch was another man, this one in his mid-thirties and wearing a suit, his cologne the essence of a crisp morning in the mountains. His back was against the sofa, one ankle thrown across the opposite knee, an arm thrown over the cushion as if he were there to watch Sunday football. He kept checking his watch, darting glances both anxious and dismissive at the female receptionists.

Arsyen immediately recognized their types. The first was an engineer, the second a salesman. And there was no reason for Arsyen to think any more of either of them—or the other fifteen iterations also waiting in the lobby—as he had seen enough of both during his time in the Valley to identify their species by smell alone.

Arsyen had other things on his mind. He was there to conquer his job interview. For he was Arsyen, Prince of Pyrrhia.

Or rather, a former prince who due to unfortunate circumstances had been reduced to working as a janitor in Silicon Valley.

Or, as he preferred to refer to it, a sanitation engineer.

Not that he liked cleaning. He hated it. Prince Arsyen had not been raised in the Order of the Red Woodpecker—buffed and preened and rubbed and polished to perfection by handmaidens each morning—with the idea that he would leave the royal palace and clean people's toilets in America. (As a child, Arsyen didn't even know how to use a toilet, thanks to the service of his royal wipers.)

But like most everything he undertook in life, Arsyen excelled at janitorial work. He was so good, in fact, that he usually finished his work in half the time of other janitors. Previous employers had occasionally misinterpreted his skill as laziness and accused him of not having logged sufficient time with the mop. But Arsyen knew that a truly exceptional company would see it differently.

Anahata was that company, and this was no ordinary janitorial job. It paid better than any other Silicon Valley company by a full $3 an hour. If all went according to plan, in a few decades, Arsyen would save enough money to raise an army and reverse the unfortunate circumstances that had driven him from his country. His future, and the future of his adoring minions, depended on the outcome of this interview.

A recruiter entered the room, and the crowd of hopefuls looked his way. His casual good looks and affable demeanor struck Arsyen as an effective ambassador for a company whose public image was one of approachable superiority.

"Arsyen Aimo?" the recruiter read from a sheet of paper.

Prince Arsyen, Arsyen silently corrected him.

The recruiter used a badge to push past the security doors, and Arsyen's mouth moved in a silent *Wow* as he entered the building. The cheerful but simple lobby area had not prepared him for this. The recruiter stopped—a seemingly well-rehearsed pause of ten seconds—to let Arsyen take it all in.

The building was a light-filled air hangar with expansive skylights and shoulder-height cubicles of varying geometric configurations. One could see across the entire building in a glance. Colorful beanbags were sprinkled here and there, and sleep capsules lined the walls, emitting the faint lullaby of snoring engineers. Each corner and space was maximized to project a sense of possibility, and employees seemed to congregate wherever the mood struck—a beanbag suddenly the appropriate place for a conference call, a foosball or ping-pong table a surface to plop one's computer.

"Extra. Ordinary," said Arsyen, the English emerging from his tongue like an insult rather than a superlative.

The recruiter didn't respond—his smile was stretched too far across his face to allow any spillage of words. He simply nodded and then motioned for Arsyen to follow. They made their way toward the opposite end of the building, then exited into a sunny courtyard and an immense stretch of pert, healthy grass that should never have been able to grow in California's desert landscape but seemed the natural complement to the bright, white buildings encircling the lawn. Palm trees swayed to an invisible breeze, casting the image of an island paradise in the expansive windows of each structure. For a brief moment, as they walked across a glass bridge over a small creek, Anahata's green, watery visions of itself surrounding them on all sides, Arsyen wondered which way was up. Legs and sand suddenly joined to palm trees in the reflections, and Arsyen turned, scanning the lawn for their origin. After a few seconds, he found them: a group of tanned girls in their early twenties playing volleyball on a sand court.

Arsyen studied their long limbs and sun-bleached ponytails. They leaped across the sand like lip-glossed gazelles. *I love America*, he thought to himself. But he wasn't the only one watching. Amid the palm and water reflections on the windows, Arsyen could spot a face here and there, male onlookers with cheeks pressed up against the glass.

They entered a new building, similar to the previous one, and Arsyen was ushered into a small, white room. It looked like a normal office, except all the walls were made of glass—a familiar layout in Silicon Valley. For most employees, these spaces were a symbol of transparency and openness. For sanitation engineers like Arsyen, they were just an invitation for dirty fingerprints.

The recruiter sat Arsyen at a table in the center of the room.

"We've found that it's most efficient for everyone to take a test before we invest in a conversation," he said.

"Sorry?" said Arsyen, perpetually annoyed that the English language required him to apologize when it was others who were unclear.

"You're going to take a test now. If you pass, then someone will come interview you," the recruiter said.

"And then I meet Bobby Bonilo?" Arsyen asked.

"The founder of Anahata? At your interview? Uh—"

"I give great interview," said Arsyen, rising to his feet. He placed his hands on his hips and raised his chin as his father, the king, used to do.

The recruiter's smile collapsed for a split second before rebounding.

"How about we first see if you can find the error on this page." He pulled a paper from the top of his stack and handed it to Arsyen.

Arsyen looked down and gasped at the dark incantations before him: nonsensical numbers and letters enclosed in < >.

It wasn't that Arsyen had never seen computer code before. It was inescapable in the Valley—on buses and billboards, hats and T-shirts. Valley people spoke of code like it was an act of progress, on par with a social movement. Over the years, as he mopped and scrubbed in the background, Arsyen had overheard more than a few hallway conversations in which scrawny men talked about using their code to change the world.

But knowing how to recognize code and knowing *how* to code were two very different things. Surely there was no way he could be expected to perform such a task. Arsyen grunted. It was in moments like this that he particularly missed his home country of Pyrrhia. There he would have had any number of servants who could have learned computer programming on his behalf.

Perhaps this was the right moment to inform the recruiter of his royal lineage. There had been no applicable drop-down box in the online application; no way for Arsyen to signal that he was not simply a great janitor, but someone whose very greatness had once been written into his country's constitution.

But such a direct declaration struck Arsyen as rather crass—royalty was to be recognized, not announced.

Of course, that didn't mean he couldn't help things along with a discreet nod toward his heritage. Arsyen ignored the recruiter's prompt to find the coding error—he had no clue, and in any case, such details were for clerks and commoners. Instead, he sketched a crude outline of a pointy crown across the length of the page.

"Done," announced Arsyen, pushing the paper across the table.

The recruiter glanced at Arsyen's paper and did a double take. "Well, *that's* a bold statement," he said finally, then excused himself and left the room.

Minutes later, a slightly balding man in his thirties entered carrying a brown paper bag. He was wearing a purple T-shirt with an orange cartoon character on the front; the sandals on his feet were made of red plastic. Arsyen was surprised by the ensemble. From what he had seen during his time in America, most sanitation engineers dressed inconspicuously, their very livelihood dependent on being able to make dirt—and themselves—as invisible as possible to the general population.

This man looked more like a court jester.

"Hi, I'm Roni," he said, setting Arsyen's test on the table and extending his hand. "You got a résumé?"

Arsyen shook his head. No one had ever asked him for a résumé before.

"I get it, I get it," Roni said. "I think they're dumb, too. I mean, a piece of paper—it's like, so corporate, you know? We don't need 'em. Let's just talk like equals, like regular guys who went to Stanford together."

He sat down in the chair opposite Arsyen.

"So, how long have you been an engineer?"

Arsyen felt his heart jump. It was the first time someone had properly called him an "engineer."

"Four years," he answered, and then paused. Now was the time. He cleared his throat and lowered his voice, consciously making it as booming and sonorous as the Aimo name deserved. "I am also... prince."

Roni chuckled. "Yeah, I've heard that one before. Actually, most of the engineers here think they are kings."

"But there only one king," said Arsyen, making the sign of the red-breasted woodpecker.

"So true, so true," Roni said. "And what a king we have here at Anahata."

Roni's gaze floated skyward, as if communicating with an otherworldly being. Arsyen also looked up but saw nothing more than a halogen lamp with a sticker touting its energy efficiency.

Roni snapped back to life.

"Now, where were you before this?"

"Galt."

Roni's eyebrows leaped up in a flash, but then, equally quickly, were dragged downward—a clear attempt by their owner to anchor his admiration. Galt was one of the Valley's hottest startups, famous for having created a bunch of apps and tools that eliminated the tedium of journalism, research, essays, and speeches by reducing all thought and opinion to easily shareable, bite-sized chunks. Everything they did was about minimization—making the world "easier to digest." Some people predicted Galt was the next Anahata, though personally, Arsyen had found the company lacked any creativity or vision and was always asking him to take a second pass at the men's stalls.

"Galt, eh? Well, that explains this," said Roni. He pointed at the crown Arsyen had sketched across his test, lassoing most of the page's code.

"Pretty ballsy to suggest all of our code is a mess," Roni said. "I would respectfully disagree, but I applaud your moxie. You must be good at debugging."

Arsyen's face pruned. "Bugs," he spit. "I kill them every day."

"Awesome. Me too, me too. Obviously, there's no coding in a P.M. job, but people here will respect you a lot more if you have an engineering background."

Arsyen didn't know what Roni meant by "P.M. job." Was it a powerful mopper? A plumbing manager?

Roni dipped his hand into the brown paper bag and slowly pulled out an enormous sandwich. Arsyen watched as he slowly removed the plastic and unfolded a paper napkin, square by square, until finally smoothing it before him. Roni paused and bent his head toward his sandwich, lifting his hands just slightly in prayer. And then, suddenly, the hands disappeared, the plastic wrap was on the other side of the table, and the sandwich was half hanging out of Roni's mouth. Turds of tuna fell onto the napkin below.

"Let's get going, shall we? I only ask one big question in my interviews. I'm kinda known for that. It's all about the process, about how you go after it. It's not what you say, it's *what* you say, okay?"

Arsyen nodded.

"So," began Roni. "You're a pirate and—"

"No, a prince."

"Huh? Oh right, ha ha. Well, for the purpose of this question, you're a pirate. If you want, you can be the captain of the pirate ship. Does that work?"

"A captain is *king* of the pirate ship?"

"Exactly. Now you and your crew discover a treasure chest with one hundred gold coins, and you have to find a way to split it up."

"I give no gold. Gold is *mine*," Arsyen said.

"Well, now wait, that's the catch. If you don't give the other pirates anything, they will throw you off the ship. In order not to be killed, you have to come up with a way to distribute the coins so that at least half of the pirates agree with your proposal."

"I kill them and take gold," said Arsyen, dismissing the question with a wave of his hand.

"Not so fast," Roni said. "You're the captain, but you're outnumbered. So you can't kill them—though I like your aggressiveness.

"Now, if you get killed, another pirate will have to come up with a proposal, but then he could be killed, too, so it goes to the next pirate. And so on and so on. So it's in everyone's interest to agree on a proposal right from the start—but also maximize their profit. It's basically a distribution problem. Actually, you know, I was given the same problem when I came to interview at Anahata. Except my interviewer used the Easter Bunny and a bunch of eggs, and the pirates were actually little kids and..."

But Arsyen had already stopped listening. His family had plundered plenty of ancient treasure over the centuries, swindling mercenaries, gangsters, and, yes, occasionally pirates—stealing from the very worst of mankind to give to the good people of Pyrrhia.

"You can use this whiteboard here to work through the problem," said Roni, pointing to one of the walls. "Take your time."

"One gold coin," answered Arsyen. "You give pirates one coin each."

Roni's eyes bulged.

"Wow, uh, okay, that was quick. I mean, how did you... I mean, the whiteboard… Like, if there's two pirates and then you figure out… Wait, how did you do this so fast? Talk me through the math."

"In time to do math, other pirates kill captain," Arsyen answered. "Capitan use brain." He tapped the side of his head, just in case Roni wasn't sure where the brain was located. Roni seemed a bit dim. He clearly had never been a pirate or even known one.

"Oh yeah, like, totally," said Roni, regaining his composure. "I mean, yeah, it's not difficult. But, um, we still have some time left, so…"

Roni looked around the room, then jumped up from the table and scribbled something on the whiteboard.

How do you use data to make your decisions?

He stood back, shook his head, then erased it.

Describe how you would improve your favorite Anahata product.

He erased that one just as quickly.

Then he tried something else.

Automation.

He grinned and returned to the table.

"Okay, pick something in the modern home and tell me what technologies you would use to automate it."

"No automation. Hire more servants," Arsyen said.

"Huh? Uh, no, you can't have more servants," said Roni, shaking his head.

"Why? Because someone killed them?"

"Let's try this again," said Roni, his face reddening slightly, fingers pressing into his napkin. "I want a technical framework for how you would go about automating something in your house."

Arsyen couldn't resist a smirk. Everyone in the Valley wanted to automate everything, but to what end? All they were really doing was getting rid of people's jobs, which of course meant the peasants would eventually rise up and slaughter them. Technologists were so naive.

"Not all innovation so good," said Arsyen, shaking his head.

"Wrong! One hundred percent wrong!" Roni screamed. He jumped out of his chair and waved a mayo-covered finger in Arsyen's face.

Roni stood and stormed to the door. "Recruiter!" he shouted. "Recruiter!"

He stomped out of the room and began to pace, mostly muttering to himself, occasionally yelling "internet of things!" and then hitting the side of his head with his palm over and over again.

Arsyen sighed inwardly—another janitor diva. He wondered what sort of extraordinary cleaning product or technique Roni had invented for Anahata to put up with such behavior. Or maybe he was just one of those early hires the company never managed to get rid of.

A tall man with a crew cut walked by and Roni waved him down.

"Gregor!" he shouted. The man stopped but did not seem particularly pleased to see him.

Roni was gesturing rapidly, shaking his head, pointing at Arsyen in the room. Arsyen couldn't entirely make out what he was saying, but he was sure he heard the word "Galt." The man turned to look at Arsyen, and the Prince of Pyrrhia sat up straight and puffed out his chest. But the man's blank expression gave nothing away.

A moment later, both men were standing before him.

"What did you work on at Galt?" demanded the tall man with the crew cut.

"Bathrooms, hallways, computer screens. Much innovation," Arsyen said.

Roni and the crew cut exchanged glances.

"We're not going to get anything out of him."

"But he surely knows things," Gregor said.

"Do you know things?" Roni asked.

Arsyen nodded vigorously. He had enough experience in his father's court to know that it was always best to agree with an important person—unless they were interrogating you about murder or adultery.

The crew cut stared at Arsyen for a beat longer, then turned to Roni, whispering a few words Arsyen couldn't make out. Then, without a goodbye or any acknowledgement of Arsyen's presence, he turned on his heel and marched out the door.

A second later, Roni was grinning, his hand extending again to Arsyen.

"Congrats—the job is yours!"

✳

Arsyen was sure he had seen her before—though certainly not here, in the Anahata reception area, seated at a long white desk, her figure backlit by a neon "Welcome!" sign.

He studied her face—the brown hair moving in slow waves past her shoulders, the slightly raised cheekbones. Her lips moved silently, murmuring secrets and chants—things Arsyen wanted to know. His gaze moved again across her face, settling on her blue, almond-shaped eyes. And then he knew.

The woman was Xeri. *His* Xeri. But she was a Xeri scrubbed clean, stripped of her crossbow and pointy elfin ears, her dirty wolf cape and leather skirt that hid a dagger in the belt loop. With her long, gauzy dress and random assortment of beaded neck-laces, this Xeri was more flower child than assassin. And while that was less of a turn-on, this Xeri had one big thing going for her. She was much better than his *World of Warcraft* girlfriend. She was real.

It wouldn't have been such a shock had Arsyen not already re-signed himself to the idea that this breed of woman didn't exist in his corner of America. In his four years of working in Silicon Valley, Arsyen had run into plenty of her gender: ogre women, mustachioed women, circus women. But none like this: an attractive woman. It was like she was from another part of California entirely.

Minutes passed as the woman typed on her computer, pale pink fingernails knocking against the keyboard like little woodpeckers. *Tap tap tap. Tap tap tap.*

He caught a glimpse of his reflection in the glass wall behind her—a strong Pyrrhian man, with muscles as ropy as the hair on his arms, and a powerful chin whose virile charms were enhanced by the large and uniquely crooked Aimo nose. He was white like the glossy coat of the rare Pyrrhian ram.

His reflection frowned back at him. Would she find him a bit short?

Of course not. Back in Pyrrhia, the women always complimented him on his height.

"Arsyen?"

The woman was looking up at him, her smile the product of America's strong belief in orthodontics. Good humor was cheap currency in this country, but the woman's smile was different, it was angelic, it was—

Arsyen decided then he would make her his queen. Her big white teeth would be admired by all his people.

"Uh… Arsyen?"

Arsyen snapped back into focus. He had a girlfriend back in Pyrrhia who was dreaming of him and only him every night. He was at Anahata for his job—the job that would free his people from the starvation and terrors of the current regime. He didn't have time for beautiful women—at least not the ones who didn't accept cash.

"You're all set up as a new Anahata employee, or Anahatis, as we call ourselves."

The woman walked out from behind the desk and extended her hand. She smelled vaguely of vanilla.

"I'm Jennie," she said cheerfully, seemingly unaware of the mild earthquake that shook Arsyen as their palms touched. "Here's your badge. Don't lose it—it's what gives you access to everything here."

Jennie badged them into the main part of the building, a different one than Arsyen had visited for his job interview. An enormous skylight stretched the building's length; Arsyen could even see clouds moving across the blue sky above. Suspended from the ceiling by wires and blocking the sun's glare, an old NASA rocket and a fiberglass *T. rex* charged at each other from opposite ends of the building.

To Arsyen's left, running along the outside wall of one cubicle, a ticker tape documented connections made through the company's latest product, Moodify, a social network designed to connect people based on their moods, heart rates, and favorite video games. Although he didn't know much about technology, Arsyen had recently bought a Moodify bracelet. It pained him that his video game and gadget expenditures had to come out of his throne reclamation fund, but it was very important that the future leader of Pyrrhia be up to date on the latest technology and first-person-shooter attack and defense techniques.

Arsyen's Moodify bracelet glowed red—the same color, he was certain, as Jennie's. He waited to see their names cross the ticker tape in a flashing red arrow, suggesting a love connection, but the Moodify technology seemed to be broken. He turned to speak, but Jennie was already on the other side of the hall, standing before an enormous aquarium that stretched the length of the wall. Her bracelet pulsed with blue light. Arsyen shook his head and double-checked to see if his bracelet had changed colors. Maybe he just needed to stand closer. He ran to catch up with his future queen.

JENNIE

Jennie spotted the squid from across the floor, its peach mass hovering above a cluster of neon corals and sea plants. The squid was no longer part of the company tour—nowadays animals were included only if they were robotic—but Jennie liked to stop by at least once a week to say hello.

"Hi, friend," said Jennie, tapping the glass.

The squid wove its tentacles around a cluster of kelp, ripping the plant from its seabed and pressing it against the glass as if in offering.

"So sweet," Jennie giggled.

"What this?" said a man's voice behind her.

Oh... him. Jennie had almost forgotten about him. Who was he—Arse... Arsi... Ass? She glanced down at her HR form. Arsyen.

"This is our squid," said Jennie, stretching her receptionist's smile toothy and wide as she turned to face him.

As far as product managers went, he seemed particularly underwhelming—they'd already been walking for ten minutes and he hadn't even tried to lecture her about anything. How was it that Anahata could overlook people like Jennie in favor of dopey guys like Arsyen? Jennie had applied for ten internal jobs this quarter alone, ranging from online sales assistant to VP of infrastructure engineering, and hadn't gotten a single bite. Most of the time they told her she wasn't the right "culture fit." Sometimes they claimed she wasn't qualified—Jennie, who had an almost-PhD in Russian literature and fifteen online entrepreneurship degrees and had watched every single TED Talk ever recorded.

"Big fish," said Arsyen, clearly demonstrating his superior intellect. "Other fish here too?"

"Not anymore. We used to have other fish, but they just kept disappearing while the squid here kept getting bigger and bigger. So it's just him now. Some people think he ate the smaller fish, but I think he's just a misunderstood giant."

Jennie wanted to point out to Arsyen that she had just created a metaphor. She was obviously the squid, but prettier.

But instead she just smiled. Jennie knew her poetry would be lost on someone with an engineering degree.

"You can visit him whenever you want," she said. "And if you make it past the first week, you can even sign up to feed him."

"The first week...?"

Jennie did a double take.

"Didn't you read your offer letter?"

"Um..."

Jennie rifled through the HR paperwork. "Here," she said. She thrust a paper at Arsyen and tapped the middle of the page with a pink fingernail.

"'Anahata reserves the right to terminate your contract at any point during your first week,'" Jennie quoted. "And by 'any point,' they mean even during the first five minutes."

Jennie saw the panic that flashed across Arsyen's face and couldn't resist pushing things a bit further.

"I should probably fire you right now," she said. "In fact—"

Jennie ripped Arsyen's red badge out of his hand and started to walk away.

"But I—"

Jennie stopped and sighed. The truth was she had no power to fire anyone at Anahata. It was fun to mess with Arsyen, but if she wasn't careful, he could end up firing her. The only power receptionists had was over the refrigerator in the reception area.

She turned to face him.

"If you had read your contract, you'd know that I can't fire you," Jennie said.

"Phew!"

Jennie scribbled a note on Arsyen's HR form: *Employee did not read contract.* In another profession, that would have been a ding against Arsyen, but at Anahata, managers seemed to view noncompliance among their technical staff as a sign of genius.

"What you doing?" said Arsyen, lifting onto his toes to catch a glimpse of what Jennie had written.

"You'll be fine," said Jennie, waving away his concern as she pushed him out of the building and onto the lawn. "The only thing you need to do is keep your manager happy and, well, watch out for other engineers." She gestured toward a group of men sitting on a picnic table, gathered around a computer. "I can't fire you, but *they* can."

The largest man in the group turned in their direction, stretching his arms above his head. Jennie recognized him from the previous week, when she had seen him fire a new engineer for choosing a Diet Coke instead of a Red Bull from the micro-kitchen.

The engineer's mouth roared in a wide, silent yawn, and his eyes scanned the area around him, moving across the various employees walking across the grass. His gaze fell on Arsyen and a trigger within him seemed to be pulled. He threw his pale, hairy legs over the bench and began to lope toward them.

"Quick!" hissed Jennie, pushing Arsyen into the nearest building.

She didn't care about Arsyen, but she did care about her orientation success rate. To date, she was the only Anahata receptionist who had completed all of her new employee tours without having a single employee fired.

Jennie found an empty meeting room and closed the door behind them.

"That was close!" she said. "Sorry, I should have explained earlier. My badge is white, but your badge is red."

"Red is for special employees?" asked Arsyen, puffing out his chest.

"I guess you could say that," shrugged Jennie. "Most of the employees with red badges are contractors. Those are the employees we like… but not so much as to give them health care—you know, like cafeteria workers and security guards. The other people who get red badges are like you—provisional employees who need to pass their first week. Anyway, the point is you'll need your badge to get into buildings, but the rest of the time you should hide it in your pocket."

Jennie poked her head out the door. The engineer was pacing the hall. She shut the door and turned to face Arsyen.

"Never show fear. Engineers can smell it a mile away. Half of succeeding here is just acting like you're right about stuff even when you aren't."

Jennie glanced at Arsyen's HR sheet. He was assigned to Building 7, which housed some of the company's coolest projects, like Social Car and Builder. Maybe she could butter up to him and he could get her a job there. Though, on second thought, Arsyen seemed a little creepy and could misinterpret her intentions. The last thing Jennie needed was another work drama. A few weeks earlier she had made the mistake of hooking up with Niels Smeardon, Anahata's SVP of sales. She had done everything he wanted—told him that his penis and sales strategy presentation were the biggest she had ever seen; she even let him balance his computer on her back so he could send a few urgent emails right after they had sex. And all of that had gotten her nothing but a reassignment by the HR team to the main reception area, far away from the sales buildings.

Jennie continued to stew about her Niels hookup as she began to rattle off other campus facts to Arsyen. Sales were in Buildings 10 to 15, Operations from 15 to 20, anything supporting those teams from 20 to 27, and facilities and janitorial staff in Building 28. She saw Arsyen nod when she mentioned the janitors and wondered if he was one of those social activist employees, the type who made six figures but liked to spend the majority of his work hours railing about The Man and trying to make the cafeterias go full vegan.

Jennie found those employees a bit annoying—they were always complaining about the juice selection in the reception area—but she still preferred them to people like Niels. He had taken home more than $100 million dollars last year in executive pay but hadn't even offered to order her a car ride home.

"What do you do at Anahata?" asked Arsyen, interrupting Jennie's thoughts.

Was he just trying to make conversation, or was he questioning her competence? At Anahata, one could never be sure.

"I'm a campus guide and do some reception work," Jennie said. "It's a really important role, because if you don't have someone like me who shows new people around, they may never understand Anahata and could get lost."

She paused and searched Arsyen's face for a reaction. It was totally blank, as if he wasn't even listening to her.

"Of course, I mean 'getting lost' both figuratively and literally," continued Jennie, feeling anger build in her stomach. "Many of your lot only understand the latter point, not the former, and so you see, that is why we humanities majors are so valuable here."

Arsyen nodded but now seemed fixated on the Moodify bracelet on his wrist.

Had he even heard a word she said? He was like the rest of them—full of himself, convinced of his own brilliance, sure that a lowly receptionist was completely irrelevant to the mighty things he had to do during his day. But what did he know about the world, anyway? Coding didn't teach you about culture. It didn't teach you empathy or emotional intelligence.

"I was a Russian lit PhD before I dropped out to join Anahata, so I know a lot about what's going on in the world," Jennie said. "There are people starving, people who don't have clean water. So after Anahata, that's what I'll do—change some of those things. Or maybe I'll do it here. I haven't figured it out yet. The point is, do *you* have a social conscience? A big purpose, Arsyen?"

Arsyen looked up.

"Yes," he said. "I will save my people and kill very bad dictator."

Good lord. This tour was proving even more tedious than her last one—an engineer who made whale sounds out of his nose while they hid in a broom closet. She leaned out the door.

"All clear."

She popped her head back in and pointed at Arsyen's badge to remind him to hide it in his pocket.

They made it safely to the other parts of the campus, each building revealing a well-orchestrated surprise for Anahata's new employee. Building 3 had frozen yogurt machines in each cubicle. In Building 4, there was a service for engineers who wanted someone to tuck them in at night in the campus beds. Building 2 had moving walkways that would reverse direction every fifteen minutes—a challenge to either time one's movements precisely or exercise by moving against the current.

"Past that door is the volleyball court," said Jennie, pointing just beyond the reversible walkway, "and to the right is the swimming pool. Our founder, Bobby Bonilo, wanted to set an example for the rest of the Valley that health and fitness should be an important part of an employee's well-being."

"Like Galt," Arsyen said.

Jennie shot Arsyen a glance. What kind of idiot joined Anahata and spent their first day talking about its biggest competitor?

"Anahata did it *first*," she said sharply. "We were the first to make health a priority. The first to say you should drink lots of water and get lots of sleep. Galt copies everything we do."

She made another note on his HR form: *Cocky. Insulted Anahata.*

Yet another point racked up for Arsyen. This guy had to be one of the more arrogant employees she had ever met. He'd probably be a big success here.

ARSYEN

They stopped in front of the medieval-themed cafeteria in Building 5, and for a moment Arsyen was transported back to Poodlekek, standing in a cave next to Sklartar, his manservant.

But what had first looked like Sklartar was now, at second glance, clearly a robot, and there were no bodies scattered at his feet. Nor were there any henchmen to wait on Arsyen, or maidens to help feed and clothe him. And there was certainly no one to help clean up after him. To think if his people knew that Arsyen was now cleaning the toilets of America!

It was never supposed to be like this. If the peasants hadn't gotten so mad about the potato tax, if the neighboring country of Embria hadn't sensed weakness and attacked from the north, Arsyen would still be in Poodlekek now, having his bottom wiped by the royal wiper, occasionally exerting himself at a game of croquet.

But the Embrian barbarians had surrounded his family's palace, with Arsyen narrowly missing execution as he snuck across the border and into a U.N. refugee camp. The Pyrrhian military successfully restored the country to order, but just as Arsyen was prepared to return, General Korpeko declared a coup and foisted the helpless Aimo family from power.

Arsyen was bounced between various immigrant detention camps, eventually ending up in California, where he was released into the wilds of Silicon Valley. There, he found work as a janitor in Stanford's chemistry department. Then, from there, on to a few small startups and eventually Galt. And now Anahata, where he would finally make his mark.

Arsyen glanced over at his future queen.

Jennie's mouth was moving again. It seemed to move a lot. Arsyen knew that women liked the opportunity to speak, but beautiful women were most beautiful when they were silent.

"And so you can see," she was saying, "that the composting techniques developed in Russia in the early twentieth century had a profound impact in how we compost now in Palo Alto."

"Yes," said Arsyen, looking down to see if their Moodify bracelets had finally synced.

They still weren't working.

Jennie stopped in front of another building. It was an echo of all previous buildings they had toured: an enormous white complex with a plain, charmless exterior. "Your new home," she announced.

Hadn't Jennie said janitorial services were in Building 28? This one had an enormous black "7" painted near its entrance.

The metal doors banged open, and a large group of men walked out, laughing about something. Arsyen had never seen such diversity—so many white, Chinese, and Indian male janitors all working in the same company.

Behind them was another man, also white, walking slowly across the lawn, chomping on an enormous carrot. It was the same guy Arsyen had met at his interview. He had already forgotten his name, but the man's shirt reminded him: R-O-N-I, spelled out in big block letters sewn clumsily across the chest. This was him, the king of the cleaning crew.

Roni greeted Arsyen with a wave. Arsyen turned to say something to Jennie, but she had already disappeared.

Roni signaled to Arsyen to follow, pointing out different landmarks as they made their way around campus: "Here's where you can pick up four different kinds of cupcakes each day at three p.m." "Here's the secret underground passageway that leads to the volleyball court." "Here's where you can get a full-body massage—and if you book the tropical forest room, tell them no rainmaker!"

Arsyen was amazed by the amenities, but he was even more

excited about his paycheck. With the extraordinary salary they were paying him—ten times more than the job listing had originally advertised—his reclamation of Pyrrhia drew much, much closer. This year's salary alone would purchase twenty Pyrrhian mercenary troops and several thousand horses, as well as one million sacks of flour to be distributed to the poor (eight hundred thousand if he had his portrait printed on the sacks, which could be an important revolution/coup marketing strategy).

If he kept on this path, he could reclaim the throne in just a few years. He could probably even fly Natia, his Pyrrhian internet girlfriend, out to the United States so he could finally have sex with her. Though maybe it would be better to dump Natia, date Jennie, and spend the extra money on some new video games. Being a ruler meant setting clear priorities.

They walked down a nondescript hall that dumped them into a maze of cubicles. Each contained a handful of desks, and occasionally a table. The white walls were only shoulder height, and Arsyen could easily see who was inside. The view was the same no matter where he turned: square after square of men staring at their computer screens. The layout reminded him of ice cube trays.

Roni stopped next to a poster that read "Entering a No Galt Zone!"

"Voilà!" exclaimed Roni, his arm gesturing at the cubicle before him like a game show host. Its simple layout mirrored that of every other cubicle they had passed. There were three desks—only two of which were occupied—and a whiteboard covered in code hieroglyphs.

There were two men in the cubicle, but neither turned, continuing instead to focus intently on their screens. Arsyen wondered why his fellow sanitation engineers were working on computers, and why there were no cleaning materials anywhere in sight. Perhaps cleaning happened differently at Anahata. Thoughts of unknown methods immediately filled his head, his exhilaration only slightly tempered by the sight of Red Bull cans stacked in a pyramid atop a side table. Roni grabbed an unopened can and tossed it to Arsyen. "Lifeblood," he joked, grabbing one for himself.

Roni tapped one of the cubicle dwellers on the shoulder.

"Jonas, meet Arsyen," he said.

The seated figure turned slowly, and Arsyen realized that the gangly, pimply boy before him couldn't be more than sixteen. His skin was a shifting kaleidoscope of sallow and dark blotches. Enormous glasses covered his face from the eyebrows to the tip of the nose. Through the frames, his eyes studied Arsyen, and then moved to Roni, and then suddenly seemed to register the purpose of the introduction. "Hello," he said, in a thick but familiar accent. "It is nice to make your acquaintance. Arsyen—*bish mena kakaya*?"

Arsyen hesitated. The words, the accent, the singsong of the phrase all sounded so familiar, and yet he had no idea what the teenager had just said to him. "Sorry?"

"Oh, my most sincere apologies," the boy said. "I thought from your name... you see, Arsyen is a name we have in my country, Embria. And your face could pass for Embrian."

Arsyen's left eye twitched. *Embria!* The country that had started the Fifth Great War, the country responsible for having raped and pillaged his native land for thousands of years. The rivalry between the two countries was legendary. The greatest insult in the Pyrrhian language was to call someone a *klok-klok*—a chicken from Embria.

Arsyen offered his hand. "I am from Pyrrhia," he said, proudly trilling the *r* and making the sign of the red-breasted woodpecker.

But Jonas' expression didn't change, as if it was simply an input of information, meaning no more to him than if Arsyen had said he was from Los Angeles. He turned back to his computer.

Roni pointed to the desk across the room, where a very blond head sat atop a very long body.

"That's Sven. He's from Sweden and is ex-Microsoft, but he's a bit embarrassed about that, so don't bring it up with him. He lives with his mom, which is another topic to avoid. But he's got a thousand startup ideas—that's always a safe subject."

Roni pulled the headphones off the blond mop of hair, and Sven swiveled his chair. He grinned and shook Arsyen's hand. Then he readjusted his headphones and banged his knees against the desk as he turned back to face his screen.

Roni pointed at an empty desk between Jonas and Sven. "Here's your space."

Arsyen's eyes ran across the desk. There was nothing on it but an enormous computer. He opened a drawer. No sponges, no commercial cleaning agents, no chemicals for him to mix.

"Roni, where my supplies?"

"Oh, there's a tech center down the hall where you can get everything—a mouse, big monitor, pens—if you are one of those people who still writes things by hand, that is. Anyway, take your time getting set up. I've got an important meeting to attend, but when I come back I'll get you briefed on everything."

Arsyen took a seat at his desk and studied the area around him. The floor throughout the cubicle was covered in potato chip particles—presumably from the open bag on Sven's desk. A piece of dried putty had begun a slow, snail-like trudge down the wall above Jonas' desk. Across the room, a series of dark symbols glared at Arsyen from the whiteboard.

This was the messiest janitor's office he had ever seen.

※

The first order of business was to get his cleaning supplies. Roni's instructions had seemed simple enough—straight down the hall, a right at the first opportunity, then the second left. But no sooner had he made the first turn then Arsyen found himself lost in a labyrinth of cubicles.

He approached a map posted on the wall, tracing his finger along the rows in search of something resembling a supply closet.

Arsyen felt a tap on his shoulder.

"Are you lost? New here, maybe?"

Arsyen turned to face a freckled red-headed kid not much older than Jonas.

Arsyen's hidden red badge poked into his thigh, reminding him to be careful.

"Are you an engineer?" the kid asked.

Arsyen nodded. The kid looked skinny and weak. Arsyen was sure he could outrun him.

The kid's eyes narrowed.

"Okay, then. I want to know all the words in English that have X as the second letter and N as the second to last."

Arsyen spotted an exit sign at the far end of the hall. He decided to make a run for it.

"Hey! Hey!" screamed the kid, yelling after him. "Tell me how you would make an object model of a pig!"

Arsyen dashed down the hall, the sound of the kid's plastic Crocs squeaking closely behind him. He pushed open the door, ran to his right, past the volleyball court, over a bridge made of Legos, dodged through a group of employees fighting with light sabers, and ducked into a nearby building.

Arsyen glanced behind him. The kid was nowhere in sight. He caught his breath and surveyed his surroundings.

He hadn't been in this building before. It seemed largely empty—nothing more than a series of plain white corridors. There wasn't even anyone walking about.

He spotted another building map and traced his finger down the corridors. At the end of the northwest hall was an exit door that appeared to lead in the direction of Building 7—Arsyen's building.

He headed in that direction, keeping an eye out for predatory engineers. But there wasn't a soul in sight.

Just before reaching the exit, Arsyen caught sight of a white door labeled in simple black lettering: SUPPLY CLOSET.

Finally!

Arsyen paused before the door. This was a big moment. The tools he chose here would determine the success of his first week at Anahata. A lobby broom was a good choice for one-handed cleaning and getting at some of the trickier corners of Arsyen's cubicle. But a midsize broom would be better for general sweeping.

He knew his co-workers would judge him closely for his choice. He took a deep breath and placed his hand on the knob.

GREGOR

On the other side of the door, Gregor Guntlag's gaze alternated between the doorknob, which he thought he had seen rattle, and the clock, whose minute hand was broken. It wobbled between one tick and the next, as though no longer sure of the direction in which time moved.

The existence of a clock on a wall of the world's most important technology company was itself a quaint reminder of a different era, a period in which time was measured differently, the various positions of its hands signifying official, institutionalized periods of work and rest.

That clock—the only one on campus—was a crucial addition to the Anahata board room, aka the supply closet. The company's CEO, Bobby Bonilo, had forbidden the use of any electronic devices in the room, and the clock was the only way his management team could measure the progress of their interminable meetings. According to its current movements, one minute (soon to be minus one minute) had passed since Bobby had begun his latest yoga pose. Gregor Guntlag, Anahata's senior vice president of engineering, had many projects in the works to speed up time, but to date, even he couldn't manage to accelerate Bobby's sun salutations.

"Haaaaaaaaaaaa," came a deep, raspy sound from the back of Bobby's throat. He was on all fours at the head of the table, his butt thrust toward the ceiling, the top of his white shirt falling to expose a pale back covered with moles. Bobby rested his knees on the table and sat back on his legs, a small gut spilling over his waistband like freshly baked bread. His eyes remained closed.

"Haaaaaaaaaaa." The sound intensified. "Haaaaaaaaaaa! Haaaaaaaaaaa!"

The daily management meeting was itself an exercise in yogic patience and discipline, with all five members of the team doing a generally poor job of tolerating each other.

Although they were a small group, the men spread themselves out around the table, allowing spaces of two or three chairs between them. In addition to Gregor, there was Old Al, the company's only gray-haired engineer, occasionally useful for his fifty-four years of wisdom. A few seats down sat Greg Fischer, the chief financial and corporate affairs officer (CFCAO), who ran all the departments—legal, finance, marketing, and PR—that were seen as necessary evils in helping run a large company. Equal in irrelevance was HR Paul, the head of the human resources department, who was generally regarded as a nincompoop psychology PhD with a flatulence problem. And then there was Niels, aka The Salesman.

The master engineer and the master salesman did not like each other, but today Niels seemed to be paying Gregor no attention. Gregor grimaced as Niels bent his gel-slicked head over the small notepad that he carried around in his front pocket. He found the mere existence of Niels' notepad an insult to the advances of technology and word processing software.

Gregor had disliked Anahata's new head of advertising from the instant he spotted him on campus, a plastic smile fixed on his face, fancy designer suit falling from his shoulders like a second skin. With his wingtips pointed sharply in the direction of his target, Niels had approached Gregor to suggest the engineering team fix the advertising system interface so that Anahata's advertisers could more easily place their ads online. Gregor quickly informed Niels that Anahata was about its users first and foremost, and that its users—and just as important, Anahata's engineers—did not care about an improved advertising system. Implicit in his explanation was the unwritten philosophical hierarchy of Anahata: Engineers at the top, then users, and then, long after that, cheerleaders, janitors, creationists, and, finally, the Anahata sales team.

But Niels was slow on the uptake. He kept pushing for the change, eventually escalating the issue to Bobby. Bobby, in turn, sent Gregor and Niels an email asking them to speak to each other and not bother him with such small problems. Six years later, the two men still had not managed to do so. They only met in Bobby's management meetings, where they sat on opposite ends of the table and took opposing stances in almost any argument.

"Haaaaaaaaaa... Haaaaaaaaaa... Haaaaaaa... Ha! Ha! Ha!"

Suddenly, Bobby was on his feet, arms outstretched.

"Our minds are clear," he said, opening his eyes and bowing to his management team. Bobby sat down on top of the table, crossing his legs in the lotus position. "Let us begin."

Just then, the door opened and a man entered, wearing an enormous grin.

Gregor thought he recognized this short, swarthy man, but he could not place him. The intruder also seemed confused: He scanned the room, past Gregor, past Niels, and landed on Bobby. His eyes bulged, the grin vanished, and he took a step back. His hand fiddled with the doorknob.

"Wait," said Bobby. He looked Arsyen over. "Clearly you must be smart to have found me like this. I am elusive, you know. A bit like a panther—if panthers were also progressive Buddhists." Bobby pawed the air with his claws.

The man nodded vigorously.

Gregor's tongue roamed his mouth, searching for particles of stray food. He always brushed his teeth after lunch, but today he had lost track of time while troubleshooting a server issue with the infrastructure team. The lack of order in his mouth was mildly distressing—just like this intruder, who he wished would leave. Where had he seen him before?

"I suppose you have joined us because you know of our open-door meeting policy," said Bobby, referring to a core Anahata principle that Gregor and the rest of the management team all actually hated.

"What is your name?" Bobby asked.

"Arsyen Aimo," the man said.

"Join us, Arsyen."

"But, Bobby," said Fischer, the CFCAO, "we have confidential things to discuss."

"Trust is the cornerstone of truth. If we cannot trust our employees, our house will fall upon itself." Bobby turned to Arsyen and gestured at a seat at the table.

Arsyen took the chair closest to the door, gripping its arms oddly, rigidly, as if he were sitting on a throne. Suddenly Gregor recalled where he had seen him. This was the product manager candidate Roni had pointed out, the one from Galt. They had decided to hire him just to bleed Galt of some of its top talent. Over the past month, Anahata had lost several of its best engineers to the startup.

Gregor gave Arsyen another look. He was still panting a bit; dark hairs peeked out from a very wet collar. He did not seem like an exceptional human being. Still…

"What's up first?" asked Bobby, turning to his assistant. She was in attendance that day as part of what Bobby called "radical transparency," a philosophy that, while often cited by Bobby, seemed to be in effect only every third Thursday. His assistant leaned over and showed him a list—and some generous cleavage.

"Okay, everyone," said Bobby, nodding at her breasts. "Let's show Arsyen what innovation looks like!"

Bobby's assistant opened the door, and a product manager and his engineering team shuffled toward the table in an awkward, heaving lump. They kept their heads down, shooting furtive glances at Bobby as they prepared to present their work.

The product manager coughed. "When, um, we set out to design the new interface for Rovix, we had, uh, three goals in mind."

"Why do you need a presentation to tell me your goals?" Old Al barked. "Keep things simple. You don't need two hundred slides to tell me what you're going to do."

"It's just a few slides," the product manager mumbled.

"Al's right," Fischer said. "If you can't tell us your idea in thirty seconds, it's not an idea. It's a presentation."

The product manager closed his computer.

"So, uh, there were three goals. First, to simplify the user interface. Second, to make it easier for people to share content across all of our products. And third, to ensure we had the right structure in place to eventually run ads next to the content, if—his eyes darted over at Gregor—"we ever decided that was something we would want to do."

Gregor's radar shot to attention. Had they actually just suggested putting advertising on this product? Niels' team must have lobbied for it.

"Let me tell you something," said Old Al, shaking his finger at the team. "Bobby invented the concept of cloud computing on a high school cafeteria napkin twenty years ago. Big ideas should be simple. Napkinable."

"Here," said Fischer, pulling a napkin out of his takeaway carton. "Use this. Show us Rovix on a napkin."

The product manager fumbled with his backpack and pulled out a pen. He began to draw on Fischer's napkin. Soon, the napkin had various arrows and bullet points scattered across it, in addition to a small glob of mayonnaise.

Bobby glanced at the drawing and frowned. "Arsyen, take a look and tell us what you would do."

The napkin made its way down the table to Arsyen. His nose wrinkled as his fingers daintily pinched the clean edge.

"Speak up!" shouted Old Al as he adjusted his hearing aid.

"Throw it away," said Arsyen, pushing the napkin toward the middle of the table.

Bobby's eyes lit up, and he turned to the Rovix team.

"You heard Arsyen. There's clearly something wrong with your product—I'll leave you all to figure out what that is. But remember: Big ideas have simple solutions.

"Also remember: Solutionize. Iterate. Solutionize. Iterate.

"And really remember: Sometimes failure is success, and other times success is failure."

"Thank you," said the product manager, inclining slightly in a half-bow. He glanced at Old Al and then Gregor, likely hoping for additional feedback or some indication of whether the meeting had gone well. But Gregor wasn't in the mood to give feedback, and Old Al had fallen asleep.

The assistant shut the door behind them, and Fischer belched noisily.

Gregor rolled his eyes. He found the whole lot of them to be idiots, minus Bobby and occasionally Old Al. But then he caught a similar disgust on Niels' face and recoiled. He would not permit himself to share an emotion with that man.

"Are we done?" Gregor asked. He needed to talk to Bobby, and no productive dialog could take place as long as The Salesman was around.

Bobby's assistant consulted the agenda. "We have a proposal from Niels," she said.

Niels flashed the assistant his best grin, then launched into his pitch.

"We have a huge, untapped opportunity before us," he began. "I'm talking about the chance to make over a billion dollars in the first year alone just by—"

"Niels, stop right there!" Bobby yelped. "Don't you see who is in the room? Arsyen!"

Everyone turned in his direction.

The weight of the group's gaze seemed to sink Arsyen even lower in his chair—an observation that did not displease Gregor. This Arsyen seemed to be a rather unremarkable individual. What had Galt seen in him? Had Gregor and Roni made a mistake in hiring him?

"It is inevitable that the rest of us must discuss it, but I don't know if our engineer should hear this kind of talk. You *are* an engineer, right?"

Arsyen nodded.

Gregor shook his head but didn't say anything. Product managers were such frauds, always trying to pretend they were real engineers instead of MBAs with a few coding classes under their belts.

"You see, Arsyen," continued Bobby, "we're going to talk about money. Or more specifically, *advertising*." Bobby spit out the last word like a piece of rotten food.

That'll show him, thought Gregor, shooting a smug glance at Niels.

But Niels only smiled in response. His confidence enraged Gregor—and fed his self-doubt. What if Bobby didn't really hate advertising *or* Niels? What if his disgust was just an act?

"Bobby, you make an excellent point, as always," Niels said. "But I think it would be good for engineers like Arsyen to understand how the sales team funds their innovations."

"Fine with me," Gregor said. "It's a chance for our new employee to understand who really runs this company."

Gregor looked to Bobby, but the founder said nothing. He seemed to be distracted by some dirt underneath his fingernails.

Niels introduced his proposal—a project in which Anahata would run ads on Moodify bracelets. Within minutes, Gregor was on the attack. No matter what revenue projection or partnership expansion Niels raised, Gregor countered with the Anahata commandment to never hurt the user experience in the name of revenue.

Despite his reputation, Gregor was not actually opposed to advertising. He knew the company needed to make money, and, like Bobby, he himself was a very rich man thanks to Anahata's online ads. But Gregor was willing to put additional material gain aside in the name of thwarting his nemesis.

After an extensive back-and-forth—and a lengthy digression from Old Al, who had woken from his nap to explain how advertising had worked back before the internet was invented—the battle finally puttered to a halt. Gregor wasn't sure he had won—Bobby had refused to make a decision and then closed his eyes to meditate—but the frustrated look on Niels' face was satisfaction enough.

Fischer offered a temporary détente by raising an issue they had discussed the previous week: a newly released Galt productivity tool that reduced people's lengthy business presentations into a four-sentence sales pitch, thereby shortening business meetings and helping society advance capitalism at three times the current rate. It was nearly identical to a project Anahata was set to launch the following month. That Galt had beaten Anahata to market was no surprise: The startup had lured away two of Anahata's best productivity engineers the previous fall. In fact, it seemed that all of Anahata's work and thinking had made it into the final Galt tool.

"I always said we would lose those engineers to Galt," growled Old Al, shaking a finger at HR Paul. "We knew they were getting calls from the recruiters every week, and we did nothing to stop it."

"That's not true, Al, and I don't feel like you are speaking to me in a productive manner," Paul said. "We gave them strong counter-offers, and even took one of their mothers on a hot-air balloon ride. But in the end, both said Galt was scrappier and less bureaucratic."

"We should sue Galt and show them they can't keep doing this," Old Al retorted. "They've already poached several of our top engineers, and now they're beating us to the market with products. We can't just sit by and let them do this. You know, back when I was at Bell Labs, we had a policy that—"

"My team," said Bobby, raising his palm to silence the group. Gregor glared at Niels across the room as Bobby counted aloud to five.

Bobby opened his eyes. "When a duck grows big, people forget about its webbed feet. They forget that it can swim."

Gregor tried to remember whether Bobby had used this aphorism before.

Bobby waited another minute for someone to respond, but

Gregor didn't seem to be the only one who was lost. No one said anything. Finally, Bobby sighed loudly.

"The fundamental issue here is Galt," he said. "Our engineers are leaving us for Galt because they think it's faster and more innovative. Just look at Arsyen."

All heads swiveled toward Arsyen, and the little man sunk lower in his chair.

"Arsyen, look up again for us. Good. Do you all see that—the fear in his eyes? Watching us, watching the Rovix team just now, he has clearly been asking himself why he is working at Anahata. Isn't that right, Arsyen?"

Arsyen nodded vigorously.

Gregor still wasn't convinced the guy was that remarkable, but at least Arsyen was smart enough to know to agree with Bobby. Bobby was always right in the long run.

"We could add more of those organic juicers to each building?" offered HR Paul. "Or a pet hedgehog? Once you bond with them, you'll find it much harder to leave the company."

"This isn't about giving them more amenities," groaned Niels. "Our engineers are spoiled enough as it is. You'll notice that none of the sales team has defected to Galt—despite their recruiters trying to ambush my guys in the parking lots. It's because we run a tight ship in sales. We're not out there handing out free jet packs every day like engineering does. The only freebie I hand out is my book of master negotiator tips."

Niels waved a shiny copy of the red manual he issued to all sales employees.

"The reason you haven't lost many people to Galt is that sales will be the last to go," Gregor said. "The innovative minds go first. If ten percent of our sales workforce had gone to Galt—instead of our engineering staff—we wouldn't even be having this conversation right now."

Niels looked to HR Paul for support, but his colleague nodded in agreement with Gregor.

Niels turned to Bobby.

"We need to create more of a war mentality here. Wars are very productive for unity. Every Anahata employee should want nothing more than to kill Galt and rip their little startup hearts out. People need enemies. Enemies drive us forward."

Niels scanned the room, stopping on Gregor. His eyes narrowed to lizard slits.

"Wrong," said Gregor, not breaking Niels' gaze. "Bobby's point is that if we want to remain the world's most innovative company, we have to keep our engineers. And to do that, we have to be fast. We have to let the engineers work on exciting projects, and in an environment where they and their projects are isolated from the temptations of Galt."

"Very realistic," Niels said. "Let's just put them on an island then. Get them some fruity cocktails."

Fischer and HR Paul chuckled at the far end of the table. Bobby picked at the flap of his sandal.

"An island is obviously inappropriate. For one, fresh water would be an issue," Gregor said. "But rest assured we have a plan."

Gregor shifted in his chair to face Arsyen.

"Soon there will be no reason for you or any other engineer to ever want to leave Anahata."

RONI

Legend had it that Bobby reserved his most important discussions for the bathroom because he was convinced that Galt had bugged all the Anahata meeting rooms.

While an outsider might have thought it odd, Roni knew it was simply more evidence of the founder's cunning. He was sure Bobby chose the bathroom—with its occasional disagreeable smells and sounds and the eventual, inevitable intrusion by an outsider—to keep the length of any meeting to a minimum. This allowed him more time in his day to think of greater things. It was the mark of an exceptional leader.

Roni often recalled his first and only bathroom meeting with Bobby. Eight other employees had been present, each jockeying for position. They all wanted to stand next to him, near the hand dryer, but Roni beat them to it. Although the meeting lasted just four minutes and Bobby uttered only one sentence, they were a very long four minutes, and it was one very important sentence.

Ever since that day, Roni favored that same Building 3, southwest corner bathroom. Its gentle pale-blue walls and piped-in ocean sounds were the perfect setting for his daily hour-long meditation sessions.

With the stall door closed and his patchouli candle lit, Roni would lean back on the heated Japanese toilet seat, press the soles of his Crocs against the wall, close his eyes, and insert his finger into his nose. The dry Northern California air lent itself to large, easily removable finds, particularly during the days when the region was hit by the Diablo winds.

But today no amount of nostril exploration could ease the mild anxiety building within him.

When Roni first started at Anahata, he was one of its superstars, leading a project to do real-time monitoring of all of the world's nuclear hazards. People on campus called him "Radioactive Roni," and someone even organized a Chernobyl-themed party in his honor.

He was now into his seventh year at Anahata. Roni was making a ton of money; all his needs were met. But he no longer felt a part of the in-crowd, privy to the hottest projects or latest internal gossip. He increasingly felt like the heart of the company was beating elsewhere. It was only a vague sense, but one akin to that of the young dragon slayer approaching the bridge, one careful step after another, the fog slowly clearing before him to reveal...

Was it because he had recently become a Republican?

In any case, Roni was sure something was afoot. Gregor had recently installed biometric screening at the entrance to Building 1, and conversations between Building 1 employees abruptly stopped whenever Roni joined them at the company cafeteria.

The funny thing was that if you asked most Anahatis, Roni had a dream job. He was the technical lead of Social Car, one of the hottest, most anticipated projects at the company. But Roni had been at Anahata long enough to know a quirky project from a crucial one. And Social Car just felt a bit too much like the former. Roni wondered if it was just a distraction—a deft sleight of hand by Bobby to divert attention from the true gamble of something much, much bigger taking form in Building 1.

He had made a few passes to uncover the truth. One of Roni's friends worked in Building 1. He had proved impenetrable to inquiry, claiming he was just "tinkering with the ads algorithm." Gregor had likewise stonewalled him, mentioning something about Building 1's commitment to "breakthrough enterprise software products." Roni was enough of a Valley veteran to know that when an engineer feigned enthusiasm for business software, he was either lying about the software or lying about being an engineer. And that couldn't have been more true than with Gregor Guntlag, who was well known for his dislike of business, sales, and anything connected to advancing the dirty affairs of capitalism.

So Roni had thrown himself into other projects alongside his work on Social Car. Most notably, he had become the organizer of the company's quarterly hackathons, designed to bring engineers together from across the company to detect bugs and fix core software. But while he enjoyed mentoring the younger engineers, Roni was beginning to feel like an aging school dance chaperon who furnished the pizza and Red Bull and hung out awkwardly at the back of the hall. What he was doing didn't feel tangible or significant.

Roni sighed and pumped his Crocs against the door in a pitter-patter of plastic. He sighed again, and then again and again, beginning to enjoy the sound of his breath echoing through the bathroom. He imagined an audience beyond the stall door, sitting on the blue tiles, crowding in to listen to his wise words about an important engineering topic.

"Let me tell you the truth about cloud computing," said Roni in mock tenor. "There is no cloud. It is a myth. Your data is actually in my nose. Right above the—"

Roni stopped as he heard two voices outside the bathroom. The door opened, and Roni heard a shuffling of feet.

"Hello? Is anyone here?" The man's voice was vaguely familiar.

"All clear," said another voice, the accent thick, like a knife trying to find its way out of taffy. Roni recognized its owner immediately: Gregor Guntlag.

"So, like I was saying in the meeting," the first man said. "Life extension. We aren't working on it, and I am certain Galt is doing it."

"Which is why Project Y is so important," Gregor said. "I wanted to talk to you about an issue we're having with—"

"Imagine," the first man said. "If Galt outlives us, just imagine what that means for the planet. They'll probably reduce all of us humans to tiny bugs!"

"I'm sure we could tackle it after we solved our Project Y—"

"Life extension," repeated the first man. "I want you to make me a plan to tackle life extension."

Roni thought he heard Gregor sigh.

"We can work on life extension," he said after a moment.

"Also, I want to breed animals. Did you see that article this morning on *Tech Geek*? Galt is breeding small plants that will replace animals. Those bastards. We'll show them. We'll breed animals that will eat their plants!"

"I suppose that could be better for the environment," Gregor said. "Less carbon dioxide emissions—"

"And then we'll turn the animals back into plants!" the first man said.

"I'll look into both," Gregor said. "But first, Project Y..."

"Oh, yes, I wanted to talk to you about that. I have a new idea. Project Y needs an army. We will never beat Galt if we don't have an army supporting Y. Our employees must be an army. And then that army brings in more soldiers for an even bigger army."

"An army?" Gregor asked.

"A figurative army. No, wait, an army with weapons. No, the kind of army Gandhi would have had."

"Bobby, I'm not sure I understand."

Roni's eyes popped.

It was Bobby—of course! Bobby was the only one in the company who could give Gregor orders; the only one who quoted Ghandhi and whose license plate read "MAHATMA."

Roni heard footsteps cross the bathroom, like someone was pacing.

"Yes, yes, our peaceful army *will* be armed," Bobby said. "But its arms will be technology, and therefore not arms, but also arms."

"I don't follow," Gregor said.

Bobby sighed loudly, as if it was his eternal burden to explain himself. "When we are ready to push the button on Project Y, we will need a group of engineers who will already be converts and will spread the word. And then, of course, we also need engineers like Jonas who will infiltrate the enemy—"

Roni's Crocs nearly dropped from their perch at the sound of his employee's name.

Gregor replied, but one of them was now using the urinal and Roni couldn't make out the words. He leaned forward in his seat, careful to keep his feet suspended against the door. There were more unintelligible words. A urinal was flushed. Something knocked against something else. An object fell to the ground. *The drama! What next?* He heard the faucets running, footsteps exiting, and the door closing. Roni was alone again.

Roni's mind raced across and above and behind itself, the idea of a mysterious Project Y bolting about in his head, ricocheting off his skull, toward his ear, past Jonas' name. But no matter how he fit the bits together, he couldn't make sense of it.

He started over. There was something called Project Y—maybe that was the secret thing happening in Building 1. Project Y needed to build an army. And they needed people like Jonas to infiltrate "the enemy." Why didn't they want Roni? Roni had a black belt in karate. It was from when he was twelve, but still.

They couldn't know that he was on to them. Roni stood on the toilet seat and used his Swiss army knife to quickly loosen the bolts on the ventilator above his stall. Stepping onto the toilet tank, he lifted himself into the air shaft and onto his belly. He began to shimmy his way forward in the darkness. Roni had done this once before—many years earlier, when he misinterpreted his manager's instructions to build a product in "stealth mode." He knew this shaft would eventually take him to the building's northern corner, where he could safely drop down through another bathroom.

The metal shaft felt cool against his stomach, and Roni moved through it with greater ease than he had remembered. All the apocalypse survival training he had been doing during the weekends was paying off.

But Roni was on edge. He could feel his fingers tingling, hear his heart pumping in the stifling air around him. Project Y was so close! And yet he had nothing but a trail of vague clues. He was following a thread through the dark labyrinth, the derisive laugh of his elusive dragon echoing through the air shafts.

ARSYEN

A rsyen burst into the cubicle, eager to tell Sven and Jonas all about his encounter with the famous Bobby Bonilo. But his co-workers faced their screens in silence. The only acknowledgment of his presence was an open can atop the Red Bull pyramid, which rattled left and right, then plummeted toward the carpet.

"Hello, hello!" boomed a voice from the corridor.

Roni entered the cubicle and made a beeline for the whiteboard. He grabbed an eraser and began wiping away the graffiti. Arsyen breathed a sigh of relief. Finally, they were going to clean.

Instead, Roni motioned for Arsyen to approach.

"I want to tell you about our super-duper top-secret project."

A few years earlier, Anahata unveiled a driverless car that drove itself while the passenger sat, hands free, in the front or back seat. The project gained tons of attention in the press, and even Arsyen had heard of it. But he didn't understand the excitement. His father had invented an equally effective driverless car decades ago in Pyrrhia—royal chariots, entirely voice activated, that traveled on the backs of a pack of corgis imported from England.

Roni said their team had been assigned the next stage of the driverless car project. It was called "Social Car," internal code name: "Pad Thai."

While the passenger relaxed in the car, enjoying a stress-free commute, a console would announce who was sitting in the nearby vehicles. Profile photos of the other passengers would pop up, along with additional information like profession and gender. Passengers could also easily chat and message each other directly through the console.

In short, Anahata was making the car journey a social experience.

"Or as Bobby has put it," Roni said, "we're improving human-kind by eliminating loneliness."

Arsyen wanted to ask why someone wouldn't prefer to just wait to talk to other people at their destination, but he decided that was one of those stupid questions Jennie had warned him not to ask. After all, why would the team build something that wasn't needed?

What worried him more was just how a sanitation engineer fit into the project. From the way Roni described it, Arsyen didn't see any janitorial work needed for Social Car—unless, that is, he was supposed to clean the cars before they launched.

"Roni, what do I clean here?"

"Well, the real dirty work is for them," said Roni, nodding in the direction of Sven and Jonas. "As you know, being a P.M. is more about leading than doing. Your role is mainly to keep things organized, keep everyone focused, and lead the final polishing of the product. You know, the same stuff you did at Galt. But don't worry. I'll take the lead for now, until you have the hang of things."

Sven and Jonas scooted their chairs toward the whiteboard. Arsyen noted the computers on their laps and followed their lead, but the machine balancing on his thighs felt less like a work accessory than the physical weight of his doubt. Roni had said he would be polishing Social Car, but Arsyen had yet to spot a single microfiber cloth or tub of wax. And what was this P.M. title Roni kept referring to—poop manager? Arsyen would draw the line at poop. There were some things a prince should never, ever do.

Roni cleared his throat.

"Okay, guys, to recap: Car A detects someone in Car B. But Car B is traveling at a faster rate than Car A. Do we have Car A automatically speed up—all within say ten miles per hour of the speed limit—so it can keep pace and the Car A and B passengers can speak to each other? We're more likely to have people interacting if their cars can keep pace."

Arsyen frowned. Why were his co-workers talking about car speeds?

"But what if Car B is speeding? And Car A speeds up but then ends up with a speeding ticket?" asked Sven. "That would be bad, unless…" His eyes drifted away from the whiteboard, then snapped back. "Unless, that is, the person in Car B is a woman and she turns out to be really hot. Then, if I'm in Car A, I wouldn't be so angry about the speeding ticket."

"All you care about are girls," Jonas groaned.

"You laugh, but just you wait till puberty hits. Then that'll be all you'll think about."

"Impossible. I am very capable of processing many things simultaneously."

"Well," Roni was saying, "we just make sure that when your car speeds up, it never goes beyond ten miles per hour above the speed limit. That way, you shouldn't get a ticket."

"No, I don't care about *that*," said Sven, shaking his head. "The real problem is how to decide whether the Car B passenger is actually attractive enough for Car A to risk the speeding ticket."

"Ah, got it, got it," said Roni. He turned to the whiteboard and wrote "Attraction Index."

"We'll need to work that into the algorithm, but that shouldn't be hard. We take your profile information, and from your height, weight, and so on, we assign you a wellness score. And then we combine that score with an attractiveness score that will use your photo, measured against the Symmetry Enhancement project."

Roni turned to face the group, and Arsyen noticed an ink spot the size of a baby's fist quickly spreading across his shirt pocket. Roni's white shirt was going to be ruined. Arsyen signaled with his hand.

"Oh, sorry, Arsyen, I should have explained. Symmetry Enhancement is a project we have to make all images on the web look better. That way, the world just looks nicer to people. We mainly use it for low-resolution images—"

"And porn," said Sven, turning to Arsyen. "Did you know that most women's breasts aren't symmetrical? Our tool fixes that."

Roni's face flushed, but he pressed on. "But the cool thing is you can also use Symmetry Enhancement on people's faces. We can calculate how symmetrical your face is, then make adjustments to give it better symmetry. For Social Car, we wouldn't redo your entire face, but we could just do the first part of calculating symmetry, since it's a proxy for attractiveness. That would feed into the algorithm and determine whether the person in the other car is worth the risk associated with speeding. So, if the person is significantly uglier than you, then your car slows down and tries to match up with a new car. But if the person is on par or better looking, then it's all systems go."

"We could eventually monetize the symmetry feature," said Jonas, without looking up from his computer. "For example, we could make you more attractive to other passengers if you paid to have your image adjusted."

Roni stiffened. "Jonas, let's not talk about money. Our goal is to build a great product for our users."

Arsyen was catching bits and pieces of his colleagues' words, but nothing made much sense. Meanwhile, Roni's stain was pushing into new territory, now working its way toward his armpit. But he seemed totally unaware, or if he was aware, he simply didn't care, his hands jumping about as he got increasingly excited about the conversation.

"We combine all these factors—your attractiveness, your healthiness, and so forth—and we create a matching algorithm that puts your car in touch with the people you want to meet—the people you don't mind getting a speeding ticket for." Roni paused. "I guess that means ugly and unhealthy people won't get to talk to anyone, but maybe that's a good thing for society in the long run?"

Roni turned and made a few new marks on the whiteboard, his various lines and symbols now abutting his crude car drawings like primitive weapons.

Arsyen placed his fingers on his temples and moved them in

slow circles, closing his eyes and then reopening them. The black hole on Roni's shirt gaped at Arsyen like the mouth of a hungry Pyrrhian orphan. *Save me, Arsyen!*

"Make them all disappear," he whispered in Pyrrhian. "Make them disappear."

It was a chant that had always proven effective in Pyrrhia. Servants and peasants alike vanished whenever Arsyen issued the command.

He opened his eyes. The problem was still there; dashes and numbers on the board seemed to be converging. And Roni was still talking nonsense.

"Luckily we have our new product manager here... Arsyen? Arsyen?"

Roni was pointing a whiteboard marker in Arsyen's direction.

"Arsyen, why don't you give us a P.M.'s opinion on all this?"

Product manager. So that's what a P.M. was.

Arsyen had heard the title before. There had been product managers at Galt; they worked with the engineers but were somehow different. They seemed to dress slightly better and shower more often than the engineers but were considered less intelligent.

That was about all he knew—that, and the fact that he clearly wasn't a product manager himself. Which meant someone had made a mistake. A big mistake.

They had given him the wrong job.

✸

It all suddenly made sense—the coding test at his interview, the salary that was ten times what he had originally been quoted, the total lack of cleaning supplies in his cubicle.

Arsyen's gaze shifted to Roni's eager face, crossed over to the gibberish-filled whiteboard, then to the skeptical faces of his two co-workers, who had spent the entire day hypnotized by their dark screens. They were both incredibly pale, like their faces had never seen the sun. Because, of course—they were engineers. And he was their product manager. The person who managed the product.

They were going to figure it out and fire him. And if he was fired, he would lose everything—the chance to feed all of those hungry Pyrrhian orphans, the chance to liberate his country from tyranny, the chance to speak to his girlfriend without the aid of an internet chat application. He would be back to cleaning toilets in some startup filled with malodorous men.

There was no other solution—he would just have to fake it. Besides, how hard could it be to be a product manager? For decades, Arsyen had watched his father manage a country. He could certainly manage a bunch of talking cars.

Arsyen sat up tall.

"Be clear on problem," he said.

"Right, right, I should be more specific," Roni nodded. He pointed at his drawing of Car A.

"At this point, my car has detected a cute woman around me. So, my car is going to speed up or slow down to keep pace so that I can talk to her."

"What if woman don't want to be found?" Arsyen asked. He couldn't imagine having such a problem himself, but not all men had his charm.

"You're right, we should consider edge cases," Roni said. "But realistically, what's not to like about this? After all, women love attention."

"We should consider edge cases," repeated Arsyen, not seeing any edge or cases but certain that in this world, as in most, repetition served as effective flattery.

"Let's ask women what they think *after* the beta launch," Roni said. "It would take too much time to do it now, and anyway, there's an increasing body of legit scientific research that demonstrates that women don't ever know what they want. Sound good?"

Arsyen nodded calmly, but inside he was anything but.

"Excuse me, bathroom!" he shouted, and leaped up from his seat, dashing into the men's room across the hall.

He locked himself in one of the stalls and pulled out his phone.

Arsyen looked up "product manager" on the internet and, after a few minutes of reading, felt his confidence return.

There was really no reason to worry. Product managers were apparently in charge of the big picture, deciding why a product was needed, what it would be, and how the company could bring it to life. As one blog post put it:

As a product manager, you are tasked with leading a team and bringing an idea to life. You are the visionary who must direct not just engineers but also marketers, sales teams, lawyers, and others. You are a mini-CEO, the ruler of your product!

"Just like king!" Arsyen shouted to the empty stalls.

Of course, there is one important difference: You have no direct authority over anyone, and you must lead through influence.

"Hmmph, more like queen," Arsyen grumbled. But then he reconsidered: Other than the receptionists, he had yet to meet any women at Anahata. He probably didn't need to worry about being treated like one of them.

Arsyen skimmed a few more blogs, trying to memorize the P.M.'s language—words like "action items," "B2B solutions," and "use cases," and then something mystic called a "roadmap," which as far as Arsyen could tell had little to do with either roads or maps. There was an even greater obsession with "alignment," a concept Arsyen struggled with as his translation app told him that the equivalent word in Pyrrhian was *pokaya*, meaning to place the chicken coop parallel to one's home.

Suddenly there was a banging on the stall door.

"Arsyen? You in there?"

It was Sven.

"Listen, you've been in there long enough. Only senior engineers get to work in the bathroom. Roni has some sort of roadmap question for you, so come on back."

Arsyen washed his hands and returned to the cubicle, armed with new vocabulary.

When Roni asked Arsyen about prioritization, Arsyen asked, "Is this on the roadmap?"

When Sven suggested adding images of attractive women to the car dashboard, Arsyen rubbed his chin.

"Does this align with our strategy?"

When all three looked to him for an opinion in how best to implement Symmetry Enhancement, Arsyen stood and put his hands on his hips.

"Does this align with the strategy on our roadmap?"

No one seemed to notice anything was amiss. If anything, it seemed like product managers just asked questions that other people had to answer.

"Good brainstorm, everyone. Let's break for lunch," Roni said. "Oh, and Arsyen, this is still very confidential, so let's get this whiteboard cleaned off."

Arsyen jumped up and began to wipe the whiteboard clean as Sven and Jonas scooted their chairs back to their desks. Arsyen was pleased that product managers seemed to have some janitorial tasks in their role. Maybe this wouldn't be such a stretch after all.

*

The food in Fried Fred's glistened with the shine of oil, and neon signs blinked to a loud techno beat, suggesting an urgent need to consume the dishes on offer. The Mexican stand, the Chinese buffet, even the salad bar—they all smelled of hot lard. Next to the soda dispenser, a robot butler plucked samples from a six-foot-high pyramid of calamari, popping one into Arsyen's mouth as he walked past.

"So, Arsyennnn," drawled Sven as they sat down, "tell us about yourself. Like, what are your favorite languages?"

"Well, Pyrrhian, of course. But my English not so good."

"Ha ha, very funny. I mean computing languages. You like PHP? What about Ruby?"

"Ruby? Like diamond?"

Sven wrinkled his nose. "It is *not* like Diamond," he said, turning to Jonas. "I bet this guy likes low-level languages. He likes to do his own garbage collection."

"I do not!" Arsyen snapped, and then mumbled, "I mean, I *do* collect my own garbage... here in America."

"All right then, which did you learn first, Linux or Windows?"

Arsyen paused. Windows were clear, transparent, and easy to clean. A Linux was... well, he didn't know. But in this game of one-upmanship, surely the more unfamiliar thing was the most impressive. Much like operating some types of carpet cleaners, operating a Linux was probably a skill that once mastered was then lorded over everyone else.

"Linux," guessed Arsyen.

"Correct," Sven said. He elbowed Jonas next to him. "Don't you want to ask him something?"

Jonas lifted his head and glanced at Arsyen without speaking. Arsyen began to count the number of pimples scattered across his cheeks. He got to about twenty before Jonas opened his mouth.

"What about your first video game?" he asked.

Arsyen grinned. Finally they were speaking his language.

"*League of Legends II*," he said proudly.

His co-workers leaned forward, studying Arsyen like a rare animal.

"But Arsyen," said Jonas, "if I recall correctly—and I always do—*League of Legends II* was only released a few years ago. That means you did not commence playing video games until relatively recently."

"Hmmm... disturbing," Sven said.

"Growing up in Embria, we did not have any electricity in our house," Jonas said. "But from the start, even *I* knew the importance of Nintendo, *Myst*, and the various castles and caverns where a princess could be hidden."

"But I love video games," protested Arsyen, feeling his face burn.

"The point is, you came to gaming very late in life—you never learned the fundamentals," said Sven, wagging his finger.

"My father helped me pick the locks of rich people's houses so that I could play their game systems," said Jonas, his eyes watering. "We were caught, and they cut off his hand."

"You see?!?" Sven said. "People like Jonas' dad almost died so that their sons could have a better future, all while you were out playing hopscotch or some other primitive offline game. You have no sense of history or sacrifice!"

"But I love video games," Arsyen repeated.

"That's not enough," Sven shook his head. "By the time *League of Legends* came around, the world had completely changed. Video games had ceased being platformers. Techno was birthing thousands of deformed children in Europe. In some parts of the world, people were already learning to text, and their thumbs were growing ganglia. People's brains had begun to function differently! You clearly came of age in a different world—one that doesn't know latency or patience."

"I am disappointed by this conversation and am done speaking for now," Jonas said. "Please carry on by yourselves."

He stabbed his fork into his pile of noodles, then began twirling them with great concentration.

Arsyen felt as though he himself were in a video game, his life meter, a flashing red heart, beeping at low levels as he desperately searched for a wizard or magic plant to replenish his strength.

He silently cursed his mother. As a child, Arsyen repeatedly asked her for a video game console, but she refused, claiming the nobility should focus on croquet, not cartoons dancing across a screen. She was lucky the king hadn't allowed Arsyen to send her to the dungeon.

Arsyen breathed deeply and closed his eyes, willing his heartbeat to slow. If he could just keep his P.M. job long enough to become a permanent employee, he could eventually have his army behead Sven and Jonas.

Arsyen lingered over the image of a guillotine snapping Jonas' neck until he felt his pulse steady. He opened his eyes. His co-workers were staring at him, expecting something. Arsyen needed to redirect the conversation—make them do the talking rather than him. He turned toward Sven, who was clearly an easier target than Jonas.

"Roni says you have startup project?"

Sven brightened and reached for a fry on Arsyen's plate. "Two, actually. The first is called Fingerbell. It's like a dumbbell, but on your mobile phone. You try to move an animated weight up the screen by using one finger. With each level, the resistance increases and it gets harder to move the weight."

"But why—"

"Because there's a real obesity problem in this country these days. Fingerbell is about revolutionizing exercise—starting with your fingers."

"How it make money?"

Sven threw up his hands. "What world do you live in, Arsyen? Jonas, are you listening to this?"

Jonas ignored them. He now seemed preoccupied with separating his noodles into individual pods on his plate.

"Here's how it works," said Sven, leaning in. "All you have to do is come up with an idea for a startup, build it, and get users. The important thing is that your users are growing—even better if you can tell everyone your growth is exponential."

"It is rare that anything is truly exponential," said Jonas, suddenly looking up. "Most growth is linear, but then most people are stupid." He lowered his head again.

"Next," said Sven, "a venture capitalist sees all this growth and they start doling out cash like it's candy. You get rich before you've even proven your product can make money. Then a big company like Anahata comes along and buys your startup. Sometimes it's just to acquire your employees—you can make millions of dollars if you just tell people you employ experts in A.I. and machine learning. Computer security, biohacking, and micro-algae are also good areas. Worse comes to worst, you just tell people you're making robots—there isn't a single CEO in the Valley who doesn't get a hard-on over robots.

"Now, if you're really lucky, the company isn't after your employees but your actual product. They want to buy it so they can kill it and keep you from competing with them. That's where you really get into the big money. And, yeah, it kind of sucks that all your hard work and years of no sleep and sex will be destroyed, but hey, you're rich now, and you can go and invest money in things you really care about, like food security cameras or currency for sea animals or—"

"Bikek," said Jonas, looking up. "Bikek is the capital of Embria. It has a temperate climate, and in its surrounding mountains one can grow delicious apples in the winter. Embria boasts a modern railway system, as well as three national highways and—"

"No one wants to hear about the transportation system in your obscure country," said Sven, rolling his eyes.

Jonas scowled, but Arsyen saw an opportunity to score a point with his co-worker.

"Your English good, Jonas," said Arsyen, trying out his Magnanimous Leader smile.

Jonas nodded, his eyes lifting slightly from his tray.

"His English gets better each day," Sven said. "It's like training a machine learning model. Correct him once and he doesn't repeat the mistake."

"That is the goal," Jonas said.

"You come to America for school?" Arsyen asked.

Jonas shook his head, his gaze still fixed on his tray.

"There is a video about it online," interjected Sven. "Basically, Jonas was like a mad-scientist teenager genius working out of his parents' apartment. He built a computer by looking at the stars and calculating from the astrological patterns how he could construct a mainframe."

"Sven…," began Jonas, lifting his head.

"And then there was a documentary filmmaker from the BBC who happened to be in town filming the plight of some rare yak in Bikek. He was staying at the hotel across the street on the day Jonas hooked his computer up and started a fire that nearly burned down his apartment building. Overnight, Jonas became the most famous boy in Embria, and Anahata, which has its Progressa program—"

"Progressa?" asked Arsyen.

"Progressa brings technology to poor people like Jonas," said Sven. "They are begging for food and water, and Progressa shows up with a computer and—"

"That is incorrect," Jonas said. He turned toward Arsyen. "Progressa is the philanthropic branch of Anahata, designed to tackle the world's biggest humanitarian problems."

"And so young Jonas got on a boat—" began Sven.

"An airplane, actually."

"An airplane, and came to the United States of America. Where loving Anahata taught him to program."

"We will not discuss my situation further," Jonas said. "Arsyen, I suggest you ask about Sven's other startup idea if your hope is to have a conversation."

"Oh, yeah," Sven said. "This one's almost as good as Fingerbell. It's gonna make me rich."

He pulled out his mobile phone.

"I wanted to solve a problem that all of us have: getting rid of things we don't want to do. Like, what's one thing you wish someone else could do for you?"

"Kill evil ruler of my country."

"Riiiight," Sven said. "Maybe something a bit more day-to-day?"

"My laundry?" Arsyen offered.

"Great," Sven said. "Now what if I told you I could make that problem disappear with one simple app?"

With an abracadabra flourish of the hand, Sven tapped a button on his phone. The word "Dogtown" emerged, written in light blue across a black background. Underneath, a cartoon dog with a bone in its mouth looked out lovingly from the screen, its tail wagging back and forth.

"We all have problems we don't want to deal with ourselves—like laundry. So what I've done is create an app that helps you outsource *everything*. You list your problem and then send it out into the Dogtown community. Whatever dog—that's what I call our members—wants to do the task, he responds to 'fetch' it for you, and you work out the details. Then you pay him in dog food."

"Dog food?"

"Well, money. On the app, money is called 'dog food.'"

Arsyen liked the idea of outsourcing his battle to reclaim Pyrrhia. Someone else could just go off and do it for him, leaving Arsyen to play video games and hang out in California until Pyrrhia was ready for him. The laundry scenario, however, seemed complicated.

"So, someone come to my apartment, wash my clothes, wait while clothes dry… seem easier for me to do."

"You just need to embrace the concept of outsourcing your life," Sven said. "There may be a few people in your house, but once you accept that they are there to perform a function that ultimately benefits you, they are just there—like moving furniture. I mean, I just used Dogtown a few hours ago, right, Jonas?"

Sven waved a fry below Jonas' nose, and the teenager looked up.

"This morning, Jonas was slurping his Red Bull so loudly I could hear it through my headphones. So I sent out a call on Dogtown to ask someone to take care of it for me. A guy in San Francisco saw my request, I gave him Jonas' email address, and the guy emailed him telling him to shut up. Worked like a charm."

"But he sit next to you. You can just tell him or send him email," Arsyen said.

"I consider myself a pacifist. I don't like conflict."

Arsyen nodded but didn't really understand. Conflict in the

janitor community was always solved through direct conversation. And sometimes mop fights. But never through an app. What kind of person would think it was better to argue over the internet rather than speak directly?

"By receiving an email, I was able to process the information quickly and stop slurping," Jonas said. "If Sven had stopped my work to speak with me, I would have found it quite disrupted."

"Disrup*tive*," Sven corrected.

"Disrup*tive*," Jonas repeated. "Technology is disrup*tive*, but I, Jonas, do not like to be disrup*ted*."

"Very good," Sven said. "Now if we can just tell that brainiac processing center of yours to incorporate some contractions into your English, it will be flawless."

"We have discussed this previously," Jonas sighed. "Contractions are not elegant. Moreover, many times they are grammatically incorrect. I will not have my speech sullied by—" Jonas' eyes caught sight of something in the distance.

"He is here," Jonas whispered.

Sven turned and gasped. "What do you think he will eat?"

"Who?" Arsyen asked.

"Bobby Bonilo," they answered in unison.

Arsyen scanned the entrance and quickly pinpointed the object of their attention, not because the figure was remarkable or distinguished in any way, but rather because the effect of the man's presence was universal. The cafeteria fell silent. Those waiting at the stands of Fried Fred's pushed themselves against the buffet rails to allow ample room for the man to pass. Mouths froze in mid-sentence. Hamburgers were forgotten on their plates.

It was the second time that day Arsyen found himself in the presence of Anahata's elusive founder.

Bobby stopped at the Mexican food stand and surveyed its offerings. He dipped a finger into the guacamole bowl, and the chefs held their breath, waiting for his verdict. Showing no reaction, he then continued on to the sushi bar, then the Asian fusion stand, at one point looking as though he was set to take a dumpling. Then he abruptly turned on his heel and walked three steps to the salad bar. Arsyen could hear Jonas' legs shaking under the table.

Bobby circled the salad bar once clockwise, then stopped and changed direction. Finally, he picked up a bagel, nodded as though in communication with the tub of cream cheese in the buffet, and glided out of Fried Fred's.

As soon as the door closed behind him, the cafeteria exploded in sound.

"Wow, do you know who that was?" Sven asked Arsyen.

Arsyen nodded.

Frankly, he didn't get the fuss. Sure, Bobby Bonilo's story was impressive—he had started Anahata from his college dorm, convinced a rich guy to invest in his idea, and, a few years later, became a trillionaire. But Bobby's physical appearance was utterly ordinary, with a pale, slightly puffy face falling into a neck that connected to the gently disintegrating body of a man approaching middle age. He looked nothing like the pictures Arsyen had seen in magazines. There, Bobby's chiseled face seemed straight out of a cologne ad. He was always dressed in white T-shirts that showed off massive biceps, and in more than one article, a small glow circling the top of his brown, curly hair gave the impression of a celestial aura.

"Everyone so quiet. Do people not talk to him?" Arsyen asked.

"Well, you *can* talk to him. But he speaks in puzzles," Sven said. "Not everyone is capable of understanding him. So, if you're going to talk to him, you just better make sure that what you have to say is really, really smart. Like the smartest thing you've ever said."

"Bobby *is* Anahata," Jonas said. "He created it, built it, runs it. He is a genius. And seeing him here is a momentous occasion. Most of the time he is in Building 1. That is the locked building. It is said, 'No one goes in, and no one comes out.'"

"Though of course they do," Sven jumped in. "But it's really only the senior engineers that are allowed in there. I heard Bobby decided to get rid of all the chairs and desks in Building 1. He said they stopped people from thinking. So everyone works standing up, roaming about and having their thoughts collide in the hallways. It's supposed to encourage innovation and collaboration. And phones—there are desk phones—though of course they are placed on the floor since there are supposedly no desks. Bobby apparently had them installed to encourage people to *speak* to each other."

"I heard that all responses to questions in Building 1 have to start with 'yes,'" Jonas added. "You are not permitted to say no unless you have said yes first, because Bobby believes that if you start from believing things are not possible, nothing will ever be achieved."

"It's one of the ten Anahata commandments," Sven said. "They're like the company's guiding principles. One of them is to always start with the word 'yes.' And the rest, well, there is one about speed, and another about innovation... and putting our users first... oh, and changing the world. We must improve humankind!"

"Humankind?" Arsyen didn't recognize the word. Did Anahata want to make humans be kinder to each other? That sounded like something a silly communist would dream up.

"Bobby believes that with every product, we should be able to ask ourselves what serious world problem we are solving."

Arsyen immediately thought of Moodify and the scores of Anahata products that seemed to exist just to waste time and have fun.

"Really? *Every* product must solve world problem?" he asked.

Jonas shrugged. "That is for the marketing and PR team to figure out. We build the product, and then they communicate to the public how it improves humankind. So, for example, Anahata's search engine..."

"Is democratizing knowledge," said Sven.

"And Anahata ads..."

"Are enabling opportunity for small businesses."

"Anahata Maps..."

"Are making it possible for poor children like Jonas, who have no access to food or clothing, to discover faraway places on the internet."

The men bussed their plates. Outside, the sun was blinding. Arsyen, temporarily disoriented, veered to the left.

"Oh, Arsyen," said Sven in a singsong. "I wouldn't go there if I were you."

Arsyen turned. The path to his left looked exactly the same as the path to his right.

"Going left is always a bad idea," Jonas said.

"But what if I come from—"

"Never ask questions the rest of us know the answer to," Jonas said. "Such inquiries are a sign of weakness unless employed as rhetorical devices, or if, in their pointed framing, they are designed to undercut one's interlocutor."

"Stay close to us, and remember to keep that red badge hidden," Sven said. "Just for this week, of course. No one gets fired after the first week. It's, like, too mean to fire people after they've worked here for a week."

"Yes, Sven and I might form an emotional attachment to you by then, and it might hinder our productivity for us to lose a team member," Jonas said.

He paused, then took a step toward Arsyen.

"To be clear, that attachment has not yet formed."

"Plus," Sven added, "you could steal all of our secrets and take them to a competitor like Galt. Anahata will do anything to keep you from going to Galt."

"In the meantime," said Jonas, "do not go anywhere without us. You are safe while you are with us. That is, unless *we* choose to fire you."

RONI

Roni found himself staring dumbfounded once again at the hairy little man before him. For the past three days, Arsyen had been talking about sponges, complaining about the brand they stocked in the micro-kitchen. "Anahata should disrupt sponges," he was saying. "Align sponges with roadmap."

It was typical product manager speak—big vision statements with little understanding of the technical difficulties. Did Arsyen know just how complex modern sponges had become over the past twenty years?

Whenever Arsyen spoke, Roni just nodded in response. As a technical lead, it was his job to let product managers like Arsyen think he cared about their opinions. Still, Arsyen's opinions often seemed particularly random and difficult to endorse.

"I make manifesto," Arsyen announced to the team that morning. "As good P.M., I know manifesto key to successful product."

He began to read aloud.

Social Car is Anahata technology to eliminate loneliness. Every day we drive somewhere thinking we go somewhere. But really, we go nowhere, because part of journey is lost to us all. That is human part.

By using latest cutting-edge innovation technology, combined with old social networking, Social Car connect you to people in other cars. Thanks to Social Car, you make conversation with them and begin life-long friendship. Because relationship is in cloud, you do not have to worry about catching sex disease or awkward moment where you realize other person is missing arm. The person is real and not real, like your journey, like life.

Roni's brain started to spin. This Arsyen was such a mystery. He spent half his time in the bathroom, and when he did materialize, you couldn't be sure whether you were about to hear the stupidest or most brilliant idea of all time. One moment he was suggesting they attach mops to the wheels of Social Car in order to clean the road while driving, and the next moment he was busting out an amazing product manifesto. It reminded Roni of his first day on the job at Anahata, when Bobby smoked pot with him and the other NASA recruits, dropping some crazy science on them all about unicorns and space elevators. Both sounded totally stupid until you realized Bobby was a genius.

Perhaps Arsyen was also a genius.

If he was, that helped Roni, too: Managing a genius was always a good career move.

"That's pretty deep," Roni said to Arsyen. "Life is like an empty journey unless you have Social Car. It really makes you realize how our technology is changing humankind for the better."

"I had never thought of the one-armed-person use case before," Sven said.

"It is statistically very unlikely that you will meet a one-armed person while driving," Jonas said.

"Maybe in the past, smart-ass," Sven said. "Now that cars don't need drivers, you may see a whole bunch of armless and legless people out on the road."

"But there should also be fewer armless people on the planet since driverless cars are safer. Car accidents cause 8.18 percent of armlessness in the United States," Jonas said.

"But—"

"Guys, guys, let's stay focused," Roni said.

"I also have other idea," Arsyen said. "I think about your problem—classic product management problem. I see problem many times in B2B solutions. I give you example from Pyrrhia social media roadmap. Sometimes when we in countryside, I have boys wash my car. But they lazy. They throw soap on car and then put water on car. But the car not shiny. It because they didn't start at beginning—with water, in the cloud. I tell them, 'Wash car first or I feed you to dogs,' and finally they do it right. It's like… software as a service for internet of things."

Roni frowned. Arsyen's brain was moving too fast for him.

Arsyen turned to the whiteboard and drew a rough sketch of two cars.

"You all talk about what happen with Social Car when you *on* the road," Arsyen said. "But what about *before* you get in car? Start at beginning of problem—not in middle like little Pyrrhian boys. Social Car can tell me who around me now. But what if I can tell Social Car who I want to meet when I first get in car?"

"You mean, program it to take you to an address or someone's house?" Sven asked. "Welcome to the modern world, Arsyen. Cars already have that. It's called a GPS."

"No, this not about taking you to friend's house. It for people and places you *don't* know. Say you want to meet other engineers. Well, Social Car take you to *Star Trek* convention. Or say you want to pitch businessman on your startup. Social Car take you to hotel bar or fancy-person strip club. Then, once cars close together, you can begin conversation with your target."

"I see, I see, so it's a more targeted way to meet new people. Kinda like a business networking tool?" Roni asked.

"Yes," Arsyen nodded. "Business networking tool… in the cloud. Social. B2B. Alignment."

"I beg to differ," said Jonas, looking up from his computer. "You are not describing a business networking tool. This is what one would call a hookup app."

Roni studied the drawing on the whiteboard. It looked like two rectangular men in suits.

"He's right. It's totally about meeting hot girls!" Sven jumped out of his chair and hopped to the whiteboard, grabbing a pen and adding a pair of breasts to the roof of one of Arsyen's cars.

"*Ohhh,*" said Roni, as the idea came to life before him, his businessmen transforming into busty coeds.

"A user inputs into Social Car what he wants in terms of age, gender, and sexuality," Sven explained. "Social Car does the rest. All it has to do is scan the profiles from all the other Social Car–enabled vehicles. And we give them pickup lines to help kick-start the conversation."

"Great idea," grinned Roni, slapping Arsyen on the back.

"Also, I think about woman problem again," Arsyen said. "You know, about woman who not want to be found. I think I have answer: We give her choice to turn off Social Car."

"You mean, let women *choose* whether to let people find her?" Roni asked.

Arsyen nodded.

"Are you crazy!?" Sven cried.

Roni shook his head. How could this be the same employee who had authored that manifesto?

He reached into his backpack and grabbed Arsyen's HR form (damn HR, always wanting him to use paper!). No genius would ever propose listening to users' opinions. As Roni made a little tick on the form, he saw a cloud of worry pass over Arsyen's face.

"If girls get to choose whether to use the feature, then we're only going to have a bunch of dudes on Social Car," Sven explained.

Roni nodded. "People get confused by choice—it's our job to tell them what they want. Besides, you've got three guys in here saying they love it. What other proof do you need?"

But it was clear Arsyen was no longer listening. He was staring at the HR form in Roni's hand, as if worried he had done something wrong. For that alone, Roni made another tick. The fact that Arsyen could even believe he had done something wrong once again indicated his inferiority. Geniuses weren't ever wrong, even when they were.

Which was also why Roni needed to be right about having hired Arsyen.

ARSYEN

Jonas cornered Arsyen later that morning.

"What do you want me to do about those pickup lines?" asked Jonas, standing between Arsyen's desk and the cubicle entrance.

"Pickup lines?"

Arsyen stood. He had learned it was best to minimize his interactions with Jonas. The boy was too smart, always staring just a bit too long and hard when Arsyen spoke about roadmaps and priorities.

He took a step to try to move past him, but Jonas shifted to his left and again blocked Arsyen's path.

"The feature we discussed yesterday," Jonas said, "the one that helps Car A and Car B start a conversation. How should I proceed?"

"Well, I just think we should look at roadmap and—"

"What's your obsession with roadmaps, anyway?" asked Sven, entering the cubicle. "I thought you came from Galt. Since when do startups have a plan or roadmap or really any strategy at all?"

"I, I—"

"So what do you want me to do?" Jonas said.

Arsyen frowned. Why was Jonas suddenly talking so much? And why hadn't he taken care of that enormous pimple on his nose?

"Arsyen?"

"Put it in the cloud," Arsyen said loudly, "NOW." As an afterthought, he put his hands on his hips and sneered slightly, mimicking his father.

Jonas didn't seem to notice Arsyen's power pose. "Something

that is already in the cloud cannot be put in the cloud again," he said.

"We create innovative double double cloud," Arsyen said.

"You are not clear," Jonas said.

Such insolence! Arsyen gripped the sponge in his pocket, imagining he was squeezing Jonas' neck. He slowly released it and felt the tension ease in his shoulders.

"I set up meeting to discuss," he said. "I bring many action items."

"Meetings are where all good things die," Sven groaned. "Let's just figure it out now."

"Must go to bathroom!" Arsyen yelled. He darted past Jonas and out the cubicle, making a beeline for the bathroom a few feet away.

Safe within its blue walls, he took a deep breath and stared at himself in the mirror. The sharp line of his chin jutted outward with authority; his mop-trained muscles nearly intimidated his own reflection.

"You can do this. You *must* do this," Arsyen told himself, making the sign of the red-breasted woodpecker.

He marched over to the cleaning closet, where he found a jute broom and some detergent pods. He decided to spend the rest of the day working on his croquet strokes. After all, if Jonas couldn't find him, he couldn't get mad at him. There was nothing unprincely about avoidance if it was strategic avoidance.

✳

Twenty-four hours later, Arsyen returned to his cubicle and informed Jonas and Sven that he wanted Social Car to change colors depending on the mood of the passenger.

"I also want you to design car so it clean itself. There should be automatic vacuum and air-freshener function."

"Cool, that's, like, robotics," Sven said.

"Yes," said Arsyen, remembering from his online research that adding a robot to one's roadmap was the touch of any good Silicon Valley product manager. "Every car come with broom robot. Robot Broom. Broom Robot. Bro-bot. With robot's deep learning sweeping dirt into neural net."

"*Arrrsyen*," Jonas growled. "You cannot send us in one direction and then another. This is a totally different idea from the hookup feature we discussed two days ago."

"Car color and clean very important to user," said Arsyen, shaking his head.

It was even more important to Arsyen. He had spent the entire night thinking up ways to postpone the team from settling on a clear direction. If he gave the engineers something new to consider, Arsyen wouldn't have to flesh anything out until after his trial period was over. And once he was a permanent employee, he'd have plenty of time to learn how to be a real product manager.

"I want purple and green cars," said Arsyen, invoking the Anahata colors. "Now, sorry, but HR team needs paperwork from me. Back later."

Arsyen made his way to the video game console down the hall, holding his sponge in front of him like an offering. He had discovered that Anahata's engineers let him roam wherever he wanted if he was carrying cleaning supplies, clearly uninterested in firing someone whose work they didn't wish to perform themselves.

He returned late in the afternoon and was relieved to see Jonas transfixed by his screen.

Sven waved but didn't look up. He was studying a bunch of cartoon dogs that were lined up vertically on his phone. Each "dog" had the face of a real human being.

"How Dogtown going?" he asked, hoping to score points with the nicer of his two co-workers.

Sven sighed and explained that he had run into a snag. A local journalist had posted something in praise of Dogtown, and as a result, a few thousand people between San Francisco and the South Bay had downloaded it to their phones. While that should have been reason to celebrate, it instead led to a supply-demand imbalance: There seemed to be far more people who wanted to perform disagreeable tasks than there were people who needed disagreeable tasks to be performed for them.

"There are too many guilty liberals on Dogtown," Sven moaned. "I've essentially got everyone bidding on the same tasks." He showed Arsyen the long list of white faces volunteering to perform menial tasks for people of color. "I tried to get someone to pick up a tub of ice cream for my fake Asian female profile last night, and the bidding war was so intense that I ended up getting it delivered for free. It's even more exaggerated if I use my Latino or African-American profiles. Every white person in San Francisco seems desperate to run errands for free just to prove they're really progressive. They even want me to design badges they can put on their profile pictures to prove to everyone else they're not racist."

"But that a good problem, right? You rework power balance. Fight the Men!" Arsyen cheered.

"I prefer to leave saving the world to Anahata. I just want to create a bidding system for errands. I'll pay you to go pick up my dry cleaning. I don't want to know who you are, what you do, or what you look like. Just pick up my damn dry cleaning."

Just then, Sven's phone rang. His eyes rolled as he picked it up, mouthing "mom" to Arsyen. He muttered a desultory greeting in Swedish as he left the cubicle.

Arsyen heard something move behind him and turned to find Jonas standing there, arms crossed.

"Despite your lack of guidance, I went ahead and programmed part of the hookup feature," said Jonas, pointing to his screen. He had chosen a handful of key attributes to generate the pickup lines—car type, model, color, passenger gender and age. He showed Arsyen a list of computer-generated interactions between Car A and Car B.

I think women in Cadillacs are interesting and compassionate.

I did not know women between the ages of eighteen and twenty-four liked Cadillacs.

Where did you buy your 2015 blue Cadillac ATS? It is the best of affordable luxury.

I want to put my key in your Cadillac.

Arsyen reread the pickup lines. They didn't strike him as particularly compelling.

"Seem okay," Arsyen said.

"Okay?" Jonas said. "I ask you for use cases and you disappear. Then I show you what I have done and that is all you say?"

"You very good at job," Arsyen smiled. "You better than roadmap."

Jonas' face tightened. "You said you were at Galt before this and that you had also worked at Stanford and other startups. Is that correct?'

Arsyen nodded. He noticed that the enormous, pulsing boil from the previous day had heaved its way farther across Jonas' nose.

"I spent last summer memorizing all the computer science professors and students in America's top ten PhD programs. I also memorized the names of everyone in the San Francisco, Palo Alto, Mountain View, and Cupertino phone books in the event I might meet them one day. I do not recall your name from any of these exercises. "

"Maybe you forget name?"

"It is next to impossible that I would have forgotten a name, and even less so, a Pyrrhian one."

Arsyen shrugged.

"What was the name of one of the products you built?"

Arsyen tried to think of his video games and gadgets, or any of the Valley software he had heard about, but instead his head filled with images of his old Stanford broom closet, the supplies under his kitchen sink, the soaps in his bathroom.

"Clorox," he blurted out.

"Clorox?"

"Cloroxy," said Arsyen, scrambling to remember his product management reading. "Young, new, hot startup, Cloroxy. Problem remover. Removes all problems. We get power users. We make API. We use social graph and provide real-time solutions for gamification. Machine learning explosion."

"Arsyen, I know you are lying. In fact, I have proof that you are lying."

Arsyen lowered his head. The game was up.

"I will expose you," Jonas said. "You will not make it past this week."

Arsyen remembered then what his father had said right before surrendering to the Embrian king: It is ignoble to fight an obvious defeat. *Bish lena, bish lena.*

He knelt to grab his backpack, and a piece of paper on the ground caught his eye. It was a blueprint for something unrecognizable, almost like a sea creature, with intricate blue lines intersecting at right angles, forming tentacles radiating from a central oval body.

Arsyen crawled out from under the desk and studied the thin blue paper again in the light. He decided it wasn't an animal but an arm, with fingers extending to the edge of the page. The fingertips were purple and green, just like the Anahata logo.

"Where did you find that?" snapped Jonas, drawing closer. He reached for the paper, but Arsyen swept his hand behind his back. He was keeping this for himself—it was all he had to show for his one week at the greatest company in America.

Jonas' face hardened.

"So this is how you want to play it?" His pimple pulsed with anger.

Arsyen shook his head. One day he would have Jonas decapitated, but for now, there was no point in further conversation. He moved to the side, but Jonas blocked his path.

"You know I know. And I know you know," Jonas said.

Arsyen shifted to the left and again tried to move past him.

"You do not seem to understand." Jonas' scrawny arm executed a surprisingly strong push against Arsyen's shoulder, and he stumbled back into his desk. "You cannot tell anyone about this. This is an incredibly important part of the project."

"The project...," Arsyen repeated Jonas' words, his mind racing to keep up. Jonas was worried Arsyen would say something about... *something*. The blueprint? Social Car?

It didn't matter—this was an opportunity.

"Don't fire me, and I keep your secret safe."

"Fine," said Jonas. "Your incompetence is a small price to pay."

Arsyen clapped his hands.

"Thank you!"

Visions of piles of cash, a new apartment, and long lunches with Jennie filled Arsyen's head.

"We will not discuss this again," Jonas said. "Put the paper on my desk and I will see it is returned to its rightful place."

Jonas stomped back to his computer and threw on his headphones, turning his techno to its highest volume as if to ensure no other thoughts could trespass.

※

Arsyen couldn't make sense of what had happened with Jonas, but he spent the final day of his trial week trying to thank him for what he hoped was his complicity. But Jonas had a funny way of showing his support, muttering "imposter" and "fake" each time Arsyen drew near.

Fearing the worst, Arsyen began to browse job sites for janitorial jobs. None came close to his extraordinary Anahata salary. It would take him decades to save enough money to raise an army and storm the imperial palace. By then, his nemesis, General Korpeko, would be waiting for him in some fancy laser-shooting wheelchair, and Arsyen would be done for before he could even dismount from the only old, decrepit donkey he was able to afford.

A little red icon blinked at the bottom of his computer screen, desperate for his attention. Although he had ignored its persistent signal for days, Arsyen clicked it this time.

It was his Anahata email account.

More than nine hundred messages were waiting for him—from mass email lists to product mocks and notes from Roni. Arsyen didn't know where to start. He opened the message at the top of his inbox:

On the subject of engineers' shoelessness.

He saw that the message had been sent to the random@anahata.com alias, which Jennie had explained was an open forum where anyone in the company could post anything they wanted about any subject that wouldn't fit into the other company lists (of which she said there were about sixty thousand, running the gamut from ana-hatanews@ and bug_testing@ to westernbuddhists@, fatahatas@, tallahatas@, and cafeteria_complaints@). Although the message had been sent at eleven o'clock the previous night, there were already two hundred responses. Arsyen scrolled to the original message that had kicked things off.

```
To: random@anahata.com
From: Chuck Smoop (smoop@anahata.com)
Subject: On the subject of engineers' shoelessness

A plague is upon us, Anahatis! Every time I go to the
cafeteria, I notice an increasing number of barefoot
employees. It doesn't seem to matter to this dirty band
of marauders that they are bringing their foot diseases
close to the food I eat. They seem to revel in this act
as though it were a Dionysian orgy of verucas, fungus,
and foodstuffs.

Do they lack money to buy shoes? Am I punishing the weak
for something they cannot change?
```

No, my friends. They are simply… engineers. It seems the "launch" of shoelessness started as a simple 1 percent rollout, with our engineering friends limiting the cool breeze between their toes to just our cafeterias.

But now, over the past two weeks, these barefoot creatures have taken their practice beyond our hallowed food halls. Now I see bare feet in the bathrooms. I see bare feet in the meeting rooms. I see bare feet in my nightmares. My brain is getting athlete's foot just thinking about it.

Please, engineering colleagues, please can you wear your shoes? It is not so much to ask.
- Chuck

To: smoop@anahata.com, random@anahata.com
From: Charles Chen (cchen@anahata.com)
Subject: Re: On the subject of engineers' shoelessness

Chuck, you seem to be assuming that because your feet are disgusting, everyone else's feet are too. Grow up. My feet are pristine. I would eat off my feet if I were more flexible. It is my right to take my feet where I will, in whatever state I wish them to be.

Smell my feet. They smell like roses.

Charles Chen

To: cchen@anahata.com, smoop@anahata.com, random@anahata.com, hr-all@anahata.com
From: Rob Joobs (joobs@anahata.com)
Subject: Re: On the subject of engineers' shoelessness

I can't believe I work at a company that allows this.

There should be a policy against it. Adding the HR team to this thread to clarify.
- Rob

To: joobs@anahata.com, cchen@anahata.com, smoop@anahata.com, random@anahata.com, hr-all@anahata.com
From: Mahali Chowdhury (mahalic@anahata.com)
Subject: Re: On the subject of engineers' shoelessness

I came to this company because it promised me freedom. And now you bureaucratic, idiot salespeople are trying to take that freedom away from me.

My Anahata contract says I must show up to work at a reasonable hour, perform tasks as described by my manager, and not do various illegal things like pirate software or look at porn on the job. Nowhere in my work contract does it say I am required to wear shoes. I could further build out the argument as to why your logic is ridiculous and explain why this would never legally hold up under current Anahata employee guidelines, but I have too much real work to do and I suspect your brontosaurean sales brains wouldn't understand what I wrote anyway.

Mahali Chowdhury

To: mahalic@anahata.com, joobs@anahata.com, cchen@anahata.com, smoop@anahata.com, random@anahata.com, hr-all@anahata.com, legal-all@anahata.com
From: Susan Jacobs (susanjacobs@Anahata.com)
Subject: Re: On the subject of engineers' shoelessness

+ Legal team so they can tell us whether or not this is legal.

Thanks,
Susan

To: mahalic@anahata.com, joobs@anahata.com, cchen@anahata.com, smoop@anahata.com, random@anahata.com, hr-all@anahata.com, legal-all@anahata.com, recruiting-all@anahata.com, susanjacobs@anahata.com
From: Gerry Manhelmer (manhelmer@anahata.com)
Subject: Re: On the subject of engineers' shoelessness

If you want to complain about bare feet, then I should be able to complain about the different hiring standards used for our sales team. I know for a fact that you all have easier hiring standards than we do in engineering. No matter what your mothers may tell you, you are at best "above average." Adding the recruiting team to this thread to confirm this is true.

One of the great travesties of the past century was not that apartheid occurred. It's that it didn't occur involving the right populations. Salespeople should be quarantined.

Gerry

To: manhelmer@anahata.com, mahalic@anahata.com, joobs@anahata.com, cchen@anahata.com, smoop@anahata.com, random@anahata.com, susanjacobs@anahata.com, hr-all@anahata.com, legal-all@anahata.com, recruiting-all@anahata.com
From: Pete Joffe (pjoffe@anahata.com)
Subject: Re: On the subject of engineers' shoelessness

Speaking of apartheid, I was on safari in South Africa last year, and I remember being taken to a village out in the bush. The villagers had lived in the same place for centuries and knew everything about the world surrounding them. And yet the one thing they didn't understand, and no number of UN officials could convince them of, was that their practice of building their huts with all their livestock in the center posed a serious health risk and was responsible for many of the eye and skin diseases they had contracted. The purpose of the livestock in the center was to protect the animals from lions and other predators, and the villagers believed their sustenance was more important in the end than a worm in their skin.

So the question is do we try to educate our engineers? They are a much more primitive people than those villagers (who also differentiate themselves from our native group here in their abilities to bathe themselves, hold conversations with the opposite sex, play sports, hunt game, and survive in the wild).
- Pete

To: pjoffe@anahata.com, manhelmer@anahata.com, mahalic@anahata.com, joobs@anahata.com, cchen@anahata.com, smoop@anahata.com, susanjacobs@anahata.com, random@anahata.com, hr-all@anahata.com, legal-all@anahata.com, recruiting-all@anahata.com
From: Petra Nichols (petra@anahata.com)
Subject: Re: On the subject of engineers' shoelessness

Pete, can you tell me where you went on safari? I've been wanting to go and am looking for recommendations.

Thanks,
Petra

To: pjoffe@anahata.com, manhelmer@anahata.com, mahalic@
anahata.com, joobs@anahata.com, cchen@anahata.com,
smoop@anahata.com, susanjacobs@anahata.com, random@
anahata.com, hr-all@anahata.com, legal-all@anahata.
com, recruiting-all@anahata.com
From: Tico Yamada (tyamada@anahata.com)
Subject: Re: On the subject of engineers' shoelessness

Pete, I find your email really offensive. I'm adding a
whole bunch of other people to this thread to confirm
my opinion.

Tico

To: tyamada@anahata.com, pjoffe@anahata.com, manhelmer@
anahata.com, mahalic@anahata.com, joobs@anahata.com,
cchen@anahata.com, susanjacobs@anahata.com, smoop@
anahata.com, random@anahata.com, hr-all@anahata.com,
petra@anahata.com, legal-all@anahata.com, recruiting-
all@anahata.com, freespeech@anahata.com, libertarians@
anahata.com, anarchists@anahata.com
From: Gary Truman (gunsandfreedom@anahata.com)

+freespeech@
+libertarians@
+anarchists@

tico — your email is the kind of sentiment that is dragging this company to an early grave and sending our
engineers to galt. you're ready to shoot anyone for ex-
pressing anything that might possibly be construed as offensive. is that how the internet (or anahata) was built?

NO!!

```
the internet was entirely built on offensive content,
porn, conspiracy theories, spam, and gambling.

don't kill what made our company great.
don't kill free speech.
don't kill pete or safaris.
```

✳

The thread continued for hundreds of messages, cutting across racism, poverty, travel tips, sales IQs, and various engineering grosseries, but frequently returning to the issue of bare feet—the battle line falling clearly between sales and engineering. Sales currently seemed to have the upper hand, if only because they woke up earlier. The engineers' ranks wouldn't fill out until noon. This gave sales the chance to pile on the anti-engineer vitriol, with little more than a whimper in response.

Arsyen heard Jonas stirring to his right and turned to discover his co-worker sniffling as he read the same email thread on his computer. Jonas lowered himself in his chair and stretched his legs toward the wall, where his shoes sat unoccupied. Using his toes, he dragged the shoes toward his chair.

"I wasn't made to wear shoes," Jonas whimpered. The boil on his nose sizzled under his tears.

Arsyen felt a sudden flash of pity for Jonas. Even a boy genius needed to know what it was to run in the fields, to wear shoes—or not wear them—to do as he wished. Instead, Jonas had been forced to work in America at age fourteen, doomed to live as a preteen among a bunch of adults who could drink, date, and surf the internet without parental controls.

Arsyen turned his fingers to the keyboard and began to release the poetry that filled his head: a story of injustice, of choices, of freedom, and Pyrrhian military history. But after five minutes, he hit the table with his fist. His English simply could not capture the words that came so naturally in his native tongue. He deleted his message and started again, settling on something much simpler.

```
To: engineering_all@anahata.com, sales_all@anahata.com,
warriorone@anahata.com, thedungeonmaster@anahata.com,
papage@anahata.com, thedude@anahata.com, sevendwarves@
anahata.com, robobo@anahata.com, coolhands@anahata.com,
kapuscinski@anahata.com, ilovejuice@anahata.com, ninjas@
anahata.com, doris@anahata.com, marionetti@anahata.
com, nihilists@anahata.com, tyamada@anahata.com, petra@
anahata.com, romansch_speakers@anahata.com, pjoffe@
anahata.com, furries@anahata.com, manhelmer@anahata.
com, swingers@anahata.com, mahalic@anahata.com, joobs@
anahata.com, swing_dance@anahata.com, cchen@anahata.
com, impressionist_painters@anahata.com, smoop@anahata.
com, gunsandfreedom@anahata.com, libertarians@anahata.
com, anarchists@anahata.com, freespeech@anahata.com,
existentialists@anahata.com, random@anahata.com, hr-
all@anahata.com, legal-all@anahata.com, recruiting-all@
anahata.com, everyone@anahata.com
From: Arsyen Aimo (arsyen@anahata.com)
Subject: Re: On the subject of engineers' shoelessness

Sales team suck.
- Arsyen
```

*

"Hooray, Arsyen!" Jonas cheered, throwing his shoes across the room.

A few minutes later, Arsyen received an email from Roni.

"Awesome response. You're a real Anahati now! And congrats—the team's just spoken. You've made it past the first week!"

A few minutes later, someone from the HR team appeared next to Arsyen's desk to hand him his permanent badge.

Arsyen floated through the rest of the day. He walked taller down the corridors and lingered crossing the lawn, flicking his new white badge as he walked, no longer afraid of any passing engineer. He even tried his hand at firing a red badge–carrying newbie, which was even more delightful than he had anticipated.

At home that night, Arsyen cradled the badge in his hand and spoke to it of handmaidens and orphans and all the wonderful things he would one day do for his country. And also which video games he would buy.

Above the profile photo, Arsyen drew a pointy crown on his head in thick black marker.

It was just like being a real prince again.

GREGOR

Gregor Guntlag moved across his office in efficient strides, enjoying the precise cadence of his combat boots thumping against the floor. From crew cut to coccyx, his spine descended in a long, straight line that leaned forward, diagonal to the floor, as though in constant battle with gravity.

At the moment, however, Gregor's problem was less physics than numbers. Ugly, unsettling numbers. While few people on the Anahata campus knew of its existence, Gregor's top-secret Project Y was the only endeavor that now mattered at the company. Everything else was an afterthought; a blip in the company's glorious ten-year history. Were the project to fail, it would mean the end of Anahata. A victory, on the other hand, would ensure the success of Anahata, the web, and all things good for decades to come. It would be Gregor's finest achievement, the greatest project to which he had ever put his name. He could not allow it to fail.

Yet by the numbers, it *was* failing, and not for any of the predictable reasons that often plagued brilliant Anahata ideas—an inability to find willing commercial partners, or criticism that Anahata was violating some silly law. Such problems, governed as they were by ignorance and reactionaries, were far outside Gregor's control. In fact, his current inability to limit these kinds of interference was one of the main reasons Gregor found Project Y so exhilarating. If it succeeded, he would be able to protect his engineers from the ignorant masses, letting them build and create their dreams unencumbered. There would be no more defections to Galt, no more debates in the media about Anahata's relevance. Project Y would definitively establish Anahata as the most innovative company in the world, ever.

Gregor often found himself wondering what would have become of him had Anahata or Project Y existed in his early days as an engineer, when he first landed on the shores of Baltimore, fresh from the University of Liechtenstein, his head filled with ideas for space elevators and floating castles.

His first major undertaking tackled the many lies and inaccuracies on the internet by using software that automatically corrected inaccurate opinions, comments, and blog posts. But the service never found any mainstream appeal—as one venture capitalist told him, "The internet wasn't built for facts."

Next, he embarked on a project to replace the planet's slavery cages (or zoos, as they were also known) with robotic animal sanctuaries. After four years of working out of his one-room apartment in San Diego, surviving on little more than instant noodles and bananas, Gregor was forced to admit defeat.

But it was there in San Diego, standing next to a dumpster, ready to trash his metal monkey parts, that he met Bobby Bonilo. The future Anahata founder tossed him a quarter, thinking Gregor was homeless. But then Bobby saw the wires sprouting from the monkey's tail in Gregor's hand, took in the faded computing slogan on his T-shirt, and in a split second seemed to understand all of Gregor's dreams—and their crushing defeat at the cruel hand of pragmatism.

Bobby had been the first to recognize Gregor's genius. "Humans cling to the past. They will work tirelessly to destroy the most important advances of society," he had said. "As a visionary, you must know that your ideas are ahead of their time. They must only come to light when the world is ready for them—or when you have too much power to be stopped."

Project Y was just that—beyond its time, beyond any earthly concept of innovation. By that measure alone it would have failed in a normal environment. But Anahata now had what Gregor then lacked: boundless capital, a deep pool of engineering talent, and the power of a large country. Moreover, there was no public opinion standing in the way of Y. Its secrecy had been closely guarded, and Gregor was determined to keep its existence quiet until it was too late to be stopped.

Instead, the hurdle Gregor now found before him was a far more potent nemesis: the devil himself, Niels Smeardon, breathing fire and online advertising in the path of Gregor's engineering team.

Niels was the reason two Project Y product managers had come to Gregor's office that afternoon.

"For the past week, we've literally been twiddling our thumbs," one said. "Every step we take is blocked by sales. We go left, there they are. We go right, there they are."

"And why can't you dart around them?" said Gregor, annoyed by the metaphor and his part in it.

"For example, we're ready to run a simulation of Y at Shanley Field. But sales has the field all booked up for the next six weeks with various internal conferences—"

"Motivational Go! Fight! Sell! conferences. Conferences… with Powerpoint," spat the other product manager.

"Also, we need to be able to turn off advertising in one part of the world to free up some servers for Y testing. It would just be a low-volume region that we'd turn off, like Eastern Africa, but sales refuses. I was told it was escalated to Niels and he stopped the whole thing, saying the entire world deserves to benefit from Anahata advertising and that under no condition should Eastern Africa not receive our glorious ads for even a single day."

Gregor snorted. He looked out onto the field below his office, where a group of sales employees were playing rugby. These were the men who sold Anahata's internet ads—pithy phrases and punchy slogans advertising cruise ships and cancer treatments. They believed in dress shirts and strip clubs and golf and triathlons. He was sure he could see Niels among them, dressed in one of his shiny custom jerseys, kicking up mud clods simply to remind the earth of his dominance.

"I will fix the Niels problem," said Gregor, steadying his voice and watching Niels' spiky blond hair attack the sky as he ran down the field. The two product managers would never have guessed that Gregor's body was raging inside, his blood cells taking up arms, their spears pricking the subcutaneous layer of his skin, ready to fight.

"Anything else?" he asked, turning to the two men.

"Things are still very quiet in the rest of the engineering community. The distractions have worked really well."

Gregor nodded. When planning Project Y, he and Bobby had devised a list of "distractions"—projects like Social Car and Genie—that if leaked would capture internal, public, and media attention and let the Y engineers continue to work in secrecy on the company's big bet.

"Go back to work, and don't worry about this anymore."

The duo left smiling.

Gregor remained by the window, watching the field. To any other observer, Niels might have seemed the ultimate captain, rallying his team to the win, throwing slaps and high-fives. But it was all an act. Niels was a man willing to knock down anyone who got in his way. Gregor had kept Project Y a secret from him for this very reason. Niels would destroy it for the very fact that it was Gregor's baby. And if Niels succeeded in sabotaging Y, it would be the end of everything.

The problem was that Gregor had no power over Niels. They were equals, if not in brain power, then at least according to Anahata's organizational chart. Only Bobby could tell Niels what to do. And while Gregor and Bobby dreamed up the idea for Project Y together, the founder had since taken a step back, tasking Gregor with making it a reality. This would have been fine were it not for the fact that Bobby seemed to have a weird affection for Niels, never suggesting that he really liked the guy, but also taking care to protect him from Gregor. He had even heard that Bobby and Niels occasionally did yoga together.

Gregor paced his office, Niels' gravelly voice and sales aphorisms trailing behind him: "With courage comes determination." "Leadership is knowing when to lead." "Those who win are those who win." He caught sight again of Niels on the field, this time tripping an oncoming opponent, the stunned player falling to the ground. Niels was halfway down the field before the man could even lift his face from the dirt.

Gregor needed Bobby's help to get past Niels for good. It wasn't simply a matter of getting a server or access to the field. Gregor needed Niels out of the picture, completely won over to the idea of Y, or contained so that he couldn't thwart it.

He opened his messenger service. Bobby had said he would be busy much of the day at a colonics retreat but in fact seemed to be online.

Gregor: *We need to talk about Y. It's behind schedule. There are roadblocks.*

Bobby: *You should come to colonics retreat. Good for removing roadblocks.*

Gregor: *These are sales roadblocks.*

Bobby: *Flush out roadblocks.*

Gregor: *Do I have your permission to do whatever it takes?*

Bobby: *Small things cloud the big ideas, threaten rain. At retreat now. Can't talk.*

Bobby's online indicator switched off.

Gregor sighed and leaned back in his chair. He stared out the window for a long time without moving, the sky above him clouding with dark thoughts.

＊

The four leaders of Gregor's "distractions" projects were all long-time Anahatis. Any one of them could be trusted to help recruit the army of engineers Bobby had requested.

Which is how Gregor ended up in one of the company parking lots, the key to a driverless car in his hand. Nose upturned, he held the car key several inches away from his body. He believed keys were an outdated method of accessing one's property, which was why he had an engineering team working on a simple identification solution that would require just a small incision in an individual's pinky.

Gregor unlocked the door and settled into the front seat.

An unfamiliar *beep boop beep* came from the dashboard, and five red lights flashed in the center console as the Social Car software booted up. Soon, the dashboard glowed Hal-like in the early light of evening.

"Welcome to Social Car," a female voice said. The dashboard flashed again, and Gregor was presented with a series of options on a large screen in the center console:

```
I want to meet…
- man [specify age]
- woman [specify age]
- programmer [specify which languages]
- designer
- venture capitalist
- engineers
- other
```

Why would he want to meet someone?

"Other," Gregor muttered.

Two faces, numbered "1" and "2," popped up on the screen. Gregor didn't recognize them but assumed they were the pictures of Social Car team members.

"Number 1," he said.

"Sven Svensson is a quarter-mile away," the voice said. "Shall I read you his profile?"

Gregor had no interest in getting to know his employees. The better he knew them, the harder it was to eventually fire them.

"Just drive me to Technology Way."

"Driving to Technology Way," the woman's voice confirmed.

After yielding to two other cars, Anahata's driverless car made its way out of the parking lot.

"There are three people near you now," the voice said as the car turned onto Processor Street.

Gregor's eyes flicked to the dashboard. Now a third, more familiar face stared back at him. He recognized Roni Herman, the team lead. Roni was a bit past his prime, already in his early thirties, but still a well-liked figure on campus. In reviewing the distraction projects and their leaders that morning, Gregor had thought Roni could be an interesting candidate to join the Project Y team.

"Take me to Roni Herman."

The software beeped its assent, and a few minutes later, Gregor's car pulled alongside Roni's.

"Speak to Roni," Gregor said. The dashboard beeped and a moment later confirmed that Roni had accepted the communication.

"Hello, Gregor, hello!" Roni's eager, nasal voice filled Gregor's car. "How do you like Pad Thai?"

"What?" Gregor never ate Thai food. He didn't like the feeling of spice running through his body, raising his body temperature.

"You know, *Pad... Thai*," Roni repeated. Gregor glanced over at Roni's car, which was keeping perfect pace with his own. Roni climbed into the back of his car, searching for something. A moment later, he put a piece of paper against the window. On it was written in big black letters: "PAD THAI=SOCIAL CAR CODE NAME."

"What would happen if I were to pull you off Social Car?" Gregor asked.

Roni didn't answer immediately. Although Gregor refused to make eye contact, he imagined Roni was panicking, afraid he was about to be kicked off his project. Although Gregor volunteered at a community garden, gave millions each year to humanitarian crisis organizations, and voted only for socialists, he did like to cause a bit of microsuffering now and then. He felt it kept the engineers on their toes.

"Oh, well, you know, I don't know how things would go if I came off it," said Roni, the panic painted across his face in bold pinkish strokes. "I've really led the team from the start and—"

Gregor frowned. In a company where sales strutted with their chins to the clouds, Gregor preferred the men who slouched. Roni could at least display a bit of faux humility.

"Slow down," Gregor told his car. He'd ditch Roni and go talk to the Genie team lead instead.

But Roni's car slowed to keep pace with Gregor's.

"Pretty great, right?" Roni said. "That's the speed-detection system we built this week. You can try to slow down, but my car will slow with yours so we can keep chatting. We've still got some bugs to work out, but I'm confident we'll launch before the end of the quarter."

What?!

The end of the quarter was far too soon for a Social Car launch. Gregor needed all of his distractions running up until Project Y was ready. He couldn't kill this project—it was too well known and popular on campus—but he certainly couldn't let it launch anytime soon. He needed to slow it down—like by removing Roni from Social Car and making him his Y evangelist. Gregor inhaled deeply.

"Have you heard of Project Y?" he asked.

Roni gasped. "I've heard... things, you know, but not all the details."

"It's our best shot at building the world's greatest company. And the most important thing right now is for us to have strong leaders. People who can motivate others. People who can help articulate a vision."

Out of the corner of his eye, Gregor saw Roni bouncing in his seat. "At many times during my career I've shown leadership and created visions and—"

"Your vision isn't required," Gregor said. "What you'll need to do is spread the word, win people over, recruit new team members—and eventually spread the project to all of Anahata's engineers."

"I organize the quarterly hackathon," Roni said. "We now have 2,000 Anahata engineers around the world who code the entire weekend over a livestream feed in exchange for beer."

"That's what we're looking for," Gregor said. "It's a big job. It's historic. I need you to move over to Building 1 ASAP."

"Building 1? Oh, yes! I won't let you down!"

Gregor gave a small nod from his car.

"Oh, oh, one thing," Roni said. "What do you want me to do about Pad Thai? Will you find a new leader for it?"

"I'll find someone new. Don't tell anyone where you are going or what you are working on."

"I'll get going right away!" Roni waved as his car turned and sped back toward campus. Soon he disappeared from Gregor's dashboard altogether.

"Take me to Innovation Drive," Gregor told his car.

As the car reversed course, Gregor contemplated how best to hinder Social Car. Putting a new technical lead on the project would undoubtedly slow it down. But he needed to throw a real wrench in the works, not simply lose a few weeks' time as someone new got up to speed.

Gregor continued to wrestle with the problem as his car made its way down El Camino Real, a street that stretched the length of Silicon Valley in an endless loop of Mexican restaurants (Casa Fiesta, Casa Grande, Casa Lupe), energy-efficient cars, and boxy computer stores. Gregor found the relentless monotony and disinterested aesthetics pleasing.

The car passed under a billboard for Mr. Fixit, a local computer-repair service. Gregor glanced up at the tongue-in-cheek, 1950s-style image of a desperate housewife ripping her hair out as a confident Mr. Fixit repaired her computer and saved the day.

Gregor rolled down the window and craned his neck to see the ad. He ordered his car to do a U-turn. The car drove past the sign again, and then once more.

By the time he passed the sign for the third time, Gregor had the answer to his problem.

"Take me back to Anahata," he said, "and drop me off at the lobby."

THE SECURITY TEAM

The next morning, Gregor found himself in a place he rarely visited: the campus security control room, in Building 28. Row after row of TV screens circled the room. Below them, men in matching purple polo shirts manned a dashboard of flashing red lights.

It appeared high-tech, but the reality was more a panopticon of the banal. On one screen, a sales employee pulled his Porsche into the Anahata parking lot, straightening his tie in the reflection of the car window. Above him, two women did yoga on the lawn. On another screen, an aerial shot captured cubicle after cubicle of workers staring at their computers.

The cameras recorded this routine and hundreds like it each day. It was a wonder that they could even keep their lenses open on alert given how mind-numbingly boring Anahata's security scene was, particularly during the night shift. In the wee hours of morning, nothing went into Anahata and nothing came out—minus the occasional nocturnal engineer. Otherwise the place was locked down with the tightest security in the Valley. There hadn't been an attempted theft in more than five years.

But that morning, there had been a break-in at Building 1—the highest-security spot on Anahata's campus—prompting Gregor to dash out of the management meeting and make a beeline for the security office.

Footage from three a.m. showed a man dressed entirely in black sneaking across the Building 1 parking lot, hovering on tiptoe like a thuggish ballerina. He jumped behind a tree, rolled through the grass, and ended up at the building's side entrance, where he pulled out an Anahata badge that had likely been swiped from a negligent engineer.

The man again raised the stolen badge to the access control reader, and for a second, the camera caught a shot of his face. He was Caucasian but looked more like a zebra, with black zigzags painted across his face.

Inside, he went past the molecular lab, the welding shop, the hard-hat zone, and the physical and intangible infrastructure teams, and then stopped in front of another office.

The man darted his flashlight around the room, splashing the walls with light. It was difficult to make out what he was doing, but from the shadows it seemed he had stopped in front of a desk and was pulling something out of his bag. The flashlight swung again. Suddenly, the scene was illuminated: The man was plugging a computer into a wall outlet.

"Galt!" Gregor gasped. This was nothing less than corporate espionage. The thief was going to plant something—maybe surveillance equipment or tampered data—then use it to gain access to all of Anahata's network.

Then the thief sat down and put his feet up on the desk.

"Wait… what is he doing?" asked Gregor, crouching to put himself at eye level with the screen.

"Sir, after watching this many times, I've come to the conclusion that he is picking his nose," said one of the guards, freezing the tape for a moment to show the faint outline of a finger moving toward the man's face.

"What?" Gregor drew even closer, his face now just inches from the screen. He signaled to the guard to continue the footage.

The thief jumped up from the chair and turned off his flashlight. Within thirty seconds, he had crept out the back exit, barrel-rolled across the parking lot, unlocked a car, and driven off. One of the guards rewound the footage and froze it on the last full shot of the man's face, little more than a black-and-white blur.

Although the security team had already watched the tape thirty times that morning, their collective adrenaline rose as they watched Gregor's face for a reaction. They hadn't seen this much excitement since an engineer's pet boa had gotten loose on campus the previous month.

"Whose badge did he use to break in?" Gregor said finally.

The security head double-checked a pad of paper on the desk. "Someone named Roni Herman, who works in Building 7. As of yesterday, Roni Herman's badge was cleared for access to Building 1. The perpetrator was probably tracking Roni the whole time, somehow got hold of his badge, and then got access to both buildings. This was probably the result of months of tracking and shadowing his movements. Should we call the police?"

Gregor stared at the face frozen on the screen, a black zigzag casting a lightning bolt from the man's forehead to his neck. "Idiot," he muttered, staring at Roni's face on the screen.

Gregor stood.

"Idiots," he said loudly, looking at the security team. "There is no need to call anyone."

He turned on his heel and clomped out the door.

The security team looked at each other and shrugged.

"Man, I will never understand engineers," said one, shaking his head before switching his attention to the cameras trained on the well-endowed girls in the customer support department.

NIELS

Niels began each day with a run. The Northern California air was just crisp enough to feel clean and pure, and the occasional headwind produced a surmountable challenge—the kind of easy and achievable goal-setting that Niels liked for warming up to his workday. He followed his workout with a long shower, the rainforest setting gently splattering purified water on his head while a speaker piped in a soothing recording of a woman's voice appraising each inch of his body.

Your muscles are so big.

Your abs are very flat.

Your Adam's apple is prominent but tasteful.

But that morning, Niels could focus only on Gregor Guntlag. The overly German German had hated him since day one and seemed intent on turning Bobby against him.

Bobby and Gregor were both nutjobs as far as Niels was concerned, but he was used to working with crazies. Fifteen years of working in the Valley and he had never worked for a CEO or founder who wasn't a sociopath or narcissist. They thought the world's problems existed in part to keep them intellectually stimulated, and that all those problems—malaria, corruption, congressional deadlock, death, you name it—could be solved by technologists. Their lack of focus was confused for genius. One moment they would be asking the entire company to dramatically change course, and the next moment they'd be giving equal attention to the color of the lampshades in the lobby. And despite their staunch atheism, they all believed their success was somehow mythically predestined.

It was an absurd worldview, but one that Niels admired for its selfishness. Managing and manipulating these egomaniacs was an art he felt he had perfected.

With persistence and patience, Niels had worked on Bobby for six years, helping him understand that Anahata needed money to be successful and that Niels was the best lever he had to produce it in large quantities. As a result, Bobby generally left him alone. Gregor, on the other hand, had been less susceptible to Niels' charm. He did everything he could to sabotage Niels, always playing the contrarian in any management meeting and sending out his engineering lackeys to turn off a sales production task here and there. It was nothing sufficiently significant to warrant an outcry to Bobby, but just enough to annoy Niels and make clear that Gregor and his foot soldiers were behind the job.

So Niels was surprised by the peace offering that had appeared the previous night in the form of a blue chat bubble on his phone—a chat message asking Gregor to come over to "work things out and bury the hatchet."

It was a shocking olive branch from Anahata's head engineer, and in retrospect, Niels realized he should have taken a screenshot of their exchange. Unfortunately, since Anahata chats were not stored (the result of Gregor and Bobby's joint paranoia about government surveillance), this historic exchange of civilities would have no record.

After an evening spent trying to discern Gregor's motives, Niels had finally replied that, yes, of course he'd be happy to talk. But the whole thing smelled fishy. Perhaps Gregor wanted something that belonged to sales. If that was the case, it meant that Niels had already achieved Master Negotiator Rule #1: *Always* have the upper hand. (Viewing even the most casual encounters as an opportunity for personal gain was key to Niels' life philosophy. An ex-girlfriend had once accused him of dealing with their relationship like a business negotiation. Niels said he didn't understand how she could possibly think that anything in life was *not* a negotiation. He came away triumphant, although the woman did break up with him shortly thereafter.)

Niels was confident he could work the meeting to his advantage. In fact, this could be the opening he needed to get Gregor to agree to put ads on Moodify bracelets.

In any other company, the management team would have salivated over the Moodify bracelets, with one billion dollars in projected profit in the first year alone. But not Gregor Guntlag, whose perennial argument against anything Niels wanted was that it wouldn't be good for Anahata users. Niels believed that *not* giving people advertisements was bad. If they didn't know something existed, how could they know they needed it? Only advertising could tell people what they needed to need.

Typically, Bobby hadn't even listened to the discussion. He caught just the tail end of Gregor's rebuttal and seemed to defer the decision indefinitely with a wave of his hands. If you asked Niels, Bobby gave his head engineer far too much rope. Gregor was holding the company back from billions of additional revenue. And what did he do to make up for it? As far as Niels could tell, Gregor was simply there to execute Bobby's big ideas. All of Gregor's own projects had been massive failures. He was good at implementation but had no vision of his own.

Niels stepped out of the shower and surveyed himself in the bathroom mirror. He was forty-two but didn't show a single gray hair or wrinkle. By almost any measure, he was the picture of excellence in aging. He gave a quick, indulgent flex of his muscle and a flash of bleached teeth. He remembered that the Anahata employee he banged a few weeks back had commented on his nice smile. He racked his brain for a split second, trying to remember her name. She was that sexy hippie receptionist who kept asking him for career advice as he tried to take her clothes off. Janine. Jane. Jennie. It didn't matter. It was probably a bit stupid to hit on someone who worked at Anahata, but he wasn't going to worry about it. He always could have her fired if things got uncomfortable. So far, he hadn't even run into her on campus.

Niels threw on his favorite Prada slacks—the ones he wore to close a deal—and finished getting dressed for work. He took a final look in the mirror and flashed his teeth. Never underestimate the power of a killer grin.

※

Master Negotiator Rule #36: Arriving a few minutes late to a meeting communicates dominance. *You* will wait for *me*. Punctuality is for the meek.

And so, despite having changed his outfit three times—should he go business casual? slouchy engineer? weekend triathlete?—then having spent two hours circling Gregor's neighborhood, Niels made sure not to appear at Gregor's doorstep even a minute early.

Three minutes after the appointed time, Niels arrived at the address and did a double take. He checked the house number again: 414 Tuscany Drive. This was it.

Before him was an immense silver gate—the kind of gate that only the truly rich, and truly paranoid, possessed.

Niels pushed a button on the intercom. Someone picked up, but instead of a "hello" there was simply a buzzing sound, followed by the slow opening of the gate, revealing a long driveway abutted by row after row of towering pines.

On some level, it made sense to Niels that Gregor would live in the wealthiest neighborhood in Atherton, itself the wealthiest city in the Valley. He was, after all, one of the earliest employees at Anahata and had made billions of dollars when the company went public. But Gregor was also the man who wore faded decades-old shirts every day, ate the same bland lentils at every lunch, and drove a beat-up Jeep to work. Niels had assumed he'd eschew a fancy house and live in austerity in a small condo in crime-ridden East Palo Alto, or perhaps an inconspicuous cottage in the slightly smelly, middle-class part of Mountain View. Anything but the estate that was emerging before Niels' eyes—a sprawling mansion the style of which Niels could only describe as nouveau-chateau, and whose inhabitants Niels would ordinarily assume to be a transplanted Texas blonde and her bejeweled poodle.

The house was ostentation at its American best, its climbing spires and ornate Mediterranean palacio flourishes the odd manifestation of new money's dream of old Europe. At the end of the driveway was a large marble fountain—six white swans spouting water onto a central lily pad. Rising up behind the fountain was a large marble staircase that led to the front door. Two long, peach-colored wings branched out from the entrance, each ending in a tall, Rapunzel-like tower.

Gregor was waiting for him at the top of the marble steps, dressed in his typical uniform of white T-shirt, khaki pants, and combat boots. In his hand he held two beers, one of which was immediately thrust at Niels, as if Gregor was following a textbook instruction on how to relate to American men. The beer was warm, likely pulled from the pantry just minutes before. Even if this was all just a plot to get something out of him, at least the guy was making an effort. And in any case, it was kind of fun to witness Gregor's visible discomfort in his role as host.

If the garish exterior of Gregor's palace had thrown Niels' preconceptions, the interior only reaffirmed them. Once inside, Niels could see nothing in the house beyond white walls and a single overhead light in each room. The few windows in existence were so high up from the floor that they reminded Niels of a cathedral... or a prison. There was no artwork, no photographs, no sign of a woman, pet, plant, or any possible sign of life.

"You're not one for decorating, are you?" said Niels, turning to Gregor with a smile designed to communicate friendliness.

"I like simplicity," Gregor said. "I don't really like... *things.*" The word lingered in the air between them.

"Except for an enormous house," Niels smirked.

"I only bought a large house so as to have a strong fortress in the event of an anthropogenic risk," Gregor replied.

"An anthropo-what?"

"Hostile artificial intelligence, nuclear holocaust, fossil energy exhaustion, the collapse of everything."

"Ha ha... oh..."

Niels stifled his laugh; Gregor wasn't kidding. The engineer's face was as smooth as his walls, giving up nothing. He seemed to be staring at an imaginary spot just past Niels' shoulder, avoiding eye contact.

"You like wine," Gregor said.

"I do."

"Fischer said you took him on a wine tasting in Napa a few years ago."

"I didn't know you liked wine," Niels said. "I would've invited you along."

"No, you wouldn't have," Gregor said. "And if you had, I would have said no. We aren't friends."

Niels coughed. Being a salesman, he wasn't used to such direct displays of honesty.

Gregor's eyes briefly flicked away from the wall, settling on Niels' shoulders. "Do you want to see my wine cellar?"

Gregor led him down a white hall and through a massive, empty kitchen, at the far end of which was a wide, floor-to-ceiling steel door. Gregor pushed a button, and the door slowly slid into the wall, revealing a flight of stairs leading into darkness. In the seconds before their descent, Niels recalled an article he once read in a tech magazine, in which a successful Valley engineer kept a dungeon underneath his home, holding secret orgies while his nuclear family, clothed in matching pastel cottons, lived happily and unknowingly in the rooms upstairs.

But when Gregor turned on the lights, the illuminated space below revealed nothing more than a simple wine cellar, with row after row of bottle racks, and in the center, two chairs and a wooden table.

Atop the table was a decanter filled with wine, and next to it, an empty bottle.

Instead of a toast, Gregor spent thirty minutes detailing each wine purchase in length: how much it had cost, what was said about the vintage, and when he was planning to open a particular bottle. He had built an elaborate wine management system that scanned the bottle's label, then input each detail—including age, composition, and position in the wine cellar—into an algorithm that determined the ideal "drink date." When the date approached, Gregor was sent a notification at two-week, one-week, day-of, and then hourly intervals, alerting him of the impending deadline.

"One time I received a notification while on a course of antibiotics," said Gregor, leaning in just slightly and lowering his voice. "I had this bottle I needed to drink and was worried it was going to go bad. I had to save it until I was well again. It was very upsetting."

"You don't have to drink the bottle right that very same day. It's not like milk."

"But then I would get no benefit from such a complex system," Gregor said.

He grabbed the bottle of wine from the wooden table and passed it to Niels, who let out a low whistle of appreciation. It was a Chateau Margaux—the holy grail of red wine. Niels couldn't help but grin. He was going to crush his enemy at the negotiating table while trying one of the world's most highly regarded wines.

Niels believed that learning to appreciate wine was an apprenticeship akin to golf—at first difficult to acquire, but then indispensable for business and generally agreeable as a pastime. And he had, in fact, come to love the taste of it. Chateau Margaux was a real bragging right, and he had never held its deep ruby on his tongue.

Niels sat down on an uncomfortable wooden chair. One of the spindles was split in the middle, and the raw edge pushed into his spine. He suspected Gregor had never been inside a home furnishings store in his life, that he didn't see the inconsistency in offering up one of the world's most expensive wines in such a dank and uncomfortable setting. For all his engineering brilliance, Gregor would never even have made it past the sales team's entry-level "Hospitality & Negotiation" training course.

Gregor poured the wine from the decanter and handed a glass to Niels. The men studied the wine and took in the aroma, each eying the other over his glass.

But the deep tones of the Chateau Margaux transformed them. Niels loosened his tie, Gregor slouched just slightly in his chair. It was an exceptional wine. And after they took their first sip, Niels had the sudden realization that this was the first nondisagreeable experience the two had shared since Niels joined Anahata six years earlier. Gregor even tried to offer a slight smile, pushing it onto his face as though it were a heavy wooden beam. But at least he was trying.

Niels did not say a word—Master Negotiator Rule #33: Approach silence like a battlefield. He who speaks first shows his hand.

Niels sipped his wine slowly but decisively. He imagined his Adam's apple bulging then receding, like a heaving warrior ready to break through enemy lines. A warrior with rippling abs and a weathered loincloth that barely covered his forceful manhood. He could crush this wine glass with just a slight clenching of his fingers. It would shatter at his feet, taking with it all of Gregor's dreams and—

"Do you read any philosophy?" Gregor asked.

"Not really," Niels said. "I mean, college, but that was a long time ago."

"I thought so," said Gregor.

Niels wanted to tell Gregor that he had graduated summa cum laude in economics from Yale, that he had been a Rhodes scholar, that he had won a Cambridge debate on the virtues of Adam Smith—but he held back. It was best to let the conversation advance smoothly toward the negotiation point.

"For centuries," Gregor began, "people have tried to create the perfect society. To achieve what we see flickering on Plato's cave. To transpose the ideal on our reality."

Niels imagined Gregor sitting on his white couch, within his white walls, reading Greek philosophers after a hard day's work.

"Many people have tried to create a community of like-minded individuals, with the aim of a peaceful and collaborative rule—a utopia, if you will. You may recall the Rappites...?"

Niels didn't.

"Or the Oneida community."

Again, Niels drew a blank.

"In any case," Gregor said, "all of these attempts ultimately failed."

"We weren't made to live on communes," Niels shrugged. "People are fundamentally selfish."

"Or... perhaps it's just a few bad seeds."

"A few bad seeds are enough to ruin the crop."

"Yes, Niels!" exclaimed Gregor, his chair rocking underneath him, a flush of pink invading his face. "That's why we get rid of the bad seeds!"

Gregor took a deep breath, and the color was sucked back into his body. He coughed, then continued.

"We know how to do it. We know how to build the perfect society."

"On campus?"

Gregor leaned forward in his chair, putting his hand awkwardly on Niels' shoulder. In a sharp whisper, his eyes blazing, "Niels, we're going to the moon!"

It took Niels a few seconds to realize what he had just heard. He moved to speak, but Gregor's hand stopped him, his words spilling over his palm and rushing at Niels.

"We've figured out how to build the perfect society—and from all angles, from actual technical infrastructure to the societal structure. We've figured it all out!"

The Master Negotiator faltered and a laugh escaped from him, rudely punctuating Gregor's plan. Niels couldn't help himself—with just one simple, absurd phrase, six years of intimidation had evaporated. Gregor wasn't anyone to be afraid of. He was simply insane. And that was surely to Niels' advantage, though he knew one had to proceed carefully with crazy people. They could be unpredictable.

"Slow down," Niels said. "Are you joking with me?"

"We have been working on the project for a year," Gregor said. "Fifty engineers working in secret in Building 1. We're building a colony on the moon."

"You mean you have a spaceship and everything? How are you dealing with gravity? Wait, never mind, don't answer that. What I mean is, since when did Anahata get into the business of humankind?"

"Anahata has always *only* ever been about humankind. Everything we do is done for—"

"Yeah, yeah, I know, everything we do is to improve humankind. But I mean, a *society*, Gregor. There are no synergies with our current business. How do you know how to construct a society?"

"Actually, a society is a lot like software. You build it on solid principles, then you iterate. Then you solutionize, and you iterate again."

"What makes you think you can solve what centuries of wise men have failed to do?"

"Because we have something they don't have," Gregor said. He pushed his chair closer, and Niels couldn't help but lean forward. The broken wooden spindle leaned with him, pushing into his back. But he did not move to swat it away; his eyes were locked on Gregor, their faces almost touching.

"Algorithms," Gregor whispered.

"You have got to be kidding me," Niels snorted. "These are humans we're talking about, not robots. You can't predict and control human behavior with algorithms."

"That is an emotional reaction to what is a very logical project. And, yes, an algorithm could have predicted that you would respond that way. Even irrational behavior is rational when seen as a larger grouping of patterns. And as you can imagine, this project is built on patterns of success. Project Y, we call it. It will save Anahata—and, as a result, humankind."

Niels shook his head. He had come to ask Gregor to slap some silly ads on a dumb bracelet; Gregor was telling him they were going to build a moon colony. If Gregor wasn't crazy, then Niels was stupid for asking for so little in return.

"Let me get this straight. We're wasting tons of company money for a totally altruistic endeavor? There's not a single business purpose in all of this?"

"Obviously there's a business purpose," Gregor said. "That's where it all started."

Niels smirked—now they were speaking his language. The company always talked about saving the world, and sometimes really did believe in it, but Bobby always made sure there was a monetization element involved—and that Niels was in charge of ensuring the project's economic success.

"Tell me more," said Niels, leaning back in his uncomfortable chair.

"Project Y is fundamentally about protecting our employees and our company from outside threats," Gregor said.

"So this is about beating Galt."

"And any future Galt. We have the world's best engineers, and if we lose them, we lose everything. But if we build them a utopia, they will never have any reason to leave."

"Don't you think the company's already done a pretty good job of building a worker's paradise?" Niels said. "If anything, we've made all these engineers into self-entitled, smoothie-guzzling cult members who will never have any reason to leave. Where else could they have job titles like 'Evangelist,' 'Security Warrior,' 'Protector of All Things Internet,' and 'Debuggenator'?"

Gregor shook his head. "It isn't enough anymore. Free food, massages, and light-saber aerobics were revolutionary when we first started the company. But nowadays, every startup has them. The smaller companies can offer faster career mobility, wider remit, and most important, by dint of being small and under the radar, they can innovate wildly through illegality. Just think—when was the last time we were able to get away with selling a user's private data or violate someone's copyright? Those golden days are gone. We simply can't compete. And Galt knows it. Everyone knows it."

Niels couldn't disagree. Galt was a real threat, particularly in the Valley, where the average shelf life of even the most successful tech companies was just a decade or two. Anahata was already ten years old. Practically ancient.

"So, if you build a colony on the moon…"

"The better way to state it is, if we build an isolated utopia—which just happens to be on the moon—then we will secure the future of this company. No more Galt headhunters. No more Galt stealing our great ideas."

"And you'll just lock the employees up there on the moon? Give them a one-way ticket?"

"Imagine—a planet full of geniuses!"

Niels shook his head. "Surely there are easier ways to do this. What about raising employees' salaries or giving them longer vacations? Going to the moon seems extreme. I see no value add to the company."

"*Value add*?" Gregor sneered. "Your statement is not made true by its redundancy. There is indeed value. It's only by tackling what seems impossible that you can ensure no one else will do it. Galt can compete with bigger salaries and fancy perks, but they won't be able to compete with a moon colony. Plus, we're building a utopia that no engineer will ever want to leave. We'll be unstoppable! All other utopian societies have failed—it's a big problem that no one's solved. It's a huge opportunity for us."

"Or the sign that we will fail like all the others," Niels sighed. A moon colony was crazy even by Anahata standards.

"Our utopia will be different. We've spent several months analyzing the best combinations of political thought, philosophy, and technological advances necessary to achieve a better society. We've also looked at societal failures through the centuries—Rome, Byzantium, and so forth. What was consistent throughout was a lack of individual purpose. As a society progresses, it becomes more specialized, and while its citizens become ever more dependent on each other, they have no relationship with the tasks they perform. They are cogs in a wheel they never wanted to build."

Niels remembered late-night pot-filled conversations in college that sounded a lot like this. He fiddled again with the wooden spindle digging into his back. When the first ad appeared on Moodify, he'd send Gregor a new chair as a snide gift. Nothing was more insulting to a rich man than to send him a better version of what he already owned.

"We will take the best sampling of society and give people roles that fit their skills," Gregor continued. "The man born to be a mechanical engineer will be a mechanical engineer. He who cooks well will be a cook. There will be no *anomie*—I guess you don't know the philosopher Émile Durkheim? But in any case, every man will have his place. Every man will work together, for himself and for the greater good of the group."

Niels put one hand behind his back and began to twist at the base of the wooden spindle, trying to wrench it free from the chair. It wouldn't budge no matter how hard he tried. He could feel the sweat forming amateurish circles under his expensive shirt.

"This goddamn chair—"

He looked up and saw Gregor studying him, expressionless.

"I mean," Niels said, "how are you going to transport all of mankind to the moon?"

"Oh, no," Gregor said. "That would just be bringing along the bad seeds and all their earthly problems. There is a full selection process. The bulk of the group will be engineers, of course, as they perform very well across every factor we've determined necessary for success. You see, we have calculated a target percentage for every category of person and skill type that we need in order to have a high societal success rate."

"Argh!" growled Niels, the spindle behaving even more egregiously than before, pushing on his spine, scratching at his well-buffed skin. Such a crappy chair had no place in his existence. He worked way too hard and earned too much money to have to sit in chairs like this.

He scooted to the edge of his chair, but the spindle followed him, digging into him, pushing him forward and downward as though he were Gregor's supplicant. Unacceptable!

Niels leaped to his feet.

"Sit. Please," said Gregor, leaning across and pulling the spindle out of Niels' chair in one single, swift movement.

"As you may have guessed," said Gregor, laying the spindle next to the bottle of wine, "sales employees won't be as likely to be admitted to the moon colony given the high bar, but that doesn't mean they don't have a shot. If you help us, I can even imagine we'd raise the percentage of acceptance for the sales employees. Provided, of course, that they pass the necessary tests."

Niels snatched the spindle from the table and pointed it at Gregor. He thought the move looked intimidating, menacing even. But then he glanced down and realized he looked more like an orchestra conductor. He threw the spindle to the ground.

"You always get so upset when I speak in a factual manner about the sales team's IQ," Gregor continued. "But you should listen objectively to this plan, because there's a part that you're going to love."

Gregor paused, then drew out his words. "I... will... let... you... monetize."

Niels eyebrows shot upward in genuine surprise.

"Monetize the moon? You'll let me do that?"

"Yes."

"But… you never let me monetize," said Niels, sitting down. "What's the catch?"

"I'll let you export the moon minerals," Gregor said. "You and your team will go down there and pull them out and—"

"Minerals!" roared Niels, rocketing out of his chair. "My team sells internet advertising, Gregor, not minerals! Internet advertising!"

"Well, before they can sell the minerals, they need to get them out of the ground, so the selling part is sort of a moot point at this stage."

"You want my sales team to become miners?"

Gregor looked puzzled. "Oh, I hadn't really thought they would be the miners. But now that you suggest it, it's not a bad idea. The skill sets do overlap, I suppose. The 'core competencies,' as you call them, are the same—dirt digging, rubbing elbows with worms, hunting for gold—"

"Gregor!"

"One thing," said Gregor, holding up his hand. "I don't want you to get too excited. We can't export minerals right away. It really doesn't become economical until we build the space elevator, and that's not on the roadmap until late next year."

"Space elevator?!? You are going to sink this company!"

Niels knew it was time. He jumped onto his chair and stomped his feet. He waved his arms in the air again, willing his face redder and redder, sputtering a few expletives to express his outrage at Gregor's ridiculous plan. While not all business meetings required such theatrics, almost one hundred percent of Niels' negotiations involved either throwing a pen or stomping away from the table. He found it was often the best way to force a rapprochement from his opponent.

"Sit down," said Gregor calmly, pouring them both more wine. "You have nothing to be concerned about. Project Y is highly economical. By retaining our best engineers and protecting our most secret projects, we save hundreds of millions of dollars each year. And that's before even calculating the potential upside from building the world's first functioning utopia. Ultimately, we think this could generate tens of billions of dollars of new revenue."

Niels slowly lowered his arms, but he wasn't sure what to do with them. Feigned outrage was a tried-and-true technique—why hadn't it worked this time? Just the previous week, Niels had used the same approach on the CEO of the world's largest advertising firm, and in a matter of minutes the guy agreed to make his own car a surface for real-time Anahata ads.

He decided to continue standing on the chair. Niels threw his hands on his hips and puffed out his chest, then clenched his fists to make his biceps pop.

"So you're going to put a whole bunch of male engineers alone on a planet, huh? Sounds to me like this will last up until you have your first system downtime and your engineers are no longer able to stream porn from Earth."

Gregor said nothing for a few seconds, as if it took him a moment to understand.

"Oh," he finally said. "No, we've thought of that already. There will be women."

"I mean *real* women, not robots and avatar women. Or holograms," said Niels, referring to the recent Anahata prom, for which Bobby had commissioned Japanese nurse holograms to accompany dateless engineers.

Gregor waved him away, but Niels wasn't sure whether he was ignoring him or missing Niels' swipe entirely.

"Our engineers have found ways to solve all of the many dangers that could befall a young society—famine, natural disaster, war. You think they can't solve the simple problem of women? History has shown that if you give an engineer a problem, he usually can solve it. Again, that's why our society will primarily be made up of engineers."

"Most of your engineers can barely dress themselves," sniffed

Niels, staring down at Gregor from atop the chair. "Besides, I heard what happened last year at your winter retreat—hardly the outcome one would expect from superior beings."

"I don't know what you mean," said Gregor, but the hint of a grimace suggested otherwise.

As part of a team-building exercise, Anahata had put its engineers into teams for a virtual trek through the Amazon. Along the way, the engineers were met with various obstacles—wild animals, tree loggers, and angry environmentalists.

"You know exactly what I'm talking about," Niels said. "Your engineering teams abandoned sick and injured teammates just so that they could make it out of the Amazon first. A bunch of the employees got fed to anacondas."

"We didn't use real snakes," Gregor protested.

"They left their teammates to die."

"Only in a virtual world!" Gregor's face burst in splotches of red.

"Your moon colony *is* a virtual world!"

A few seconds passed, then Gregor spoke.

"I agree it would have been good of our engineers to save their colleagues. But at least their motivation was pure—to escape the jungle on behalf of Anahata. This is why they are the ultimate citizens of our new society. They will always work for its greater benefit and not be led astray by the petty distractions that affect so many other people. Distractions like…"

Gregor's eyes flashed.

"Distractions like pots of gold."

It was clearly a dig. But last year's sales incentive—in which Niels had promised a pot of authentic gold doubloons to any sales team member who doubled their quarterly returns—had proved to be a brilliant motivational technique. Anahata had tripled its profits that year thanks to a bit of luck o' the Irish. Niels wasn't crazy; he was shrewd. And that, he believed, was the difference between him and the man seated below him. There was no reasoning with insanity.

"What do you want from me," Niels asked, throwing his hands up. He was no longer certain of his next move. Should he come down from the chair? Or maybe it was best to speak to Bobby directly, though that also carried risks.

"Stop blocking my teams from testing on Shanley Field," Gregor said. "Free up the servers in Eastern Africa. Basically, get out of our way. In exchange, I will give you full transparency into our plans and eventual access to the moon minerals."

"No, I don't like this," Niels said. "It's not right for Anahata. And what will the rest of the world think when they find out? Our shareholders will freak out and the stock price will tank."

"It doesn't matter. By the time they find out, we'll be gone. On the moon. And once we're there and things are up and running, it will be easy to prove that the model works."

Niels sighed and shook his head. He was used to arguing over dollars in well-lit restaurants, not debating with a psychopath in his wine dungeon. It was time to play the Bobby card.

"I think we need to talk about this—seriously talk about this at a very, very long management meeting."

Gregor's face tightened. "There is nothing to talk about. Bobby agreed to this a long time ago."

"Then Bobby's going to need to come talk to me if he wants those servers in Africa. I'm not going to let you thwart the part of the company that makes all the money and funds your crazy ideas."

Niels got down from the chair and took a step toward the stairs.

"Wait! We're not done!" Gregor yelped.

Niels suppressed a grin. Clearly, all was not lost. He counted to five in his head, and slowly, slowly turned toward his prey.

"Maybe there is a way…"

"I'm sure we can find a compromise," said Gregor, the slight tremble in his voice confirming Niels' hunch.

Gregor was afraid Niels would turn Bobby against him. It never ceased to amaze him the things grown men feared. Niels feared no one.

"I want ads on Moodify," Niels said.

Gregor's face scrunched into a sour ball, then unfolded into a scowl before disappearing underneath his skin. A second later, it was as if his face had never hosted any expression at all.

"Listen," said Niels, "you let me put ads on Moodify and I'll support you one hundred percent in the moon colony project. Shanley Field, servers in Africa—I'll even give you a few sales guys who can wash your engineers' laundry on the moon."

Niels held out his hand, but Gregor made no move toward him. For a minute, the two men stared at each other without moving.

"Putting ads on Moodify bracelets is bad for our users," Gregor said.

Niels shrugged. "Okay, I'll just discuss this with Bobby tomorrow and—"

"Wait," said Gregor. He jumped out of his seat and moved quickly toward Niels. "There is something I have to show you."

Gregor took a few slow steps backward toward the stairs, as if his gaze could freeze Niels in place. He then turned and bounded up the steps, letting the door slide gently behind him.

Down below, Niels crossed his arms and yawned loudly.

But once Gregor was gone, Niels began to rub his temples. Why hadn't he just gone into banking instead? Greedy capitalists were so much easier to negotiate with than engineers.

ARSYEN

Five miles away, Arsyen Aimo was also thinking about money—namely, that thanks to his huge new salary, he was once again on the winning side of capitalism and ready to upgrade his entire life.

Part of that upgrade definitely involved getting a new girlfriend—preferably an American one with excellent teeth.

Of course, he already had a girlfriend, Natia, though that had happened somewhat by accident.

A year earlier, he had signed up to an online dating site as "Rick," a blond surfer from Santa Cruz. Rick resembled an underwear model, with a chiseled body, defined jawline, and a strong nose echoing Arsyen's own good looks.

The first woman he met was Natia—herself masking as a Romanian grad student at Berkeley. Between her confusion of Los Angeles as a Northern Californian city and Arsyen's own English mistakes, they quickly called each other's bluff and soon were speaking to each other in Pyrrhian.

They struck up a fast virtual friendship—not more than that initially, as they were both too practical to imagine dating someone thousands of miles away. Arsyen took pains to conceal his true identity. From his experience, once a Pyrrhian woman knew she was in the presence of an Aimo, all hopes of reasonable conversation dissolved in a puddle of sighs. Instead, he told her about living in America, about drive-through pharmacies and the endless array of flavored sparkling water, and the importance of sanitation engineers like Arsyen, who fixed the various clogs, stains, and crumbs that could slow the infrastructure of a fast-moving startup.

She in turn wrote to him about her life in Poodlekek, Pyrrhia's capital. Natia worked as a switchboard operator for the national telecommunications firm, a graying dinosaur that was slowly moving Pyrrhia into the 1980s. She belonged to a political philosophy group, which met weekly to discuss why Marxism failed and whether man could subvert machine in a post-capitalist society. Arsyen found her little intellectual forays rather cute. There would be no need for political philosophy once royal reign was restored, but why discourage Natia from stretching her feminine brain in the meantime?

She was particularly passionate in her dislike of General (now President) Korpeko—the source of the Aimo family's undoing. He was a "despot," she wrote, "hell-bent on pushing sports and false achievements instead of encouraging the true prosperity of the nation."

Among her many gripes was Korpeko's obsession with the little-known sport of curling. He believed it was Pyrrhia's ticket to international fame—sufficiently obscure as to ensure little competition from wealthier countries. Korpeko had replaced all the bike lanes and gutters along main roads with curling courts, and no vacations or trips outside the country were allowed during the first week of February, now known as Pyrrhian Curling Week. Arsyen's stomach tightened each time he imagined Korpeko's curling lanes snaking across Pyrrhia's unmarred hills.

"It sounds nothing like the rich cultural life that once flourished under the royal family," Arsyen wrote to Natia, thinking of the literary salons and long afternoon croquet matches his family hosted at their summer palace for the Pyrrhian elite. The king had generously ensured that vivid accounts of the affairs were published in all of the country's newspapers so literate citizens could vicariously enjoy the experience.

"Do you remember the photos of them playing croquet atop their verdant courts?" Arsyen asked. "It was far more dignified."

"Yes, I suppose if you consider hitting a ball a more civilized activity than rolling a puck," Natia replied.

Natia's lack of appreciation for croquet was one of the many shortcomings Arsyen had been forced to tolerate as a lowly janitor. Another was the mole on her cheek—it was just a little too big for his liking; he often found himself covering it up with his thumb whenever they did video chat.

Luckily, product managers didn't have to put up with such defects. When product managers discovered problems, they fixed them. And that's exactly what Arsyen planned to do.

With a fat new paycheck now coming his way, Arsyen was better equipped to find himself a beautiful American girl—someone like that hippie receptionist, Jennie. Then, when the time was right, he would return to Pyrrhia bronzed and wealthy, with his beautiful queen and her good orthodontics on display. Natia and the other women of Pyrrhia would weep at what they had lost, only able to take comfort in the possibility of becoming one of Arsyen's bathing maidens.

So it was decided: Natia was out. The only question was whether to write her a breakup email now or first play his video game.

Arsyen opted for the video game. And there he was, a half-hour later, stuck on his couch, glued to his screen, when the phone rang.

It was the chief strategist of the TRC—the Throne Reclamation Commitee.

"Have you heard the news? A train went off Golden Bridge and fell into the lake."

"Mmm-hmm," said Arsyen, drawing his sword and piercing the heart of a castle guard. "It was probably a drunk conductor. Our trains are flawless."

The national rail service had been one of the great Aimo accomplishments—christened by his father as "locomotives of progress and prosperity." The king even had a toy train replica built to travel over their palace moat and directly into Arsyen's bedroom. He wondered if that train was still there—particularly the first-class carriage, outfitted with miniature foodstuffs. As a teenager, Arsyen often threw the train's gold-plated bison fries at his manservant Sklartar when the old man wasn't moving fast enough.

"They say you could hear the screams of the children as the train flew through the air," the strategist said, "that the flames moved across the sky like a rocket."

"Huh," said Arsyen, his thumb pumping up and down on the console button as he sliced through the head of one of the king's henchmen. Tragedies often befell poor nations. There wasn't much point in getting worked up over a handful of dead bodies.

The felled henchman rose, holding his head in his hands. He was coming back for more. As Arsyen pumped the console with his thumbs, the phone fell from his ear. No matter, if the news was that important, he was sure to hear from the TRC again. Nothing was going to interrupt his game. He had made it through his grueling first week at Anahata and deserved some downtime.

Arsyen glanced at his email on his way to the bathroom a few minutes later and saw that Natia had written. She too was obsessed with the train accident. She claimed the government had stopped any media from reporting the event, fearful that the news could put a damper on its bid to host the International Curling Championships the following year. Government workers had already begun repairing the bridge, and no effort was being made to dredge up the train. Meanwhile, the police were arresting anyone they believed was spreading rumors. All internet services were blocked in the capital, and Natia had been forced to travel outside the province to get to any café with open access. "If they find out I am here, they will arrest me, or worse!" She wrote. "Help us get the word out about what happened. Hundreds are dead!"

Arsyen had assumed the TRC had been talking about ten people. Hundreds of people elevated the train wreck to a national disaster—the kind of thing worthy of a future king's attention.

"What would a king do...?" Arsyen wondered aloud, imagining himself laying his healing hands upon thousands of maimed

Pyrrhians, their bodies draped in rags—rags he would eventually replace with velvet robes!—as they lay prostrate before him. They shielded their eyes from his divine light, and chanted his name to the ground below them. *King Arsyen. King Arsyen.*

He shook himself back to reality. His dream was still far off. Whatever happened in Pyrrhia now would certainly be repeated in a year's time, with a new set of mothers rolled out to despair over the loss of their children at the hands of Korpeko's corrupt and negligent government. He needed to be patient and let these minor catastrophes accumulate. At the point of ten train wrecks, the time might finally be right for a royal coup.

But in the meantime, Arsyen could at least give a nudge toward revolution and have some quick fun with Korpeko. If working in technology had taught him anything, it's that the internet loves a troll.

While working at Galt, Arsyen had learned about GaltPages—a popular tool that aggregated everything people had to say on all the different Galt apps. He even half-started his own GaltPage a few months earlier to promote his Aimo Air Freshener—a custom pink mixture he invented out of cleaning supplies so he could cover up the persistent stench of body odor that permeated the Galt meeting rooms. Its cotton candy scent would one day make Arsyen millions—provided he could figure out how to keep it from combusting.

He hadn't gotten very far with his page back then, but Galt seemed to have made its product easier to use since he last tried. He could easily repurpose his early work to suit Natia's social justice needs—the fluffy pink plume of cotton candy in the page's background no longer suggesting a sweet scent but rather an artsy take on a nuclear holocaust. And, Arsyen told himself, there was a potential bonus to be had in all of this: If enough people were interested in what he posted about Poodlekek, he could collect their contact info and sell them his air freshener once all the furor died down.

Arsyen had worked in the Valley long enough to know that

the key to social media was virality, not sincerity. So he renamed the page "Justice for Poodlekek" and posted Natia's text about the accident, calling for action. He then posted the link to Justice for Poodlekek in the comment section of every Pyrrhian blog and newspaper article he could find and wrote a review of Korpeko's government on the restaurant review site Help!. Then he added pictures of Golden Bridge to his Photomatic account, using the retro and futuristic filters, as well as a bleaker one with a sprinkling of decapitated bodies.

Arsyen leaned back in his chair and put his hands behind his head. It was an awfully nice thing he had just done for Natia, and it would hopefully assuage her disappointment when he broke up with her in favor of dating Jennie.

He returned to his video game and quickly forgot about the page. But a while later, passing by his computer on the way to the kitchen, he saw that the previously blank comment section of Justice for Poodlekek now hosted a long list of responses. The view count was already in the thousands and climbing with each minute. Arsyen did a double take: People seemed to really be upset by this train thing. And not just the train, but about Korpeko and his government as well.

The streetlight has been out for two weeks.

Why is there no bison milk on Mondays?

Arsyen squealed with delight. His people seemed so unhappy! He hit the refresh button again and again, each new complaint augmenting his euphoria.

Korpeko will drag our country into further poverty!

I hate curling!

Arsyen couldn't resist posting a comment under a fake name.

This never would have happened when the Aimos were in power!

Someone replied immediately.

That's true. King Aimo would've made us play croquet until our fingers fell off.

Arsyen laughed. That had indeed happened to a few unlucky peasants who had trespassed on the royal croquet court.

As the minutes passed, complaints about bison milk were replaced by complaints about potholes, potholes by accusations of corruption, corruption by torture.

Arsyen did a small jig before his computer, then paused—first to check out his flexed biceps reflected on his computer screen, and then to update his page with a new message.

My people, we must take action!!

Of course, Arsyen knew President Korpeko would put it all down. That's how it happened in Pyrrhia and the rest of the poor world. People protested and waved hand-painted signs, and then, if they weren't disappeared by the government, they trudged back to work on Monday.

But Arsyen's well-meaning but rather stupid Pyrrhian subjects couldn't see that far ahead. Instead, the misery of Pyrrhia wrote itself across the Justice for Poodlekek page. The decay of the streets, the decay of the nation, the decay of everything, really, but the country's gleaming curling lanes. The page's followers swelled into the thousands within minutes. Soon they were asking about the creator of Justice for Poodlekek, calling on him to lead them forward.

It was terrible timing. He still had six levels to go in his video game.

"Men of action take action," Arsyen said to himself, repeating a poster he had seen outside one of Anahata's sales buildings.

He composed a short note to Natia:

My dear Natia, I have made a GaltPage to help you spread the word. Also, I am sorry but I think we will have to break up because I am not going to be able to come to Pyrrhia anytime soon.

Arsyen paused. What if Natia showed up one day in California without that unfortunate mole and wanted to sleep with him?

He began to type again.

Let me know if you ever come to California. Keep in touch!

Then he left the house to go grab a burrito. He needed some fuel to keep him going if he was going to conquer the six-headed henchman later that night.

NIELS

Whatever Gregor Guntlag was trying to prove, Niels was determined to ignore it. He would meet Gregor's final, desperate plea for cooperation with the same dismissal with which Gregor had treated Niels' chair-jumping antics.

Niels pictured Gregor lugging the mysterious proof of his superior world order down the stairs, his combat boots thudding against the wooden steps, then stomping to the table. What did he want to show Niels? A philosophy book? A line of code? A diorama? Regardless, Niels' expression would remain placid, unmoved, mouth silent in Guntlagian style until Gregor's desperation grew to the point where Niels would only need to repeat three words: "Ads on Moodify." Maybe he would even agree to let Niels put ads on employee T-shirts and the meeting-room chairs.

When had Gregor left exactly? Half an hour earlier? An hour? It was starting to seem like an awfully long time to leave someone waiting in a basement.

It was obvious what Gregor was trying to do. He had locked Niels in the cellar in order to assert his dominance and put Niels on edge. But these kinds of mind tricks and one-upmanship were old hat for a Master Negotiator. After all, Niels was the man who had challenged a quadriplegic music executive to a game of rugby; the man who hid *E. coli* in an opponent's entree so he could pitch him on a business proposition as the other lay prostrate before the toilet for six hours. This wine cellar act was amateurish.

That said, why would a grown man lock a work colleague in his basement? Was that something Germans found funny? Or maybe

Gregor was in fact Austrian. The Austrians were famous for their appreciation of basements. For a split second, Niels' body tensed as he imagined Gregor descending the stairs in a pair of leather pants.

Niels closed his eyes, took a deep breath, and opened them again. He couldn't help but respect his opponent for planting these seeds of doubt. Five minutes passed, then ten. Niels felt splinters from the chair making inroads into the back of his arms. Shapes emerged from the shadows, then receded. Another twenty minutes passed.

Niels knew he shouldn't panic, but the shadows, the quiet, the unpredictability of his opponent all began to cloud his confidence. The longer he sat and paced and sat and paced, the more Niels became convinced that the taciturn Teuton was planning to leave him there all night, returning only once confident that he had broken the Master Negotiator.

Niels needed to plot his escape. From his shirt pocket, he pulled out the pen and pad of paper that he always carried with him. In a world of internet intangibles, Niels found reassurance in last-century items.

His high-level plan of attack was fairly easy to map. First, Niels needed to get himself out of the basement, and second, he needed to stop Gregor's moon colony plan. (Third, he needed to destroy Gregor, though that was a longer-term goal that would require a separate strategy and PowerPoint deck.)

The question, of course, was how to go about these things. Niels considered the obvious—he could call another member of the management team. But as soon as Fischer, HR Paul, or Old Al showed up, Gregor would have some story ready and they would all have a good chuckle over Niels' paranoia. Word would get out around Anahata, and even his own team would eventually find out about his panicked call for help. Exhilarated by the scent of weakness, the salesmen would circle him like the killer sharks he had trained them to be. It would be the end of him.

Instead, Niels sketched a mountain. At the base, he wrote, "Me." At the summit, he wrote "FREEDOM." Then he paused, realizing that he had failed to capture the full complexity of the situation. So he drew a second mountain next to the first. Now he had a mountain range. At the base of that second mountain, Niels wrote, "Gregor announces Moon Colony Plan." At the top, he wrote, "I DESTROY the Moon Colony Plan!!!"

After a few minutes, and a few trees and shrubs added to his drawing for good measure, Niels had the entire route mapped, from base camp to summit. He was ready to go. He leaped out of his chair and did fifty jumping jacks, followed by one hundred sit-ups, enjoying the rush of blood through his body. Niels would save Anahata from the worst decision it could ever make, and possibly even get Gregor fired in the process.

The first step was simple. He would ring Bobby and suggest that he pick Niels up at Gregor's house for a midnight yoga class. Bobby was a sucker for yoga invites and had stated on numerous occasions that he wished the management team would chant together. Niels, for his part, thought yoga was the lazy man's excuse for exercise, but like golf and wine, he saw value in its acquisition. Yoga had not only helped him meet several lonely housewives, but had also distinguished him as the only member of Bobby's team who could execute *Chaturanga Dandasana*—providing a reasonable excuse for him to seed business ideas over sun salutations.

Niels pulled out his phone, selected Bobby's number, and was soon hit by his mountain's first boulder. There was no reception in Gregor's basement.

He was not used to being knocked down so early in the game, but like a true sales champion, Niels rose quickly. "Only losers lose," he whispered to himself, quoting one of the motivational posters in his office. He did five pushups with one hand, then jumped to his feet.

Niels tapped his phone's email application and began to type:

Bobby, have just heard of a killer nighttime yoga studio in Mill Valley. Fantastic kombucha bar. I can get us in. Can you meet tonight? I'm at Gregor's—stuck in his basement actually, funny story. Come grab me and we can head straight to the studio.

He paused. Would Bobby sense desperation? He needed to make his message appear as normal and Niels-like as possible.

Also, Gregor told me all about Project Y. Fascinating idea. I have some ideas about how we can monetize.

Niels smiled. He could feel his bed and a good night's sleep within reach.

He pushed "send" and immediately began composing a second email, this time to HR Paul. Gregor's insanity needed to be recorded somewhere—even if in the short-term Niels had no intention of compromising Anahata's public reputation and Niels' own financial stake in the company—by outing its head engineer as a psychopath.

Niels decided to attach a photo of himself in the basement. He raised his phone camera to get an angle that captured both the rows of wine bottles and the staircase leading up to a locked door. Then he hit "send" and took a swig of the Chateau Margaux—it would make for great bragging rights at next month's HBS Successful Man Golf Tournament.

Niels opened the email application again, and his face fell. His email to Bobby hadn't gone through. In its place was a time-out message—the data connection just wasn't strong enough. Niels tried to send again, and then again and again, from different parts of the basement. But each time he was met with the same result.

The Master Negotiator was hit with a strong dose of reality—there was no phone connection, only a very weak data connection, and he was trapped in an Austrian psychopath's basement.

Niels scanned the room. Aside from the bottles of wine, it was absolutely empty. The staircase led to the locked door on the first floor, but otherwise there were no windows and no way out. He couldn't go to work. He couldn't make money.

He couldn't make money!

"No!!!" he screamed, kicking over one of the chairs. He bounded up the stairs and began pounding on the door. "Let me out! You can't do this!"

Niels pounded for several minutes, but there was no answer from the other side.

Niels crumbled on the top step and was at first shocked, then horrified, then just miserable to discover that the wet feeling on his face were tears, actual man tears. His body shook, and he began to feel cold. He wanted his mother, or the ex-girlfriend he had cheated on, or even just that hippie receptionist he had slept with.

Or even God. Niels clasped his hands in prayer, unsure whether the gesture was necessary for the Almighty to hear him. Did God have to listen to him? Didn't God love rich people?

Just in case, Niels apologized extra hard for ignoring Him the previous four decades and promised that he would be good from now on. He wouldn't sleep with receptionists, he'd mentor inner-city entrepreneurs, and he'd teach the homeless how to code. He'd get rid of moon colonies and pop-up internet ads, and he'd fix piracy on the web once and for all. Above all, he'd be a good citizen and son and follower of whatever religion God turned out to belong to.

He looked down at the useless mobile phone in his hand. Tears had formed pathetic puddles across its surface, distorting his Flitter application, which now seemed to sprout wings from the "f" of its logo. Niels stared at it for a few seconds, watching the "f" heave under his tears, like a bird dreaming of flight.

And then it hit him. Flitter—Galt's popular thought-sharing tool—was famous for working in the lowest-bandwidth parts of the world. They were always bragging in the press about how someone had used their tool to escape an oppressive regime. It drove Bobby crazy—he thought Anahata should have a monopoly on freedom and hope.

Niels didn't care about any of that. In fact, he had zero interest in Galt or Flitter or in reading anyone's thoughts other than his own. But a year earlier, he had tried to convince Galt to run Anahata's ads on their apps and opened a Flitter account, Niels_1973, to show them he *really* cared about their product. But eventually the deal fell through, and other than a few half-hearted fleets about some Anahata sports matches, Niels' account lay dormant for months. He had practically forgotten he even had it installed on his phone.

The likelihood Flitter would work in the cellar was low, but Niels had nothing to lose. He fired up Niels_1973 and, hands shaking, expressed his panic in fewer than one hundred thirty-five characters (the limit set on any Flitter message):

Help me! Trapped in basement at 13 Willow St, Atherton.

Niels hit "send," and in a split second, the post was successfully transmitted. Niels jumped up from the step, pumping his fist in the air. "Yes!" he cheered. He sat back and waited.

And waited.

And waited.

Twenty minutes passed, and there was no response—no "we're coming" or "hold tight, buddy!" For a moment, Niels wondered whether his message had indeed been delivered—or fleeted, as the Flitterati would say. But he could see there were millions of other live fleets coming in from the rest of the world—fleets about politicians, fleets about celebrities, fleets from companies hawking their products, and fleets from celebrities hawking those same products. Clearly someone was getting through to someone.

The problem, Niels quickly realized, was that no one was listening to *him*. He had only two people following his fleets: agefshgr_74 and tina_xxx. Niels didn't even know who they were or how they had found him in the first place.

"Failure is not an option," Niels whispered to himself, repeating the Smeardon family motto. He took a gulp of Chateau Margaux and reminded himself that the important thing was that Flitter worked. The next step was simply to make it work better for him. He needed something more eye-catching—something that would get people so excited that they would want to refleet his message to all of their friends and followers.

He quickly settled on *Tech Geek*, the Valley's hottest tech gossip site. Including the @techgeek Flitter handle was his best bet to be seen by someone following their account. So Niels tried again, decades of Chateau Margaux life force moving him into a new world of confidence:

@techgeek Love your hard-hitting tech analysis. Also: Help me! I'm a prisoner of #Anahata.

THE SOCIAL MEDIA MANAGER

U p in San Francisco, *Tech Geek*'s social media manager stared at the fleet from Niels_1973 and groaned. Of all the Galt apps, Flitter definitely had the most crazies. There was something about giving people just one hundred thirty-five characters to express themselves that made them even more desperate—fueled by the hope that a bite-sized thought would be small enough to penetrate the world's scattered attention.

It wasn't just weirdos like Niels who drove him crazy. It was the number of people who didn't properly understand Flittiquette. They exhibited a poor use of hashtags, a tendency to refleet every compliment or inane statement made by a follower, and an inability to craft something eye-popping in one hundred thirty-five characters.

Social media was a twenty-first-century art, and a true *amateur* ("in the French sense," he explained to anyone who would listen, "meaning a lover of social media") had to spend time honing his craft. He often reflected that his title should have been Master Craftsman of Social Media. Or simply God.

Because as far as he could tell, there was no job with more prestige. Sure, he told his friends, he could take a high-paying social media job at a big corporation, but that wasn't his style. He didn't want to be the guy fleeting "Not feeling fresh? Try the new #Summer_douche in fresh lavender." He had done his college senior thesis on Che Guevara's influence on scatological pop art. He could hardly sell out to the agro-chemico-industrial complex to be their social media plaything. He was part of an #online #revolution #disrupting #everything.

That's why he was at *Tech Geek*, by all accounts the heart of the universe—or, at least, his universe, and the universe of anyone who mattered to him. *Tech Geek* was where all things tech and Valley were beating, throbbing, iterating, de-duping, compiling, normalizing, and randomizing. As far as he saw it, if you did social media for the Valley, you were, in many ways, *the* Valley. In fact, he liked to think of himself as a modern-day William Randolph Hearst. The decisions he made—whether to refleet someone's comment, post a piece of news or gossip about another company, or (shock!) ignore it altogether—these were the things that made and broke powerful men and their companies.

So it annoyed him when fools like Niels_1973 would fleet things that were clearly false, just in the hope of grabbing his attention. It was irresponsible and a waste of his time. Niels_1973 was probably the same guy who had tried to send a "tip" to *Tech Geek* a few months earlier that Anahata had discovered Atlantis and was refurbishing it so that Bobby Bonilo could have an underwater pleasure kingdom. Or the guy who had fleeted that Anahata was suggesting its lowest-performing employees take performance-enhancing drugs. Granted, the latter proved to be true, but the source had missed a crucial detail. Anahata was randomizing who would get the drugs so they could analyze the effectiveness of the trial—a piece of research that would be helpful for the entire scientific community. #detailsmatter

Niels_1973: @techgeek Love your hard-hitting tech analysis. Also: Help me! I'm a prisoner of #Anahata.

He reread the fleet and shook his head. He spent several minutes contemplating the various punishments he could mete out, finally deciding to block Niels_1973 from his list altogether. It was an extreme punishment, but he couldn't condone such outrageous, attention-seeking behavior.

Then, feeling like he had done yet another great service for the world, *Tech Geek*'s social media manager called it a night and made his way to bed.

NIELS

It took total isolation from the outside world for Niels to discover what millions of Galt fans around the world already knew: There was no longer any point in real conversation when you could just communicate in short phrases and poop emojis.

As night gave way to morning, Niels found himself deeply focused on a handful of celebrities and their preferred hair products and was closely following the reports of a burgeoning relationship between two contestants on a popular reality TV show. His concern for smooth hair and the couple's happiness grew stronger as he finished off the bottle of Chateau Margaux, then opened a 1787 bottle of Chateau Lafite.

Niels' innumerable fleets about captivity, despair, and Anahata had gone unanswered despite variations in text, creative spelling, and attempts at haiku. Despite hours of nonstop fleeting, there were still no refleets by his two followers, and still no acknowledgment from *Tech Geek*. Nor had he gained any new followers who could potentially spread the word on his behalf.

Ever the mountaineer, Niels devised a new plan, with a new mountain range that showcased the complexity (but also the conquerability!) of his current situation. This was one of his favorite mountain-range models to use at work. It had switchbacks and a very large boulder. The point, he often told his team, was to not get distracted by the boulder and to stay focused on the switchbacks.

Flitter users were switchbacks.

No, they were boulders.

Well, whatever they were, they weren't the point. The point was, he had been foolish to think that people on Flitter would care about *him*, Niels Smeardon. What they cared about was the content he himself had been sucked into—the celebrities, the gossip, the life-style guru tips. The trick was to make these idiots care about him through his connection to the people they worshipped. They were like lichen growing on top of the boulder. Or maybe the sign at the bottom of the mountain marking the trail. Or…

"I don't need mountains," Niels growled. "Mountains need ME."

He crumpled the paper and tossed it to the ground, then immediately started fleeting again.

His first pass was a flop, despite referencing the biggest pop star on the planet—the sexy blonde singer named La Lala who was known for hitting high notes while writhing on the floor with pythons.

#OMG LaLala making new video with #Liberace! A duet with a legend!

The only reaction came from Tina_xxx, who removed herself from his list of two followers. No one else responded to his fleet.

Niels sipped some wine and took a few minutes to study the most popular tweets about La Lala. Then he tried again.

#LaLala sings at #Nashville high school, discourages #bullies. Wears pythons in school uniform. Such an #inspiration!

Niels doubted La Lala had ever been to Nashville. But no matter, within minutes, he had been refleeted. There was even a string of responses, most of them from Lala fans in Nashville asking where she had sung. Niels responded:

My friend said #EmersonHigh. She wore Band-Aids instead of clothes!!

Within a few seconds, he had two new people following his account. He stretched his fingers and typed his next set of messages.

#LaLala wears no makeup to remind us that talent is more important than beauty.

#LaLala pythons remind us that in every snake is a beating heart.

#LaLala spotted at #LAX, straddling a plane. Anyone have pictures?

The popularity of Niels_1973 began to climb. The more inane his posts, the more misspellings and melodrama (driven more by inebriation than calculation), the more followers he gained. Niels felt his blood begin to pump again. He gave one of his *help me!* posts a go, just to see if someone would respond. But despite having amassed four thousand followers in thirty minutes, all hanging on every word he had to say about La Lala, there didn't seem to be anyone interested in helping the man behind the fleets.

Niels scratched his head, then returned to his notepad. He drew a SWOT analysis listing the strengths, weaknesses, opportunities, and threats of his pop star. When he hit the "weaknesses" box, he realized his error: La Lala skewed toward a much younger audience. Was it really plausible that a pimply fourteen-year-old fan would come to his rescue?

Niels groaned. His demographic targeting had been all wrong. La Lala fans were too young. He needed serious people. People who had driver's licenses. People who thought a bit more about the consequences of social media. People like... thirty-year-olds.

Niels flipped back to the Flitter homepage to study the most popular age-appropriate topics. What were people fleeting about on a random Monday morning? Scrolling through the list, Niels saw that most of the topics were things he knew nothing about. In addition to the perennial pop music favorites, the list included things like #bitchslap, #whatimknitting, and #blessedmoments. Niels kept scanning, moving farther and farther down the list. And then he saw it: #Poodlekek.

"Yes!"

Niels knew all about Poodlekek. It was his friend's heavy metal band in college. He was surprised they were still together after two decades, let alone had become so popular. He remembered going to their shows at the campus coffee house, cigarette lighter waving in the air as he and his then-girlfriend sang to guitar-heavy ballads about twisted love, rocky family relationships, and starving children in Ethiopia. Their fans would likely be Niels' age, the kind of people who would take seriously his cries for help. And Niels had plenty of interesting things he could fleet about them to get people's attention—like the lead singer's bad case of the Herp. Women would totally refleet that.

But first things first. He needed to build a new fan base. Niels kicked off his first Poodlekek fleet with a bit of nostalgia.

Raise your lighters for #Poodlekek

ARSYEN

Arsyen rose from his bed, ready to conquer an American woman.

It would not be his first attempt. He had made several passes at courtship since arriving in the United States, but most women were too intimidated by his overwhelming virility.

But Jennie, the Anahata receptionist, struck Arsyen as the confident type. She shook his hand without averting her gaze and even scolded him during their campus tour when he complimented Galt. He liked a sassy lady with good teeth.

He had the day all planned out. After lunchtime, he'd surprise Jennie in the reception area and give her his Aimo Air Freshener. Then, after a bit of chitchat, he'd suggest they head to his apartment for some video games and sex. It would be the perfect first date.

The only potential hiccup was keeping his words straight. He wondered whether Sven would practice his English with him that morning.

But Arsyen had no such chance. Sven greeted him as he entered their cubicle, waving a hand bloodied by jelly doughnut. Jennie—*his* Jennie—was standing next to Sven.

She spotted him and smiled. "Oh, hi! How are you liking Anahata?"

Arsyen shook his head vigorously. He did not have an answer prepared for this.

But Jennie seemed to have no difficulty continuing the conversation by herself, telling Arsyen something about her feminist book club. Little of what she said registered with him. He was watching her lips move, fascinated by the way they came together and then parted as she spoke just to him. They were so different from Natia's lips, which moved together in fits and jerks, all depending on the bandwidth of her internet connection.

Sven cleared his throat.

"Jane here was just about to tell us what she's doing here."

"It's Jennie," she said, turning to Sven. "And I'm here because I'm the new nontechnical technical lead."

"Huh?"

"I'm your new manager," Jennie said.

It was as if Vesuvius had exploded across the well-manicured lawns of Palo Alto. Sven's nose twisted until the rest of his face followed in a spiral of despair. Jonas' mouth froze in a perfect, horrified O.

Arsyen understood their reaction immediately: They were as upset as he was about having a female boss.

"This sounds like the kind of subterfuge the sales team would instigate, sending a nonengineer in here to sabotage our project," Jonas said.

Sven jotted some lines on a piece of paper and threw it in front of Jennie. "What do you see here?"

Jennie took the paper in her hands, and Arsyen noticed that her wrists bore the remnants of a henna tattoo. She took a few seconds to study the crude drawing, which showed a graph with a diagonal line descending from the top left-hand side to the bottom right.

"Um, a descending line?" she said.

"And what's the first thing you think of, in the context of Anahata?" Sven asked.

"I don't know… falling profits?"

"I knew it—imposter!" he yelled, leaping to his feet.

"But I'm not from the sales team. And that was just a line—"

"You could've said it was a Pareto curve, or a drop in latency, or a decrease in the number of users," Sven said. "There were endless acceptable possibilities."

"The possibilities were indeed infinite, in a figurative if not exact sense," Jonas nodded.

"You had so many options, and yet what's the first thing that comes to mind? Money. You are from sales. Out with you!" Sven's finger pointed toward the hall, its edict winding across the floor and out the exit door, sending Jennie back to the reception area from whence she came.

Jennie glanced at Arsyen. *Help!* her eyes seemed to plead. It was clear she didn't belong there—maybe she had also been trying for a janitorial position, like Arsyen, and had been mistakenly rerouted to Social Car.

"Did you come to clean?" whispered Arsyen, stepping closer. He reached into his pocket to grab the air freshener.

Jennie shot him a dirty look. "You think because I'm a woman I'm supposed to clean your cubicle?"

Jennie opened her leather fringe vest and shoved her chest at Arsyen. *Feminism Happens Here*, the T-shirt read.

Arsyen froze. He was not used to such forwardness in American women.

Jennie turned back to Sven and Jonas.

"Gregor Guntlag himself asked me to do this. He said I didn't need to know how to code—just to lead. I'm a tour guide. I know how to lead people."

Sven shook his head and slumped back to his chair. Jonas pouted. Jennie's face relaxed, as if their disappointment was the first step toward acceptance.

"Now, who's going to tell me about Social Car?" she asked. "All Gregor said was that it was using the driverless cars to help you meet people. Sounds like something someone without friends would come up with."

"Sounds like something someone who can't see the future would say," sneered Sven, grabbing another doughnut and slowly ripping it down the middle, letting the red jelly drip directly onto the table.

"Great, it seems like you're the perfect person to explain the project to me," Jennie said. She grabbed a spare chair from a neighboring cubicle and seated herself next to Sven. Arsyen noted their arms were almost touching.

For the next hour, Sven walked Jennie through Social Car—from its initial history as a simple driverless car to its current state as a meeting platform. At first, Jennie scribbled madly across her notebook as he spoke, taking note of every word, code name, and milestone along the way. But as Sven progressed, her notes became fewer, punctuated by question marks, dashes, circles, and asterisks—an entire discourse happening on her page, separate to the story Sven was narrating.

"I don't get it," said Jennie after a few minutes.

Sven snorted.

"Why would people want to use this?" she asked. "I drive to get places. When I want to meet people, I go someplace where I can meet them."

"But Social Car helps you meet people before you get to that place, or it can tell you where to go to meet those people. It is significantly more efficient," Jonas said.

Arsyen kept quiet. He had never really understood the purpose of Social Car. That said, he didn't want Jennie to have a negative impression of it—she wouldn't want to date the product manager of a stupid product.

"Why not just design a car that makes me a smoothie?" Jennie asked. "Or a car that washes my hair and does my nails? Those are more useful than what you've come up with."

Arsyen saw Jonas and Sven exchange glances, as if to consider the validity of her idea.

"Because not everyone wants a carrot juice or a perm," said Sven finally. "On the other hand, everyone wants to meet someone. The use case is bigger."

"There *isn't* a use case. You're solving a problem that doesn't exist. And what about traffic jams and accidents? What are you going to do when everyone's trying to meet everyone else, and all of a sudden everyone's headed in the same direction, turning about and crashing into each other?"

Sven looked at Jonas.

"Women are *not* going to use this," Jennie said. "Even if there are one or two who do, they're going to be inundated with messages from men. They'll be overwhelmed, and they'll just turn the feature off."

"Oh, we already thought of that," Sven said. "We've opted everyone in to the service as a default and made it difficult to find the privacy settings. So we project that only two percent of users will actually manage to opt out of the service, and only a fraction of those will be women since they rarely know how to find and change their settings. So women will have to use it, and we'll have gender equilibrium. Problem solved."

Jennie shook her head. "This is creepy. Someone can see my profile and decide to keep pace with my car. Do you not see a problem with this?"

"That's just so that when you are ready to stop and park somewhere, the other driver will have kept up with you and can stop and park, too," said Sven slowly, even slower than when he explained things to Arsyen.

"You mean it's going to help offline stalking," Jennie said, crossing her arms.

Jonas turned to Sven. "She does have a good point."

"I was just thinking the same thing," said Sven. He approached the whiteboard.

Jennie's face brightened, and Arsyen brightened with her. Maybe he could suggest they take a drive in Social Car together?

"I think we can fix your problem," said Sven, grabbing a pen and starting to scribble on the board. He turned toward Jonas.

"What if we got a queuing theory expert to help?"

"I bet the original driverless car team had one," Jonas nodded. "They must have looked at the traffic jam issue when they were first scoping out the project and—"

"Traffic jams?!?" Jennie screeched. "Of all the things I said, that's what strikes you as the biggest problem? You completely missed my point! There is no way that I'm allowing your Stalker Car to happen."

The room went silent. Now was his time to strike. Arsyen rose from his chair and opened his palm to reveal the pink, heart-shaped bottle of Aimo Air Freshener.

"For you, Jennie, so I can always find you."

Jennie shook her head.

"We're killing this project," she said. "As your lead, *I* am killing this project."

Jennie stomped out of the cubicle, brushing past Arsyen and knocking the bottle out of his hand. Arsyen gasped as his sweetly scented vision of eternal love shattered into a thousand shards of pink glass. The liquid sizzled like acid on the ground, devouring an orphaned Cheerio near Sven's desk.

Sven hit the desk with his fist. "Dammit! Do you all get what just happened?"

He pushed his chair out of the way and stomped out of the cubicle, a shard of Arsyen's pink glass heart lodging itself in the bottom of his flip-flop.

✸

For Anahata's great technical minds, boredom was far worse than anger. It hovered above their cubicle like a dirty cloud, obscuring all possibilities beyond what was proximate. After Jennie stomped out, Jonas pouted while trolling message boards; Sven focused on improving his speed at the Rubik's cube. With each second gained, he let out a new sigh, as if these small victories were simply a reminder of a greater defeat.

Things were much worse for Arsyen. Sven had told him it was just a matter of time before they were all reassigned to other teams. That new team would quickly figure out Arsyen was a fake, and even if they let him stay at Anahata, he'd surely be demoted to a lower-paying janitorial role. His contributions to the Throne

Reclamation Committee would drop, there would be no Pyrrhian liberation for decades, and Arsyen wouldn't enjoy the palm fronds and promiscuous handmaidens he deserved until he was old and wrinkled.

No kingdom. No girlfriend. He'd be back to cleaning toilets.

All of this was Jennie's fault. As his father had always said, women are harmless until, suddenly, they're not.

Arsyen gazed at Natia's photo on his computer, apologizing to the bearer of its image for having lost his way. He caressed her pixelated cheek and yelped—his internet girlfriend had just shocked him.

With nothing else to do with his time, Arsyen decided to check in on his GaltPage. He saw that his previous night's post encouraging people to take action had prompted a response from more than twelve thousand people.

For a moment, Arsyen remembered the sweet taste of obedience.

He scanned the news. Images of Poodlekek captured jagged windows of abandoned storefronts and old women crying, shaking their fists. Youths in bandannas and sweatshirts huddled in front of international TV cameras, shouting slogans as the newscaster voiceover explained there had been a ten-thousand-person march in which protesters had clashed with police. Ninety people were reported dead—a number that didn't include the hundreds who had died in the train wreck.

His mobile phone rang, and Arsyen ducked out of the cubicle to take the call.

"The TRC is ready to strike," announced the Throne Reclamation Committee's chief strategist.

"But we're nowhere near ready," Arsyen said.

"The TRC has spoken!" said the strategist, and then abruptly hung up.

Five minutes later came another call, this time from an unfamiliar voice whose words were punctuated by a hacking cough.

"Korpeko has outlawed our beloved (cough) national (cough)

sport. A curling court now cuts through the Arsyen Aimo (cough) Croquet Academy!"

Arsyen rose to his feet. How dare Korpeko destroy his gleaming croquet court! Arsyen had spent hours deciding on the color scheme. He had made numerous visits to the site to ensure that the proposed spot for his statue was positioned so the sun rose from his left hand and set in the right. And now—destroyed!

Arsyen wondered how many of his supporters were out there, working with the Throne Reclamation Committee to plot his return. "Thousands," the chief strategist had once said. "Millions," he sometimes claimed.

He returned to his cubicle and gazed once again at Natia's photo. She looked very serious, with her hair pulled back and not even a trace of a smile. But she was pretty, and he liked that mole on her right cheek. It made it easy to tell the difference between one side of her face and the other. Where was she? There was no sign of her—not on his GaltPage, in the newspapers, or on email. Was she in trouble?

Arsyen's phone rang again. This time his ears filled with the sound of the old national anthem—the song that had once played each time Arsyen's father addressed the nation.

Nationhood, brotherhood, progress upon progress...

"It is time," said a man's emphysematic voice, as the music faded.

"But we don't have enough money," Arsyen protested.

"Revolutions don't need money. Without money, people are more motivated, more bloodthirsty."

Arsyen's father had often said the same thing. He inhaled sharply.

"I need some time to think."

Arsyen scanned Flitter, the Galt app that had been appropriated by the protesters. There was no sign of Natia, but one fleet did catch his attention. In just thirty minutes it had been refleeted three thousand times, as if a rallying cry for the revolt.

Niels_1973: Raise your lighters for #Poodlekek

Arsyen read the fleet twice, its simple, thirty-four-character plea underscoring the desperation of his country.

This was all moving too fast. If only everything were ready—the forty cows, the special bomb, and the ten thousand horses. The latest TRC report had shown the acquisition of only ten cows and two mangy goats. How could that possibly be enough?

Arsyen left his cubicle and found an empty micro-kitchen. He rang the chief strategist.

"Can we do it without the horses and the bomb? Like, in some sort of peaceful way, with just the cows?"

"Since when were you against violence?" the chief strategist asked. "Don't you remember the king's annual dissident hunt? You rode one of the bears!"

"Mmm," said Arsyen, remembering those winter days of crisp air and hearty stews. "But those were peasants. They don't count. And anyway, Korpeko's no fool. If the peasants are revolting, he will put them down quickly and quietly."

"That's where you are mistaken, Your Highness. It is not the peasants who are protesting. The peasants are too busy with work to have time for revolt. It is the students, the middle class, who are up in arms. That is much trickier for the government."

"I need to think," Arsyen repeated. He hung up and frowned, then returned to his cubicle. He scanned the new Flitter messages on his computer.

Korpeko must be stopped!

Down with tyranny!

The subtext was clear. "Come back, Prince Arsyen! Lead us to our destiny!"

Many of the messages linked to Arsyen's GaltPage. Surely it was not mere coincidence that he, Prince Arsyen, had become their conduit.

Arsyen turned again to Flitter, typing to his people in their native tongue.

Wouldn't it be better to have the royal family in power? #Poodlekek

A response came quickly.

Sure, if you want to die by starvation rather than in a train crash.

And then another:

Anything's better than Korpeko.

Arsyen's heart beat faster. It was just as the Throne Reclamation Committee had said. His people *were* calling for him.

He looked for another response. Instead, there was that same message again from Niels_1973. People kept refleeting it.

Raise your lighters for #Poodlekek

Arsyen studied the message closely. Unlike the other *#Poodlekek* messages, this one was written in English. It was a clever move—an English fleet would reach an international community. This person was a strategist, someone central to the movement—someone like Natia, trying to bring their domestic turmoil to international attention and put pressure on the Pyrrhian government. If there was any sort of core revolutionary committee, Niels_1973 was a part of it. He probably had additional ideas or information. Perhaps he even knew Natia.

Arsyen clicked on the sender's handle and read some of his other fleets. From what he saw, Niels_1973 had written a lot about a famous pop singer before he had started fleeting about Poodlekek. From misspelled, teenybopper musings, Niels_1973's fleets had moved to angry, passionate words about lighters and bodies and destroyed hopes.

Burn it all down! #Poodlekek

Justice for All #Poodlekek

Arsyen imagined Niels was a college student, a man who hours earlier had been listening to La Lala, carefree and young, before suddenly seeing bodies burn around him.

He might have the key to Natia's whereabouts.

Across town in Atherton, the *ping!* of a new Flitter message rang sweetly in Niels' ears.

"Yes!" he said aloud, pumping his fist in the air and draining his second bottle of wine. It was his first response since he had begun targeting Poodlekek fans.

But whether he was drunk or simply confused, the message from PrinceArsyen didn't make much sense:

Is it that bad? Can I help?

Was PrinceArsyen quoting a Poodlekek song? It certainly wasn't from any Poodlekek song he could remember. Niels hated it when he was outsnobbed by other music fans.

Then again, even as a lyric, the fleet didn't really make sense. Poodlekek songs were never about charity or helping people. It was one of the reasons Niels had liked them so much—heavy metal had been an early conduit for his misanthropy. He had even found the name of the band fitting—all about the prissiest of dogs, a poodle, getting kicked.

Niels pictured a startled poodle flying through the air above him, landing with a crash among Gregor's shelf of Chateau Latour.

He laughed at the image, but then paused. Poodlekek, or was it Poodle*kik*? Poodle*kik*. Poodle*kek*. Poodle*kik*…

What the hell was Poodle*kek*?

Niels groaned, suddenly remembering a college geography course. Poodlekek was the capital of one of those countries no one cared about; one of the places that was always poor, and always in re-volt, whose leaders were always doing crazy things like naming the days of the week after their dead pets. The hundreds of #Poodlekek fleets about violence now made sense to him. There must be some sort of revolt in the region. That was just what those countries did when they had free time.

"Arrrrrrrrrgh!" Niels kicked the step of the cellar stairs. How could he screw up his Flitter strategy yet again? How many more times would he have to start over?

And then he stopped. An invisible hook passed over Niels' face, first drawing the eyebrows upward, then the corners of the mouth, freezing in a smile.

He turned back to his phone. There was a new message.

@PrinceArsyen: *What it like there? People ok?*

Niels responded immediately.

@Niels_1973: *Shootin', lootin', and general pollutin'!*

It was the chorus of his favorite Poodlekek song: *Shootin'—boom boom—lootin'—boom boom—gen-er-al pollutin'!*

Niels hummed the song, feeling the wine dance along with him in his head. No one cared about old Niels, but it seemed like a whole lot of Flitterati cared about a bunch of poor people in Poodlekek. He'd make the most of it.

@PrinceArsyen: *Anyone hurt?*

@Niels_1973: *Can't you hear the distant cry, of the children, the women!*

@PrinceArsyen: *Horrible!*

@Niels_1973: *No food, no water, we're in for a hell of a slaughter!*

Arsyen gasped as he read Niels_1973's messages. It was worse than he had imagined. Natia, his supporters—they were all in danger. He jumped from his seat and paced the cubicle, the trumpets of the Pyrrhian national anthem marching through his head.

It was eleven a.m. in Palo Alto, but already nighttime in Pyrrhia. His country was moving into the future before him, its steps and disasters ahead of him and beyond his control. He jumped back to his computer.

PrinceArsyen: *Can I help? What do you need?*

Niels_1973: *I am a leader, kidnapped and trapped.*

PrinceArsyen: *Klok klu sto bi kek Natia Simatov? Kiki Natia?*

Niels_1973: *Speak English. Other languages danger-ous. Can you call the police for me?*

PrinceArsyen: *Police controlled by government. Natia Simato safe?*

Niels_1973: *Natia is in great danger.*

Arsyen felt his heart jump. There was no one but him who could save Poodlekek.

Arsyen spun in his chair to face the whiteboard, trying to dream up cheap and quick modifications to his forty-cow, one-bomb, ten-thousand-horse plan.

"Sven," he said, tapping his co-worker on the shoulder. "If you want to do something but don't have money, is it problem?"

Sven looked up from his Rubik's cube. "If you build something people want, the monetization will figure itself out. That's what Bobby always says."

"So if you need to kill someone but don't have money to pay person to do?"

"Figure out how to incentivize them. Give them extra points or access to a secret level or something. Maybe they win an extra life if they kill the bad guy?"

"Yes!"

Arsyen stood. If Bobby Bonilo could run his company without thinking about money, then Arsyen could certainly take back his small country without it. All he needed was vision and spirit... and two other things.

"I need guns and horses," said Arsyen. "Does Anahata have?"

Sven kept twisting his Rubik's cube and didn't look up. "Hmm... probably. Ask one of the receptionists."

Arsyen nodded and made a note to contact Jennie. He had a long to-do list and very little time. He had to get to Pyrrhia. He bent over his keyboard and wrote one last time to Niels_1973.

Coming! Stay there!

He stood, made the sign of the red-breasted woodpecker, and dashed out of the cubicle.

GREGOR

G regor knew nothing about the ventilation system in his wine cellar. Niels had been stuck down there since the previous evening—how much longer could he last? A few days? Gregor still needed several weeks before Project Y would be ready.

Then there was the issue of sustenance. Gregor had to go to work and would be able to feed Niels only twice a day. That was probably sufficient—though Niels' body might not easily digest the legume balls Gregor ate in lieu of breakfast and dinner. Even then, he had no slit or dumbwaiter he could use to pass food or water to the cellar. And if he opened the door to deliver it himself, Niels might pounce from the top step. Even if Gregor could overpower him (which was no guarantee), he'd have that same problem each time—unless he didn't feed Niels, and Niels became weak and then… but no, that was too cruel. And in any case, at the moment Niels had all of his strength and wits about him—what might he do to Gregor's wine collection? Was it bad to starve him just a bit? Gregor could feel his head spinning. He had stayed up all night and hadn't gone into work that morning—the first time in ten years. But it was already almost noon, and still he had no plan.

As much as Gregor hated it, there was only one thing left to do. He rang Bobby.

Someone picked up immediately, but there was a loud racket on Bobby's side, and Gregor couldn't hear the voice on the other line.

"Bobby? Is that you?"

It sounded like a bunch of children running about, screaming and banging cymbals.

"Bobby? I can't hear you."

The clamor suddenly stopped.

"Sorry," came Bobby's voice. "I lost control of the electric chimp, and he was throwing things from the chandelier. He's made quite a mess, and someone's going to have to clean it up."

"Listen, we need to talk," Gregor said. "I did what you told me. I removed the roadblock, but now I don't know what to do."

"Roadblock?" asked Bobby.

"The roadblock I told you about before. I removed it."

"Oh, good! I told you those colonic cleanses were effective. Though… how long were you stuck in the bathroom? I gotta say, by the time I got to the second hour on the toilet—"

"No, Bobby. I mean the sales roadblock."

"I see," said Bobby. "The… sales… roadblock."

"The sales roadblock… is locked in my wine cellar."

There was silence on the other end. Then came a groan. "Ugh, this is last year all over again. Is she an employee this time?"

Gregor sighed. Bobby was confusing him with Fischer, Anahata's CFCAO known as much for his fiscal wizardry as his trysts with the company's paralegals. Gregor hadn't had a woman in his home since his grandmother died. Bobby knew that. How could he confuse him with someone like Fischer?

"Nothing like that," Gregor said. "I'm talking about the Project Y roadblock. I had no other choice. He was going to stop it all. Stop our engineers. Stop our dream!"

"Which dream?"

"Project Y, Bobby! You have to help me."

"We do best when we help ourselves."

"He's locked in my cellar. I don't know what to do."

"You and Niels need to learn to work things out. My yogi told me that—"

"If he gets out, he will destroy Project Y. Please, Bobby. I never ask for your help, ever. But this time… it's him or me. You have to choose."

Bobby sighed.

"Okay. My thought sends itself to you."

"Bobby?"

Bobby sighed again, louder this time.

"Listen closely and I will repeat myself: I will send Progressa to deal with your cellar. In the meantime, I want you to leave now and drive to my cabin. Do you understand?"

"Yes, Bobby."

NIELS

Niels' wine buzz had long worn off, and he was left with nothing but exhaustion. He had been stuck in Gregor's basement for eighteen hours. His sales team at Anahata was well into the workday, marching forward to monetize unconquered corners of the internet.

Niels kept glancing at the top of the stairs, straining his ears for the sound of a car coming down Gregor's driveway. But there was no sign of PrinceArsyen. He had sent him the Tuscany Drive address and tried messaging him several times, but it all had gone unanswered.

Niels stifled a yawn. He was too angry to sleep. He kicked the broken chair, then the good chair, and finally the table, leaving the center of the cellar looking like the remnants of a bar fight. Niels scanned the room for something else to kick, but there was nothing left beyond wine bottles. Those weren't an option—he didn't want to stain his Prada shoes.

He sat down against the wall opposite the stairs. Once he made it out of Gregor's dungeon, he would make sure that ads were on every single Anahata product—blinking, singing, dancing, screaming at consumers to try, buy, dabble, and dip into any and everything that a human being could be offered. And then he would have Gregor Guntlag fired and thrown in jail.

Just then, Niels heard a crunching of footsteps outside the door at the top of the stairs. He drew in his breath, straining to hear what was happening on the other side. He hoped it was PrinceArsyen coming to rescue him, but even if it was just Gregor, that would still be progress.

Niels considered his options. He didn't want to do anything that would set Gregor off. Admitting defeat was fine if it would get him out of that cellar. He sat up straight in preparation for his visitor.

The door opened a crack, and a sliver of white light peeked through, a light so bright that Niels suddenly realized just how dark it had been. But even with the light pouring in from above, there was little Niels could see above the shadows now cast across the entrance. "Hello?" he called out. "Gregor?"

There was no answer, but Niels could now make out the form of two pairs of legs, shifting, conferring with each other, at the top of the stairs. The silence worried him.

"I think I've been down here long enough. You've made your point," Niels said. "There will be no ads on Moodify, and I'll help you with your moon plan."

As he rose to his feet, the legs on the stairs suddenly dropped into a crouch. He could make out the outline of two enormous frames, a pair of linebackers blocking the stairs.

"No sudden moves, Niels," said an unfamiliar voice. "There are more of us than there are of you."

It was them.

Niels took a step back, running into the wall.

"I'll do anything you say," he said, his voice collapsing at the end of his sentence.

He had never thought it would end like this, at the hands of the Progressa unit. These were the men who ostensibly brought Anahata technology to the poor but who lived in the shadows, nameless, faceless, conveniently turning up in various spots around the world just before popular upheavals, banking reforms, or natural disasters. They were also known to clean up any of Bobby's "messes."

Now Niels was one of those messes. The stupidity of his earlier nonchalance leaped upon him. His eyes darted about the basement, looking for a means of defense or a place to hide. He could grab a wine bottle, but Niels realized there were too many legs at the top of the stairs, too many Progressa men for him to take on his own.

The heavy shoes began their descent down the staircase, their large bodies blocking most of the light from the top. Quickly, Niels refleeted an earlier message, hoping one of his six thousand Flitter followers would finally take him seriously.

#Anahata building moon colony. Stop them!

GREGOR

When Gregor arrived at Bobby's cabin in Big Sur, he found his boss blindfolded, sitting in the grove behind his back porch. Laid before him were a stone, a strip of bark, a leaf, and a mobile phone.

Although Gregor didn't understand the significance of the props, he immediately recognized the ritual. It was the same performance Bobby had enacted a decade earlier, just a few days before Anahata became a publicly traded company. Summoned at midnight to a small Palo Alto park, the Anahata board of directors had watched Bobby's cryptic movements in horror, worrying in hissed whispers that he would repeat his routine at the sound of the market's opening bell. Then, as now, Gregor absorbed it as one might a nature program. He believed that watching Bobby (and watching Bobby watch others as they watched him) was the only path toward understanding the Anahata founder and his genius.

Because for all of his billions, comprehension was the one thing Bobby Bonilo couldn't buy and would probably never have.

But that's why he had Gregor, whose job it was to help translate Bobby's vision to reality. If Bobby was a genius and his ideas transformed the world, then Gregor's work was vital to human progress. If Bobby was a sociopath and his dreams lacked innovation, then it meant Gregor was a fool and his own work meaningless.

Bobby was now rubbing the strip of bark against his cheek. Gregor glanced at his watch—more out of curiosity than impatience—and realized he had been standing on the porch for ten minutes. He zipped up his windbreaker—the ocean lay just beyond the fir trees, and the air was crisp.

Gregor let a few more minutes pass, as he knew he should, then threw a rock against a nearby trunk, producing a loud *thud* sufficient to break Bobby's trance.

Bobby removed his blindfold, bowed to the grove's fir trees, then threw his hands into the air, waving his fingers as though playing a piano in the sky. He breathed deeply, taking in the forest air, then lowered his arms and slowly walked back toward his cabin.

"I've been thinking about big data," he said to Gregor as he sat down on the bench.

"What about it?"

"That it could be bigger. *Much, much* bigger," he said, his hands drawing an imaginary load of great weight.

Gregor looked at Bobby's hands. How could big data be bigger? How could there be a limit on the limitless?

"And one other thing—optical time travel. People get too caught up in transporting the physical body. And then they worry about whether *you* are *you* once your body has been reconstituted. If we just transport your eyes, you can see everything, but it's like, just your eyes. All the benefits, none of the existential dilemma."

"But if the eyes are on the body—"

"Not now, Gregor. Only big thoughts here. Big thoughts."

Bobby gestured at the forest before them.

"You know, I think differently when I'm out here. As Thoreau said, 'I lose myself in society, but I find myself in the woods…' Want some kombucha?"

Gregor shook his head. He would've preferred to talk about big data and optical time travel, but there was a much more pressing matter at hand.

"What will they do to Niels?"

"Ah, Gregor. When you know as much as I do, you also know that knowledge is not always a gift. I will not burden you with knowledge. But rest assured that Progressa will not hurt him. I was clear about that. I also asked that they teach him Spanish."

"Spanish?"

"In case we ever want to bring him back. We really need a more diverse workforce."

Bobby was always one step ahead.

"Now that I've solutionized that little problem," Bobby said, "tell me where we are with Project Y."

"With Niels gone, I expect things will be back in shape on the technical side with Project Y within a day or two. The field, the servers—we can now move forward without any obstacles. Though there is one other problem. A human problem."

Bobby's eyebrows rose. "Is something wrong with our child prodigies... or the distractions? Is there something wrong with Genie? Social Car?"

"The child prodigies are all fine. The distractions are good, too. Actually, I threw a female receptionist onto the Social Car team to slow them down a bit. They were performing ahead of schedule and could have launched this quarter, ahead of Project Y. The result was actually better than I expected—she killed the project. So that's currently serving as a distraction for the distraction. I think I will try the same technique with a few other teams."

"It's a shame women keep failing at the opportunities we offer them," Bobby sighed.

"Well, yes, that's part of our problem, actually—the women," Gregor said. "According to our predictions, our colony dies out after the first generation because we can't get the inhabitants to breed."

"How can that be? We've optimized for the best models of behavior and philosophy for the past fifteen centuries."

"Yes, but only if we can get the colony to self-perpetuate. We've run several different models, but we can't get the women to sleep with our male engineers, who of course make up the bulk of our moon population. Hence, virtually no breeding, and our colony eventually dies out. The best we can do is keep shipping women in, but that doesn't make for a stable community."

"That doesn't make sense," Bobby said. "It's biologically predestined to work."

"But it doesn't," said Gregor, remembering working through the same questions when he had pored over the data. "Our analysis suggests that the women don't find a compelling attraction mechanism present in the engineers."

"No attraction mechanism," Bobby said slowly. "But surely there is nothing more attractive than an engineer?"

Gregor shrugged. "When the data provided no clues, we tried asking some female employees what they thought of the engineers. We did a few focus groups, but even then, the women couldn't pinpoint any huge problem."

"Of course they couldn't," Bobby snorted. "The women at Anahata love engineers. Why else would they work for us?"

"There were some who highlighted hygiene and clothing issues, and the word 'nerd' came up a lot, but mainly they just found the engineers to be less desirable than other men on campus."

"What other men?"

"The sales team."

"Hmm." Bobby stood and walked to the edge of his porch, gazing into the forest. "Gregor, this is serious."

"Yes, the breeding program is crucial to—"

"It's not just breeding. I see now that there is no path to happiness in our plan. Happiness *is* the path. We have no happiness *and* no path."

Gregor tried to visualize what a path to happiness would look like but could only conjure up his driveway and its rows of towering pines.

"Our engineers must be happy if our society is to succeed. They are the keystone of our new world. If they are not happy, our society will fail. And the best way to make them happy—more in our new world than they could ever be in this one—is to give them what is impossible today."

Bobby crossed the porch and nodded to himself, stopped, then nodded again.

"We made a crucial error. We only thought about innovation and happiness through the prism of isolation, not of inclusion."

"Inclusion?"

"Our bodies are linked by desire. We must harness desire in order to transform ourselves into something transcendental."

"Transcendental?"

Bobby threw up his hands.

"*Fucking*, Gregor. We forgot about fucking. That's what our engineers need. Not just money. Not just hackathons. Not just innovation. They need girls. Preferably hot ones with loose morals."

"I guess we could look at shipping them in to the colony," Gregor said. "Once we have the space elevator, we could have a strip club furnish them directly and—"

"No, we can't just ship them in. We need Project Y to regenerate *and* we need to make sure the offspring are of the highest pedigree. So the women need to be Anahata employees who have made it past our stringent hiring process. Otherwise we'll end up with a moon colony of...," Bobby paused and grimaced. "A moon colony of normal people."

"What if—"

"I've got it!" said Bobby, rushing to Gregor's side. "How about we make the whole engineering department gay? If the men could just breed with each other, there'd be no dilution of intelligence or engineering skills..."

"But two men can't breed."

"Ugh, of course," Bobby said. "I'd forgotten that project still isn't complete. That would have made us a much more progressive company than Galt. Imagine a ten-thousand-man team of gay engineers—on the moon!"

Gregor cleared his throat. "I decided to address the attraction mechanism by looking at the greatest societies of history in order to find a correlation between philosophy and societal structure and—"

"And fucking? No, that's not the way. Philosophy is nothing more than a tree in our forest. Social structure is also a tree. But the fertilizer is the girls. If you get the girls, the engineers will come. And the engineers will be happy. And then, *then* they will make little saplings. But only in that order. Our forest must be fertile."

"A fertile forest," Gregor repeated slowly, trying to picture the happiness path leading into a lush forest. "I think the problem is still the same. The girls don't like the engineers as much as other types of men."

Bobby nodded then pressed his palms together and lowered his head. A minute later, he looked up.

"Then we must become the change we seek."

"I'm not sure I understand."

"No," Bobby sighed, "I guess you wouldn't."

The men sat in silence for a moment. Gregor waited for an explanation.

"Here's another way to think about it," Bobby said. "Some engineers will need playmates on the moon. Others, likely older, will be ready and interested in producing baby engineers. So we need to make The Engineer as a concept be sexy. It's the only way to cover both short-term pleasure and long-term mating."

Bobby began to pace. His toes jutted out past the edge of his plastic sandals. His pants bunched awkwardly around the back of his legs, stopping just a bit below the knees.

"We just need to fix the perception," Bobby muttered. "We must become the change we seek, we must become the change we seek…"

Gregor kept quiet on the bench, finding himself in a hopeless loop, with all potential solutions only leading back to the initial problem.

"I've got it!" shouted Bobby, leaping down from the porch and onto a pile of leaves. He stomped up and down in a victory dance, then looked up.

"You said the women kept comparing the engineers to the sales guys, right? So the answer is simple. We make it impossible for them to compare the two groups. We get rid of the competition."

"Like we did with Niels?" Gregor said. "We can't very well kidnap all of our sales staff."

"No, of course not. Listen. Do you know why supermodels sleep with me? Because I'm one of the richest men in the world and I excel at both tree and crow's pose. Women want my power, my status, my flexibility—it really is quite impressive. My shaman explained it once: Men want an attractive woman, but women want what we men represent. How else do you explain all the ugly men in the world married to beautiful women?"

"So…"

"So all we need to do is elevate the status of our engineers."

"We can create a higher promotion curve for the engineers so they can have better titles than the sales team?"

"Nonsense! Think like a man for once, Gregor, not a computer. We just need to de-ball the sales guys, pull the pedestal out from under them. Lower their status."

"And so our engineers become the change they seek. They become the top," said Gregor, his head slowly nodding.

"Exactly. You work up the plan. I need to get some meditation done before the sun crosses my stone circle."

Bobby opened the cabin door.

"There's one more thing," Gregor said. "What are we going to tell the sales team about Niels?"

Bobby waved away Gregor's concern. "I only want to hear about the specifics after you've fixed the problem. Remember, small clouds the big."

"But—"

"Just come up with a plan." Bobby turned. "Oh, and then call HR Paul and tell him to draft me a note I can send to the employees."

"You want us to tell people what we're doing?"

Bobby shook his head.

"If you give a man a slice of the orange, he tastes the orange and thinks he knows what an orange tastes like. You do not need to give him the full orange to make him think that."

"I understand," Gregor said.

"Transparency makes us look strategic."

"I understand."

"Good, Gregor. It is so wonderful to see you continue to grow in your role."

LESSONS IN THOUGHT LEADERSHIP

To: Anahatis@anahata.com
From: Bobby@anahata.com
Subject: Positive Changes at Anahata

Dear Team,

While Wall Street defines a company's success by its numbers, at Anahata we see it as so much more. It's about people. It's about you. That's why this week we'll be rolling out even more benefits and programs to benefit Anahatis—and humankind:

Better the World (BW) benefit, to allow employees a paid sabbatical to work full-time for charity organizations, natural disaster relief, and left-leaning political campaigns.

Marathon Care Time (MCT). We know how hard it is to balance work commitments and marathon training. The MCT benefit allows those in training to have greater support from their managers in terms of flexible working hours and special exemptions.

Anahata Eats (UEats) program, which ensures that any

uneaten food purchased by Anahata will not be wasted, but rather provided to local communities. This week, we will be serving leftover lobster and blanched asparagus to four local homeless shelters!

Horizontal Moves (HM), a new, exclusive career development program designed to help sales staff explore new roles in the company and broaden their skill set. Select sales staff will be chosen to participate in this exciting career opportunity, which will start tomorrow. We look forward to developing the program in response to your feedback.

On a final note, we would like to inform you that we will be making a small change to our organizational structure. Going forward, all of sales will report into Gregor Guntlag so that we can better align our engineering and sales goals. We think this change will help streamline processes, ensure quick decision-making, and make sure we are all moving in the right direction. We'd like to thank Niels Smeardon for all of his hard work. He has left the company for other adventures.

Onward and upward!
Bobby

✳

As documented by the HR department, there were four types of employee reaction to the memo announcing Niels' departure.

The first group never read the memo. This was primarily the engineers, who believed that anything sent to the entire company would be devoid of data and facts, given it was necessary to be comprehensible to the lowest common denominator (aka sales).

The second group responded with indifference. This was the support staff—people in departments like legal, finance, marketing, HR, and customer support—who were reminded on a daily basis that their opinions and activities were not truly vital to the company's success. They knew that a shakeup at the top wouldn't change their status in the slightest. They read the email, shrugged their shoulders, and moved on with their meaningless day.

The third group responded with outrage. This was a small number of engineers who had actually read the email and found it unacceptable that the water slide and petting zoo they had requested months earlier still had not been granted, while other employees (clearly those from sales) were being granted a marathon-training allowance.

The final group was the sales team, who immediately understood the significance of Niels' departure. With just one nonchalant email from Bobby, a new world order was imposed, one in which bits and pixels trumped money and smarts trumped designer suits; a world in which golf clubs, fast cars, and weekend "business" trips to Vegas would be replaced with gadgets, robots, and video games. They knew nothing would be the same.

In fact, the reality turned out to be worse than anything they predicted. (As any engineer would have pointed out, this was to be expected, since the ability of the dimwitted sales team to predict much of anything was genetically limited.)

A few minutes following Bobby's memo, most members of the Anahata sales team received an email informing them that they had been chosen to participate in the Horizontal Moves (HM) program and that they should report to the sales auditorium in Building 13 at eleven a.m.

Their excitement at being chosen for an exclusive program dissipated once they arrived at the auditorium. The plush purple sofas that usually welcomed them for Niels' quarterly strategy meetings had been replaced with fold-up metal chairs. There was no breakfast buffet, no robot butler ready to dispense coffee. Just a man from the HR team with a clipboard who spoke only long enough to repeat Bobby's memo and then direct the group to line up according to last name at different stations throughout the auditorium. There, he said, they would be given their new special assignments.

The employee who sold ads to fast-food restaurants was given a pair of purple Anahata sweatpants and told to report to the volleyball court, where he would start that morning as a personal trainer. The employee who sold ads to construction companies, henceforth known as HM #4002, was given sunscreen, a suit, and a life buoy and told to make his way to the pool. A former cubicle mate, now known as HM #3403, was made part of the concierge service, while his former boss, HM #2435, became an errand runner for engineers who hated leaving their desks. HM #12009, formerly specialized in selling ads to podiatrists, was assigned to give foot massages to a product manager named Arsyen Aimo. When the latter didn't show up to his first appointment, HM#12009 was reassigned to run the puppet and juggling shows in Building 4.

Before leaving the auditorium, all the sales employees were given new orange badges that clearly identified them as a different class.

The next day, Horizontal Moves staff members who showed up for the company shuttle bus in San Francisco were curtly instructed to stand in a different line from the engineering staff; HM employees who drove to work were directed to separate parking lots located at the far end of campus. These employees were still allowed to eat in the cafeterias and take advantage of the many gyms and amenities, but they were assigned off-hours when they would be less likely to encounter engineering staff.

These weren't the only changes. The soccer field was closed for sports so it could be used as an amateur rocket launcher and robot playing field. The lap pool was taken over by a group of engineers who wanted to build a salamander farm. And the Friday afternoon drinks party in the main hall—which the sales team had long viewed as their territory—no longer played hip-hop and pop music, but rather ambient sounds and repeats of *Star Trek*.

The other Anahata employees took quickly and easily to the new hierarchy. They soon began referring to the former sales employees as Horizontal Movers, or simply by those two damning letters—HM.

As for the HM staff, even they had to admit life wasn't so bad on the bottom—low stress for the same pay. Many of them spent their entire days working out, and their six-packs grew new, defined lines. Such accomplishments made them wonder whether their destiny had never been to sell things—and intangible things in a virtual world, at that—but rather just to be in incredible physical shape.

Of course, there were moments when they suddenly remembered the thrill of their old life, of hitting their monthly sales target and beating their colleagues in the number of new client acquisitions. When those memories hit, the HM puppeteers would suddenly transform their rehearsal of *Sesame Street* into *Reservoir Dogs*, the HM lullaby squad would change the engineer naptime music to death rock, and the HM physical trainers would find themselves assigning their engineering clients one thousand jumping jacks or a five-mile run. The engineers huffed and puffed, but it was of little consolation to the demoted employees; the stain of their new HM status stamped itself in blotchy red patches across their clients' faces.

But most of the time, they just admired their biceps. Life as a full-time jock was a much less stressful way to live.

✷

Anahata's PR director awoke with a start. She saw the phone jumping on her nightstand, a blue light flashing across the screen. It registered then—her phone was ringing. It was her boss, Greg Fischer. The ringtone gave him away: a trumpet heralding the release of racehorses from their starting gates.

She scrambled to sit upright, as though worried Fischer could see through the windows of her home. She was sure he wouldn't approve of her being asleep at 6:24 a.m. since he, like most nonengineers in the Valley, believed in rising early in order to achieve great things before everyone else.

Her boss both terrified and frustrated her. Although PR was one of the departments he controlled as part of his larger remit as chief financial and corporate affairs officer (CFCAO), Greg Fischer had no idea what her team did and generally spoke to her only when something had gone horribly awry.

"Yes, I'm here," she said crisply into the phone, hoping she sounded alert. "What's going on?"

"A blogger found some fleets from Niels, and *Tech Geek* just picked it up. It'll be everywhere soon. *The Street*'s already onto it. The market opens in six minutes, and we're going to take a real beating. Read it and call me back."

The phone clicked, and she was alone again.

She yawned, then quickly shuffled to her kitchen table. She scanned the news feed on her computer. The last time Fischer had woken her up with a "press emergency," it was because a gossip rag had run a picture of Bobby's electric chimp without his permission. Fischer wanted the issue recalled and couldn't understand why she was unable to make that happen.

The PR director scrolled through the headlines. There were thousands of stories each day about Anahata—half of them on gossipy *Tech Geek*—but it took no time at all to determine which story had prompted Fischer's early morning freak-out:

Anahata Moon Colony: Totally Awesome or Totally Insane?

By PJ Point, May 13, 6:10 a.m. PST

Silicon Valley types like to think big. But "let's fly to the moon!" big? That's pretty ambitious. It seems that's exactly what wacky

Anahata is up to, according to fleets posted by the company's top sales exec, Niels Smeardon (@Niels_1973), who urged his followers to stop the tech giant from going to the moon. Smeardon's departure was announced internally two days ago—shortly after the timestamp of these fleets. Could these be the ramblings of a disgruntled employee? Or could Anahata really be building a moon colony?

It's not totally clear whether the fleets are real. After all, there are very few posts before this one by Niels_1973, and the bulk of his messages are about La Lala—hardly something screaming tech credibility, though the pop starlet did once try to hump the internet at an awards show. But rumors of a top-secret project at Anahata have been floating about for the past few months, with many saying that founder Bobby Bonilo is looking to build a killer product that will serve a knockout punch to the company's main competitor, Galt.

There's also a less exciting though somewhat credible explanation: There have been whispers that the company is interested in finding new places to put its data centers.

If that's the case, well, you'd think there'd be cheaper options than the moon, but this is Anahata. And with privacy freak Gregor Guntlag leading engineering, he may just want to get Anahata's precious user data as far away as possible from any U.S. government agencies.

Have any information? Let us know!

The woman sighed and rang her boss.

"What's your plan?" Fischer snapped.

"I need to know if it's true," she said. "The moon colony. If it's not true, we'll just say it's not true. It's actually quite straightforward—*if* it's not true."

"The truth is not relevant in this case," Fischer said. "Just fix it. Deny nothing. Confirm nothing. Hold on."

Fischer's voice was muffled then, as though he had placed the phone against his shirt. She could hear another male voice in the background. A few seconds later, Fischer was back.

"I have Bobby on speakerphone. Do you need him to do an interview?"

"An interview where he denies and confirms nothing? I don't think that will help with—"

"He says he will do it provided you can get approval on the article before it's printed. The stock is going to take a dive today if this story stays up."

"I can't control the media, and I can't rewrite a *Tech Geek* article—or any article. Not in this country."

"Hold on."

She imagined Bobby and Fischer speaking in a magical, foreign tongue, with only Fischer able to translate the founder's words into speech a mortal like herself could understand. In the five years since she had taken over Anahata's PR team, she had not once spoken to Bobby directly. And this, she recalled with no small amount of resentment, despite having spun a massive copyright case against the company into a populist revolt against the music industry and pushed the U.S. government, which was investigating Anahata, to christen a new phrase in competition law: "dynamic dominance." Just last week she had managed to keep photos of Bobby in a high-end Latvian brothel from making it to print.

Fischer returned to the phone with a bark.

"Bobby wants to know in which country you *can* control what gets printed."

The PR director racked her brain. "Russia, Poland, some Southeast Asian countries—"

"Those won't work!" Fischer snapped. "We are not moving the company to Russia. The tax structures there aren't favorable at all. Jesus—think practically! What about Bermuda? Cyprus? Malta?"

"I—I—I have to admit I don't know much about the press there. They are smaller countries, so you might be able to—"

"Dammit!" Fischer shrieked. "I need a plan. Bobby and I are very upset."

"Understood. I will fix it."

Fischer hung up on her.

The PR director slumped in her chair as she reread the *Tech Geek* story, the only consolation to the inevitably long week ahead being the fact that she wasn't going to have to relocate to Moscow.

RESPONSIBLE USES OF
SOCIAL MEDIA

May 13, 11:03 a.m. PST
By Greg Fischer, Chief Financial and Corporate Affairs Officer (CFCAO)

If you've been reading about Anahata in the press this morning, you've probably read something about a moon colony we're supposedly building. We'd like to take this opportunity to set the record straight.

First, please look at this picture of the moon.

Do you see a colony on it? Neither do we.

So here's what happened.

After being asked to leave Anahata a few days ago, Niels Smeardon, our former SVP of sales, posted some messages on Flitter that ended up making it into the media. Niels is a big fan of social media and was interested in utilizing some of the marketing techniques he had learned during his career. The messages he sent were designed to increase engagement with his followers and were not meant to be construed as fact. It is well known that there is little relationship between reality and what people post on social networks.

We hope this clears up any confusion.

To: anahatis@anahata.com
From: paul@anahata.com
Subject: Important Reminder About Social Media Use

Fellow Anahatis,

You've no doubt seen things in the press today about
Anahata and a moon colony. While the story was funny,

what has happened in the market—a more than 10 percent drop in our share price—is not. Rest assured that we are working to correct the rumors that are floating about. In the meantime, we ask that you remain focused on your work—and all the Anahata fun we provide (btw have you tried out the new organic juicers?!?).

In addition, I'd like to take this opportunity to remind you of our company's policy on social media and blogs. We think these platforms are wonderful things, and we want you all to use them as you wish. The internet, after all, was built on free speech!

But we do have a few guidelines we'd ask that you respect.

There is NO blogging or posting about Anahata projects or policies, market strategies, or competitors.
Here's an example of things that are okay to post—you'll see that it's much longer than what you *can't* post!

1. All the fun things you do at Anahata.
2. Pictures of our delicious cafeteria food or of the cute animals and pets you are allowed to bring to work.
3. Thoughts about your hobbies (provided those hobbies do not cast a negative light on Anahata—for example, furry petting circles).
4. Relationship musings and advice (provided those relationships do not involve other Anahata employees).

Thanks for your cooperation!!!
- Paul Barlow, your friendly HR SVP!

JENNIE

From the Building 4 window, Jennie watched the cute HM trainer out on the soccer field as he moved closer to his client, the engineer's face straining as he attempted to lift a car tire toward his chest. The HMer got in the engineer's face and yelled some sort of insult; the engineer stumbled backward a few steps before regaining his footing. He brought the tire to the ground and looked to his trainer for praise. Instead, the HMer sent him off down the field to run sprints.

Just a week following the reorganization, the tanned, sporty sales guys already seemed like naturals in their new jobs. It was like they had been destined to be personal trainers and massage therapists; no one had to train them or teach them anything.

It couldn't have been a greater contrast to Jennie, who felt she wore her new engineering role like a little girl dressed up in her father's suit.

But she knew it had to work out. If Bobby Bonilo had a master plan for the sales team, surely he had a master plan for her.

Jennie had been studying Bobby ever since joining Anahata. She had read his autobiography, *Becoming the Me*, four times and kept a collection of all his internal strategy memos, taping the most inspirational and visionary quotes to her wall. Every time it looked like Bobby was making a highly questionable decision, it would later turn out he was solving three or four problems at once. Bobby Bonilo was always a few steps ahead of everyone. His book had said as much.

In this case, Bobby wasn't simply helping the sales team discover their natural talents. He was also achieving greater company unity. Engineers and HM staff were now coexisting peacefully. The sales employees had stopped tripping the engineers in the cafeteria, and the engineers had stopped programming their robots to chase the sales guys down the hallways. The internal email wars between the two groups had ended nearly overnight. In fact, the engineering staff seemed to have backed down entirely since the announcement of the HM program, no longer viewing their sales cum HM counter-parts as enemies, but rather officially acknowledged subordinates, children who should be encouraged and supported in their new roles.

Jennie's gaze moved across the field, pausing here and there on a bare chest or a chiseled set of cheekbones. It wasn't just HMers that caught her eye. Even some of the engineers were getting cuter. Many of them still walked with an odd, ape-like gait, but they somehow looked more... vigorous, healthy. Even Sven, horrible Sven, seemed to be sporting a new set of biceps.

"Get up, losers!" screamed a voice at the other end of the field, where a pile of arms and legs twisted about like a frantic octopus above the tire course.

She just couldn't understand why she wasn't succeeding in her new job. Of course it had seemed odd that Gregor would ask a nontechnical person to be the technical lead of Social Car. And that when he had asked her, he knew nothing about Jennie other than that she was a campus guide and receptionist.

But Gregor must have known (maybe it was in her HR file?) that Jennie was a born leader, and that leaders don't need skills—they just need to be leaders.

Jennie certainly had that. She was convinced she was destined for something world-changing, like reversing climate change or melting the polar ice caps to give clean water to people in Africa.

So, while being assigned to Social Car wasn't quite the same thing as building an endangered elephant preserve, Jennie knew not to pass on such an opportunity. This was the cosmos shaking an enormous neon sign right at her, telling her it was time for her to do great things.

But something had gone wrong in the universe. Jennie had somehow killed her own job.

Despite her lack of technical skills, Jennie didn't second-guess her decision to kill Social Car—or Stalker Car, as she now called it. She was confident it would have been a disaster for Anahata and driven women away with its creepy features.

But she also knew she had acted too hastily. After dramatically declaring halt to the project, Jennie found herself with no backup plan. Gregor was inaccessible, and Roni was completely MIA—probably on the moon colony the press kept talking about.

She tried to patch things up by returning to the cubicle the following week to brainstorm ideas but had been forced to retreat. Swivel chairs blocked the cubicle entrance. Sven refused to speak to her, and Jonas kept his eyes glued to the wizards on his screen. And Arsyen, the weird guy who tried to give her that foul-smelling perfume, seemed to have disappeared. He had left a message scrawled across the whiteboard—*KING ARSYEN!!!*—but no other clue as to his whereabouts.

To make matters worse, her friends were all thriving. Gregor had replaced all the lobby receptionists with sign-in kiosks and assigned the women to new technical projects, telling them it was a part of an HR program to "bring in more diverse perspectives."

Her closest friend, Karla, was now running a team that was building an internet hat—or, more precisely, an internet sombrero. Glasses popped down from the brim's front to help you see webpages; headphones could pop in from the sides if you wanted to listen to music or audio files. Best of all, just by nodding your sombrero in the direction of something, the hat would help identify the object before you.

Karla confessed to Jennie that she didn't really get why anyone would want an internet sombrero. "I mean, I've got my computer at home. I've got my mobile in my pocket. Why do I need a sombrero?"

"Did you ask them that?" Jennie asked.

"Of course not. They would have thought I was an idiot. You just have to trust the engineers. They're so smart, you know?"

"But did they ever think that maybe *they* would wear an internet sombrero but normal people probably wouldn't? I mean, it is… *weird*… right? Plus, what if it's too hot to wear a sombrero?"

Karla wrinkled her nose and giggled. "That's what I thought! But they pointed out that's why they made it a sombrero—better sun protection! Genius, right? In any case, the sombrero won't be around forever. Even if the first iteration is a sombrero, V2 will be a wig, and V3 will be reduced to a toupee or beret. The guys say that we just have to get the hat closer and closer to being part of the human head. Cuz like, eventually, it's just a brain chip, you know? Like an extension of your head. Though it's too bad they just can't skip right to that. I don't really want to have to go around wearing an ugly hat for two years just to show I'm a team player, you know?"

Jennie nodded.

"The guys on the team are really nice," Karla continued. "They say I take really good notes. You know, I always thought engineers were such dorks, but…"

Sven wasn't nice. Sven, with his messy blond hair and blue eyes and Johnny Rotten sneer. Sven who hated her and who never wanted to see her again. Sven who was an engineer. Sven who… who was like an architect, really, like an artist who painted in numbers.

Sven, who had destroyed her chance at greatness.

✳

The daily attention lavished on Jennie in Fried Fred's amounted to a short lunchtime victory followed by a long dismal afternoon. That day, she spent the afternoon tending to her plot in the company's organic garden and then curled up in a sleep capsule to reread Bobby's autobiography—in particular the chapters on failure (very short) and success (very long).

The sun was in its last pulses of light as Jennie made her way toward the exit. She stopped for a moment by the gigantic squid, the tank now lit for nighttime with gently pulsing pink lights from below. The squid looked so happy and peaceful bobbing in that turquoise water. Why couldn't she be like a squid?

The squid spotted Jennie and unfurled two of its arms, extending them across opposite ends of the tank, as though to give her a hug. Jennie took a step forward and put her hand to the glass. A tentacle mirrored her move. She felt a tear on her cheek. Oh, squid. Her friend the squid.

Jennie put her face to the glass, and in a swish, the squid rotated backward, exposing its mouth. It pressed its body against the glass as it chomped its jaws at her.

Even the squid didn't understand her—Jennie was nothing more to it than a potential meal.

As Jennie shuffled to the exit, her phone pinged with the sound of a new message. It was Arsyen, the Social Car engineer who had disappeared.

Hi Jenni, want chat?

She shook her head. She'd rather hang out with the mute squid than talk to that creepy Arsyen. She ignored his message and put her phone back in her pocket.

The campus had already cleared out, its lawn now empty of the voices and beeps and robots that roamed across it each day. Anahata's small green hills and winding streams now seemed like a scene from another part of America, a place where people took walks and made long-winded observations about the weather.

In her previous life, Jennie had loved to catch the campus in this state, to breathe in Anahata's freshly cut grass and optimism, but now she merely stared at her feet as she crossed the lawn.

As she passed by Building 2, a small rock suddenly flew through the air and connected with her wrist.

"Ow!"

Jennie jumped back and looked across the empty lawn, readying herself in the karate pose she had learned at her feminist book club. She looked to the left, then right, scanning for sudden movement or suspicious figures. There was nothing to be seen. Her shoulders settled back into their slump, and she began to make her way to her car.

"Psst! Over here!"

Jennie turned in the direction of the voice and saw a bush waving at her. She did a double take and confirmed that, yes, it was indeed a bush waving at her.

"It's me—Roni!"

"Roni?" She squinted at the bush. It was no longer moving.

"Sssh! Come here," he hissed, "before someone sees you!"

The bush began moving again, frantically this time, growing arms and legs, and suddenly Jennie realized it was no bush at all, but rather Roni dressed as a bush, his head popping out of an enormous fat suit, like a big green apple covered in brown leaves. When Jennie was close enough to make eye contact, Roni beckoned again with his green chin and then dropped below the shrubbery.

She pushed the brush back and found Roni crouched low on the ground. He was wearing camouflage on his lower half and had painted streaks of green and brown under his eyes to match his leafy suit. Jennie suppressed a laugh and reminded herself that this was the guy in charge of Anahata hackathons, the guy who used to run Social Car and could help her win credibility among the engineers. She needed his help.

"What's up with the outfit?" Jennie asked.

"It's just an extra precaution," whispered Roni, peering out through the bushes. "I am working on something confidential. *Very confidential!*"

So that's why Roni had disappeared, leaving no clue as to his whereabouts.

"I could use your advice, too," she said. "Social Car—"

"You *must* be quiet!" Roni hissed. "I will tell you what I can tell you. And then I need your advice. And then we can discuss your problem. In that order."

Roni cleared his throat, jumped up for a moment to stretch his legs, then hopped back down into a crouching, frog-like pose, the fat suit bobbing over his legs, threatening to swallow them. He motioned her down to his level.

"Tell me, how can I get women to like engineers?"

"Sorry? Not sure I understand."

"That's probably because I have not told you enough," Roni said. "To be clear, that was intentional."

Jennie rolled her eyes.

"Okay, okay, I will tell you more. But you must not say anything to anyone!" Roni held a finger to his lips. "We have a project that holds the future of Anahata. I can't tell you all the details yet, but what I will say is that a key component is getting women to like engineers."

"What?"

"As a first step," Roni continued, "we brought the Anahata women closer to the engineers and forced mixing of the sexes. You were an example of this—making a woman the technical lead of a project."

Jennie couldn't help but smile. She had been right. Her assignment—and Karla's, and all those other girls in Fried Fred's—it was all part of a weird experiment.

"From what we saw, bringing you and other girls into the engineering departments *did* increase male/female interaction a bit. But there are two problems. First, you women interact now with the engineers, but you're still not *dating* them, just *speaking* to them. We had not anticipated that these two actions were distinct. Second, some of the female leads—like you—are destroying ambitious engineering projects."

"But I—" Jennie protested.

"Don't take offense. We believe your failure on Social Car has nothing to do with your abilities or intelligence but a more general limitation of your gender."

It was a demeaning conclusion, and the feminist in Jennie

wanted to protest. But Roni was really just calling women failures, not Jennie specifically, and her ego was much more important to her than any larger social movement.

"That's actually *not* the biggest problem," Roni said. "Because even if I can get you girls to stop ruining our engineering projects *and* start dating the guys on your team, our approach still isn't scalable. We can't have women leading all of our technical projects if we want to be innovative. Besides, that would mean just one woman to every three to five men. Women can't reproduce quickly enough for that to be a successful ratio."

"What do you mean, 'reproduce'? Are you talking about babies?"

"Ignore the reproduction part for now," said Roni, waving the thought away with his hand. "The point is, how do I get more women to interact with the engineers at Anahata? It's a real problem. Even when we got rid of the competition, we didn't see enough uplift in dating or"—Roni smacked his hands together—"coupling."

"I'm not following you," said Jennie, shaking her head. "Babies? Competition? Coupling?"

"Forget the babies, forget the babies. There are no babies—that's part of the problem! But forget them for now. I will tell you about the competition part."

With a few grunts, Roni leaned forward in his suit, dragging his girth as he squatted close to the ground. He drew two stick figures in the dirt: one with an enormous head and the other with large arms. "Let's just say that there were two guys you could pick: a guy with a big brain or a guy with big biceps."

"Yeah, there are a few of those around here," said Jennie, a smile inadvertently crossing her lips as she thought of the squad of buff HM guys who ran drills each morning.

"Now say I've gotten rid of those guys," he said, making an X over the muscle-bound figure.

"I don't *want* you to get rid of those guys."

Roni grimaced. "Well, we did it. That's what the Horizontal Moves program is about. The sales guys are all at the bottom of the Anahata hierarchy now. And our engineers are the gods they deserve to be. The good news is that our data shows that now, when you women do talk to the engineers, you appreciate their higher status. As a result, there is a much higher success rate than in the past. We call it 'coupling.' So the coupling rate is much higher, although it still remains extremely low. Make sense?"

Jennie thought of all the women she had seen flirting with the engineers in Fried Fred's. It did make sense in its odd little way.

"So when we force the genders together, we have some good results, but generally, most of the women on campus aren't initiating conversations with the engineers. They just stay in their own buildings. So the two groups don't interact, conversations don't start, and coupling never occurs."

"You mean you want us to seek you guys out?" Jennie laughed. "Your logic is all wrong. Women aren't the hunters; we choose from everything that's offered to us. I mean, unless they're like me. I'm very assertive. As a feminist, I believe that—"

"I want to know about normal women," Roni said. "Not feminists."

"Well, my point is that the engineers need to come find us. And then they have to convince us that they are the ones we want."

"Okay, okay, I see," Roni said. "So we need a way to find the women. And then we need a way to facilitate conversation."

Jennie nodded.

"So, you are a woman. Tell me how to do this."

She shrugged. "Without fundamentally changing the engineers? Hmm… nothing occurs to me off the top of my head."

Roni's face fell, his fat suit slumping like a deflated balloon atop the caked mud.

"I should go," he sighed, casting his drawing stick into the bushes.

Without saying more, he dropped onto his belly, his face now at eye level with Jennie's shoes. He began to crawl slowly away, dragging bits of leaves with him as his fat suit bounced behind the bushes. Jennie made a swifter exit and headed to the parking lot.

As she slid into her car a few minutes later, Jennie realized that she had forgotten to ask Roni about Social Car.

"Ugh," she groaned, grimacing as she imagined the coming weeks of boredom.

Her phone dinged again with a message. It was Arsyen. The guy just couldn't take a hint.

Jenni, I need horses and guns. I have big revolution in pants.

"What guy *doesn't* have a big revolution in his pants?" Jennie muttered.

I mean big revolution plans, Arsyen wrote a second later. Which made even less sense than a revolution in his pants. This guy really needed help with his pickup lines.

She tossed her phone into the passenger seat.

And then it hit her—the solution to Roni's problem. It was so blindingly obvious.

Jennie turned her head and looked back at the bushes. At the far end of the building, with the aid of an overhead security light, she could see a bush rustling in the windless night, moving like a bloated, leafy phantom in the direction of the entrance.

Jennie jumped out of the car and ran in pursuit of the waving bush.

✳

The next morning, Jennie skipped into the Social Car cubicle with a box of bear claws and nearly tripped over a swivel chair that had fallen on its side. It seemed Sven and Jonas weren't even trying to keep her out anymore—they just didn't care.

It was obvious no work had been done in days. Drawings of robots were scattered across the whiteboard; Red Bull cans were stacked in a perfect pyramid, clearly untouched.

Jennie sidled up alongside Jonas, who didn't look up from his screen. From what she could tell, he was on a messaging forum, calling himself Wei and arguing about vegetables. To his left, Arsyen's desk was cleared off and spotless—a rarity at Anahata. Two pink sponges were stacked in the center; above them sat a note from Arsyen asking Sven to please look after them.

Jennie shifted in place just slightly so she could get a better look at her blue-eyed enemy. She studied his profile from across the cubicle and decided he actually wasn't bad-looking—particularly if he could just get rid of the dorky plastic sandals and weathered summer camp T-shirt. Then again, a costume change would probably not have any bearing on his abrasive personality.

Taking a deep breath, Jennie walked toward Sven's desk. She noticed his jaw tighten as she moved into his field of vision. She dropped her bait onto Arsyen's empty desk.

Sven's nose lifted. Jonas scooted his chair to the left to grab a bear claw from the box, but her hand blocked his reach.

"Where's Arsyen?" she asked him.

"We have not seen him in 4.6 days," Jonas said.

"No matter," said Jennie, lifting her hand. "Two people are ample resource to build our project."

"*You* have an idea," snorted Sven, eyes glued to his screen.

"Not only that. I have a project that's already been approved by Building 1."

Sven stopped what he was doing and partially swiveled his chair to face her.

"Building 1. Bobby's building?"

Jennie grinned.

"We're bringing back Social Car," she said, "but on the mobile phone."

They stared at her, and then at each other.

"I'll explain," she said. "Let's say you saw a cute girl—maybe at Fried Fred's. Would you go up and talk to her?"

"Well...," said Sven.

"Um...," said Jonas.

"Right. But if that girl was online, things would be different, right? Like Jonas, a second ago you were chatting in a forum. You had no problem pretending to be someone else."

"That's because there are no consequences online," Sven said. "If someone doesn't want to talk to you, you just move on to the next person."

"Because the fear of rejection is a lot lower on the internet, right?"

Jennie walked to the whiteboard and drew a rectangle. "This is a mobile phone," she said. Within the phone, she drew a bunch of squares with people's faces. "Now what does this look like?"

"A bit like the Social Car dashboard, I guess," said Sven, flipping open a can of Red Bull.

"I get it! I get it!" shouted Jonas, jumping up and racing to the whiteboard. "If you put Social Car on a mobile phone, you suddenly can see all the girls around you. You no longer need a car to meet or talk to them! And if they reject you, they reject you on the internet. So it is not *real* rejection. But if they like you, then you can talk to them!"

"And meet them," Jennie continued. "And because we're using Social Car technology, we'll know exactly where you are and can show you people nearby."

"Genius!" Jonas said.

"And we're going to start right here, with the girls at Anahata," said Jennie. "I was thinking we could call the project Social Me."

"Internal code name S&M," said Sven, snickering. But then his expression turned serious. "Here," he said, moving the doughnuts to the far corner of Arsyen's desk. "You're going to need a place to work."

THE GENIE TEAM

After three days and sixty-two hours of Social Me coding, five thousand Anahata employees—half male engineers, half female staff from across the company—received invitations to download and help beta test the new application on their phones. An email from the Social Me team to the lucky five thousand encouraged them to use their new app to "meet people near you now!"

"Why would I want to meet new people?" asked an engineer on the Genie team.

"Not people, idiot. *Girls*," said his teammate, showing him a row of female faces on the app. "Besides, I checked Genie and it says both of us are going to use this app." He pointed to a bunch of numbers on his computer screen. As designers of Anahata's future prediction tool, the Genie team always let their product decide their next steps. The engineer stared at the Genie prediction and shrugged. There was no point in arguing with science.

Later that evening, sitting alone in the Genie cubicle, the engineer signed himself into the app. Soon he was staring at sixteen attractive faces—sixteen girls online right then, all near him, on the Anahata campus. He touched one photo, and the girl's picture filled the screen. Her name was Sarah, and her profile said she worked in Anahata's PR department. She was twenty-six, liked electronic music, romantic comedies, and baking cookies. He didn't like any of those things, but that didn't really matter. What did bother him was the small flower tattoo near her ear. He hated tattoos.

Next was Chinmei on the HR team. HR girls were pretty slutty—or that was what the engineer's HM trainer had told him.

She liked horses and walking her dog and blah blah blah. He opened the chat box.

A Social Me prompt appeared.

Need a hand starting the conversation?

The engineer pushed the help button.

A line of suggested conversation appeared in the chat box, waiting for his approval: "Hey, Chinmei, that's such a great pic. I love horses, too!"

The engineer wasn't convinced it was such a great pickup line, but he trusted the Social Me technology over anything he could come up with himself. He pressed "send" and then stared at the phone, as if expecting a perfumed genie to emerge from the port in a cloud of smoke. But no answer came. He wondered if other men had sent Chinmei similar messages.

He went back to the gallery of photos. Laura. Alice. Julia. He stopped on Julia, who had big, curly brown locks. He opened the chat box again, asked for Social Me's help, and didn't even bother to read its pickup line suggestions, figuring it was something complimenting her hair. He hit "send." He then went back to Alice and Laura's profiles and did the same, convinced that the more messages he sent, the more likely it was that at least one girl would respond to him. (The engineer had previously worked on Anahata's email team so he knew how effective spam was.) All in all, he hit up about twenty girls.

Soon after, his phone vibrated to indicate a new message. But it wasn't from a girl—it was from the Social Me application.

No response yet? Try filling in your profile.

"Bad product design," the engineer grumbled, believing that any good product wouldn't ask him to fill anything out—it would already know everything about him.

Still, he remembered Genie's prediction that he would use the Social Me app. So he hit the "fill in my profile" button, and Social Me picked interests and hobbies for him that it claimed were high-performing with women. He was now a declared lover of art, wine, and

Asian fusion cooking. He also decided to add one bit of truth—his participation on the Genie project. It had a lot of buzz around campus, and he figured it would make him look good.

Within minutes of completing his profile, the man had his first response. It was from a girl named Emily.

`That's so cool that you knit!`

He laughed. He knew nothing about knitting, other than it was something his grandmother did. He began to type.

`I'm not very good though.`

`Oh, I can show you how to tie things together ;-)`

The engineer studied Emily's emoticon for several seconds.

`;-)`

Clearly, there was a difference between ;-) and the more straightforward :)

Was Emily flirting with him? Before he had a chance to analyze her emoji any further, Emily was messaging him again.

`So you work on the Genie team?`

He tried to think of something impressive to say.

Yeah. We predict what you're going to do in the future. I could show you how it works.

`Yeah? ;-)`

The engineer could feel his heart quicken. She was winking. Again. This was his chance.

`I can even predict what you will do.`

`Go on...`

`You'll come here to my building in ten minutes and I'll show you Genie. And then you can show me... how to knit.`

`I like to play with string. ;-) See you in ten.`

The engineer couldn't believe how fast this was happening—so many winks! His eyes darted around the empty cubicle, looking for a candle or a blanket or something that would make Emily comfortable and put her in the mood—in the mood for what, he wasn't sure, though he knew what *he* wanted.

There was nothing in his workspace but various gadgets, Red Bull cans, and the red gym shirt his HM trainer had given him. He rummaged about in his backpack until he found the reading lamp he liked to use whenever he spent the night in a sleep capsule. He set the lamp on his desk, threw the red T-shirt over it, and turned off the lights. From one corner of the room, a small light illuminated the floor in a gentle red glow. It was the best he could do. And if Emily was surprised to see this—*what if she really just wanted to show him how to knit?!*—he could just pretend he was one of those coders who liked to work in the dark.

He sat back in his chair and took a deep breath, readying himself for Emily's arrival.

Twenty minutes later, Emily was doing things to his body he had only ever seen on the internet, while Genie's future predictor compiler cast a green glow of zeros and ones across their bodies, spitting out new and promising predictions.

JENNIE

The Genie team was in an uproar, their alternating wails and accusatory shouts prompting Jennie and others in Building 7 to don noise-reduction headphones. The problem wasn't that one of their team members hadn't done any work in three days, discovered each morning in handcuffs, wearing little more than a proud smile. That was a mild inconvenience.

There was a much bigger problem—namely that Genie's future predictor tool had failed to anticipate the full success of Social Me.

In the past week alone, Genie had predicted the outcome of a major European election, the fall of the yen against the dollar, and the winner of a Brazilian reality TV show. It had announced that one Anahata engineer would go on hunger strike until his preferred brand of potato chips was restocked in the micro-kitchen; it predicted another engineer would foment a revolution in a faraway country.

It had even predicted that the Genie team members would all be invited to try the Social Me app.

But it had completely, totally failed to predict the app's success.

And three days into its existence, Social Me was an irrefutable success. While the company's stock price continued to fall and Wall Street declared that the "frivolous moon colony plan" would be the end of Anahata's reign, things couldn't have been sunnier on campus. Birds chirped in the trees and fleet-footed cupids danced down the halls, jumping from one beanbag to the next, sprinkling their magical dust on those lucky enough to have been invited to try the app. Meanwhile, those without access queued outside the Social Me cubicle, begging for an invitation.

The Genie team had just one thing with which to console themselves. While they hadn't predicted a Social Me triumph, their tool was at least predicting a Social Me problem.

The new Genie team lead, a redhead with even redder lips, delivered the news to Jennie like an arcade genie spitting out a cryptic future.

"Social Me has or is going to have a problem," she said. "When the time will come, I do not know. But expect a problem."

Noting Jennie's puzzled look, the redhead rolled her eyes.

"Look, I don't even get why we're building this product. Genie can't give concrete details, just confirmations about generally positive or negative things. I might as well tell you now that you're going to die one day. Do with the information as you see fit."

It was a useless warning, as Jennie already knew there was a problem in her hookup paradise. It was as plain as the faces staring back at her on the Social Me app.

The problem was Hot Ryan.

She had spotted him on Social Me the previous day. Hot Ryan was twenty-seven and loved going to the gym, cooking multicourse macrobiotic dinners, and taking long walks in the forest. He was everything she wanted in a boyfriend. His hair was a color Jennie was sure was called "russet," and he had the kind of slightly angular face that she was sure could only belong to a man who had experienced both hardship and love and who was sensitive—so sensitive that he felt every emotion, every loss, every moment in which his future girlfriend might leave his side. In his profile picture, he was wearing a knit sweater, sitting in front of a fireplace with a glass of red wine, inviting one lucky girl to join him for an evening of slow jams and lovemaking. Jennie could hear the fire crackling in the background, the smell of pine and winter filling her nose. Hot Ryan was dreamy, and he could be hers in a matter of seconds if she just clicked on the chat button.

"We've got another HMer on S&M," she said over her shoulder, pinging Sven the link to Ryan's Social Me profile—though not before first adding Ryan to her favorites folder in case she wanted to contact him later.

No girl wanted to date an HMer or be seen on campus with him—everyone knew they were the losers and meatheads of Anahata's employee base. But it seemed that guys like Hot Ryan had figured out how to hide their HM status from the app and were starting to monopolize all the conversations and messages from the girls, leaving the engineers empty-handed.

Sven took a look at Ryan's profile and let out a growl.

"These guys are like weeds! We get rid of one and another pops up in his place! And what's up with that sweater?"

"Jealous much?" said Jennie, turning in her chair toward Sven. She let her gaze linger on his face, appreciating the faint acne scars near his temples—the reminder, no doubt, of a painful adolescence. She liked guys who were mildly bruised—their slight imperfections tempered their attempts at arrogance. They were nothing like the sales guys, nothing like that Niels Smeardon, who had seduced her and then made her wait outside on his lawn, in the cold, until a taxi came.

Sven blushed, and Jennie realized she was still staring.

"More importantly," she said, looking down at her mobile, "how do you think they're getting onto Social Me? We restricted access to just the engineers and female employees."

"Maybe some of the Horizontal Moves guys managed to steal some of the engineers' phones and replace their pictures," Sven said.

Jonas turned in his chair. "Perhaps they are exploiting a loophole in the code."

Sven smirked. "That's like suggesting that me and my core competencies learned how to do a cost-benefit analysis overnight."

Jonas shrugged. "They must be doing something special to get into the app."

"Loophole or not, there will always be some way for a nonengineer to get on here if he really wants to," Jennie said. "We need to rig the system so that the girls *only* want to speak and meet the engineers. In other words, we need to get Jonas' profile, for example, to beat Hot Ryan."

"Our site is eighteen-plus," Sven snickered. "Jonas isn't old enough to join."

Jonas stuck his tongue out. "You really think I am incapable of hacking into my own service?"

Jennie grinned. She had indeed banned Jonas and Anahata's other child prodigies from using Social Me but soon discovered that such precautions were unnecessary. Jonas and the other boys had hacked in on the first day but, not understanding the attraction of speaking with girls, soon returned to their video games.

"Okay, so forget about Jonas. We need, like, Arsyen's profile to beat Hot Ryan," she said.

Arsyen had sent her another message that morning. This time something about being stuck in an airport with donkeys. He was the perfect example of a guy who needed Social Me to land a girl.

"The engineers will never beat the HMers on looks," Jenni continued. "We need something that makes a woman feel like there's a deeper connection with the guy she's talking to."

The men went quiet, seeming to wait for more input from Jennie. But she was already thinking about another problem, one that she did not share with her team members but had kept her awake the previous night.

Shortly after the Social Me launch, Jennie concluded that an engineer's first interaction with the app was crucial in determining whether he became a repeat visitor. Put simply, he was more likely to return to the app if he had a positive interaction with the opposite sex.

This was easier said than done. Even the all-powerful internet had its limits, and Jennie's analytical data showed that most of the engineers were needing several tries before they could land on a girl willing to talk to them for more than a few minutes. As a result, some of the engineers had already given up hope and abandoned the product entirely. If she wanted to keep her engineers on Social Me, she had to make sure that their first interaction with the opposite sex was positive—or, better yet, that it led to a full-on coupling event.

So Jennie had taken the burden of coupling events on her own back—literally—and spent the second day of the launch running from one sleep capsule to another, converting twenty engineers to satisfied Social Me users. By the end of the day, she was worn out (and slightly disgusted) and knew she couldn't do it on her own. The twenty escorts she had hired the next day made quick work of the Genie, Moodify, and infrastructure teams, and by week's end had ensured that hundreds of other Anahata engineers were reaching some personal form of ecstasy thanks to Social Me.

But she knew her escort strategy wasn't scalable and wouldn't help Roni's moon colony problem. The engineers were certainly coming back for second helpings, but once they were no longer engaged with flirty escorts but normal Anahata women instead, the conversations quickly fell flat.

Flipping through the chat records, it was clear that the men simply weren't engaging the women the right way. If they used the Social Me interest generator feature, they could start a conversation with the girls, but the moment they stopped discussing knitting, pastels, or baking, the conversation screeched to a halt. They needed a fully automated solution that would help any engineer score an offline meetup.

Jennie tapped her pen to her lips as she calculated how many more escorts she would need to make it through the week. She could feel Sven watching her and was surprised to feel her cheeks flush. Then something flashed inside her.

"Do you think you could hack into Anahata's internal HR data?"

Sven shook his head. "Impossible. Internal security is a fortress. And if we got caught…"

"You're right," said Jennie, tapping her pen against her lips. "There has to be another way."

✳

Situated at the edge of campus, its walls facing a supermarket and other landmarks of suburban Palo Alto, Building 24 was not the typical Anahata structure of white cubes and boundless windows. Rather, the human resources offices were housed in an attractive, almost historic-looking brick structure surrounded by rose bushes on all sides—a chastity belt of sorts whose thorns cut into Jennie's legs as she crouched next to Roni.

"I've never been out here before," Jennie whispered.

"Its location is no coincidence," Roni whispered back. "Nothing important happens here."

The final light went out, and the last employee left the building. Roni passed Jennie some black theater makeup. She smeared it across her face, mimicking the zigzags that ran across Roni's forehead and cheeks. He had assured her that this would work, that he had done it many, many times without detection.

Jennie and Roni crawled out from the bushes, keeping low to the ground. When he reached the door, Roni jumped to his feet, making Jennie question the whole purpose of their clandestine approach. He badged himself into the building without any problem. Human resources was not a high-security building, and any Anahata employee could get access with their badge.

Once inside, they made their way through the corridors, searching for the office of the senior vice president of human resources. At the end of the hall was a corner office with the nameplate they were looking for. "Paul Barlow," it said in blue lettering, surrounded by smiling teddy bears holding clusters of balloons. Underneath was a folksy, hand-painted wooden sign: *Come in!* There was no doorknob, and the door itself was half open, suggesting that declining this friendly invitation to enter was a much greater offense than trespassing.

Roni made a beeline for Paul's desk and fired up his computer. "We just need to break into his system and pull it out."

"How are we ever going to figure out his password?" Jennie hissed.

"Don't worry, I've done this a million times." Roni's fingers tap-danced their way across Paul's keyboard.

Within seconds, the plain password prompt box gave way to a desktop landscape of lavender flowers.

"Whoa—first try!" Jennie exclaimed.

"HR people tend to think with their hearts," Roni explained. "Emotional people don't tend to create secure passwords. In fact, it's been proven that seventy percent of HR staff worldwide use the password '12345.'"

Roni began searching through Paul's electronic files while Jennie glanced around the room. On his pale blue walls, Paul had hung several photos of himself with his elderly mother on various European vacations. There were also his diplomas: an undergraduate degree in religious studies from Harvard and a psychology PhD from Stanford. Certificates in Reiki therapy, cognitive emotional therapy, advanced Feldenkreis, and the Henry Miller Wellness Program surrounded Paul's prized degrees in a big group therapy hug. Propped against the windowsill were three books, clearly meant for display.

Healthy Employees, Healthy Company

Managing Genius

Employee Management: How to Stop Worrying About Your Duds and Start Focusing on Your Superstars

All were authored by Paul.

"I can't find anything," Roni said from across the room. "You'd think it'd be one massive online database. Maybe I'm just not looking in the right place."

Jennie's eyes fell on a chart atop the coffee table. It was little more than a manila folder marked with two alphabet stickers reading "PU" on the edge.

She opened it.

Beth Punter. Department: Finance.

There were lists of promotions, salary increases, and vacation accruals. It wasn't anything particularly interesting. But then, flipping to the second page, Jennie found a recent performance evaluation from Beth's manager, identifying Beth as a top performer in her department but denying her a promotion until she could work on a few areas: Beth was apparently somewhat bossy and not sufficiently collaborative.

So many women at Anahata seem to have that problem, thought Jennie. If only they could make the women less bossy, maybe they would get further at Anahata.

Jennie shook her head—that was a problem for another day. She kept reading.

"This is it," she gasped, jumping up to show Roni.

Roni glanced through the folder, nodding as he read the second page.

"But wait," Jennie said. "This is a paper file. Could it be a trick?"

"It's real," said Roni. "Eighty-four percent of HR employees believe that paper files are more honest and trustworthy than computer-based ones."

"Now we just have to figure out how to get more of these," said Jennie, scanning the room but not seeing anything useful. "There must be thousands of these files, and really, what we need are the digital copies."

"I know someone who can help us," Roni said. "Copy down the useful parts of that folder and get the guys to update the algorithm like we discussed. Then we'll have something to take to my guy."

✳

Twenty hours later, Jennie was standing with Roni in Gregor Guntlag's office, the second biggest office at Anahata after Bobby's. While Gregor probably thought of it as well-worn and comfy, Jennie felt as though she had just walked into a room set up only moments before, a temporary space where Gregor had halted just long enough to fire someone or intimidate any ambitious Anahata interior decorator. The office was nearly empty save for a computer on a desk, a recycling bin, and, on the wall, a solitary poster—a photograph of a Delhi slum, with the caption *Proximity Does Not Guarantee Intimacy*.

Roni had just finished his pitch for Social Me, but Gregor had yet to respond. Jennie thought he looked bored—his face was fixed in a permanent blank. Was his disinterest all an act? He had shown no interest in her as a member of the opposite sex. She wasn't used to that—and wasn't sure she liked it.

Roni cleared his throat and tried again.

"The data will make a big difference. We can show you how."

Roni nodded to Jennie. She placed her mobile on Gregor's desk so he could see the screen.

"This is Beth Punter," she said, pointing to Beth's profile picture on the app. "She's an employee in the HR department. She's on Pad Kee Mao, like thirty percent of the women on campus."

Gregor's brow wrinkled, and Jennie felt a moment of panic.

"Pad Kee Mao," said Roni, his head darting about the office as he lowered his voice to a whisper. "Pad Kee Mao is Social Me. Which used to be Social Car. Which was once known as Pad Thai."

"Today I have reviewed the projects known as Lands Ahoy, Lollipop, and Mai Tai," Gregor said, "and *killed* all of them. You would think Anahatis might want to direct more of their extraordinary creativity toward their products instead of their code names."

Jennie felt her face redden. She looked to Roni for help, but he just motioned for her to continue. She took a deep breath and reminded herself of the quote she had posted next to her bathroom mirror. *Leaders are those who lead.* She was a leader who led. Who leads. No, she led. *She did both.*

"Beth has entered her various interests into Social Me," Jennie said. "She likes baking, ping-pong, and reading. When an engineer goes to speak with Beth, we give him various prompts and suggestions to help him write an initial pickup line that will appeal to her. For example, given Beth has included baking as an interest in her Social Me profile, our engineer might tell her about the cake he baked the previous day for his mother's birthday."

"And that works?" said Gregor, raising an eyebrow.

"You'd be surprised by the degree to which women respond to a guy who mimics everything they like," Jennie answered. "The problem is that we've found HMers on Social Me, and they're getting most of the girls' attention."

Jennie noticed Gregor's face tighten at the mention of Horizontal Moves. So he was not so unflappable after all.

"We thought about trying to make the identification techniques better so that within the male employee population, only engineers would be allowed on the service," Roni said. "But there may always be interlopers. So instead, we need to focus on improving the coupling mechanism, rather than just focus on eliminating HMers. We need to make the engineers on Social Me as desirable as possible."

"So what's your plan?"

Jennie opened her mouth to speak, but Roni beat her to the punch.

"Two things," he answered. "First, starting tomorrow, we'll pump pheromones through the air vents of the marketing, HR, and PR departments—the departments with the most women. They override all the normal chemistry that would draw the women to the HM guys and instead focus them on finding good providers and long-term mates—our engineers. The Building 1 moon chemistry team has figured out how to do all of this without losing any of the lust impulses that we want to maintain. In essence, we will be able to rechannel promiscuity, diverting it from legitimate sources of lust to artificial ones."

"The chemistry team has already confirmed these pheromones will also work on the moon," Jennie said, "so we can recreate these behaviors again once we're there."

"And there's an additional benefit," Roni said. "Up until now, we've only been thinking about the heterosexual use case for Social

Me—getting the women attracted to our male engineers. But of course we also have other use cases to solve for, like homosexuality. As it turns out, the pheromones that turn the women into lusty aspiring housewives happen to react completely differently with male hormone receptors. Men in the marketing, PR, and HR departments who are exposed to our special pheromone blend will suddenly become attracted to other men, providing our gay engineers with an attractive pool of candidates as well."

Gregor's expression still hadn't shifted. "For Project Y to succeed, this attraction needs to be long term," he said. "Pheromones alone won't solve that."

"Right, that brings us to the second step," Jennie said. "Take a look again at Beth on the app. We happened to find some additional information about her—information that can improve the matching and interaction features by tenfold."

"What kind of information?"

"Birth date and relationship status, length of employment at Anahata—that kind of thing," Jennie said. She avoided Gregor's gaze.

"That doesn't sound like very valuable information."

"Well," she said, glancing at Roni, "there is a bit more than that. Like which campus cafés Beth eats at, what time she arrives at work."

"So whenever she uses her badge to access something."

"Yeah, and, um, things like career successes and failures, psychological issues."

"Psychological issues?"

"The HR files, combined with our employees' internet activity, are a huge treasure trove of data," Jennie said. "People are super confessional when they think they're just talking to a machine. We know everything about them."

"If you let us use it, we can make the algorithm much, much smarter," Roni jumped in. "Entire human interactions can be engineered from nearly start to finish. And the app gets smarter as times goes on as it learns more about each woman and what kinds of conversational topics and techniques she responds to."

"Think of it like A.I. matchmaking," Jennie said.

"Anahata data mining meets social engineering," Roni added.

"Deep-learning dating."

"Neural-net networking."

"Enough," Gregor said, "I get it."

"Right. So using Beth's file as a test case, we built this into Social Me, and all of our metrics went through the roof. Every guy who's interacted with Beth through our suggestion tool has managed to have a successful coupling with her."

"Coupling?"

"Basically, they hooked up with Beth," said Roni, grinning. "We can turn the most wholesome girls into real sluts—uh, sorry, Jennie—provided we can get the girls to ignore physical attraction and give the engineers the right data to help seduce them."

Jennie beamed. The insight had been hers. She couldn't wait to tell her feminist book club that she was subverting societally imposed attraction paradigms by making women attracted to ugly men.

"Plus," Roni continued, "the feature's activation is limited to only unattractive and low-rated profiles. That way, no HM candidates will get access to this extra help from the application. It will just be our engineers. Of course, those rare engineers whose ratings are naturally high—outliers who are good-looking or socially adept—will also miss out on this feature, but that's no big deal. They're already doing fine with the girls."

"Long term," Jennie added, "we think that by helping the engineers along with various conversation prompts, we start to train them in how to interact with women more successfully, which will help them in the offline world in all sorts of relationships. At some point they'll be able to take the training wheels off and have real conversations with real people on their own."

"In the short term," Roni said, "we keep the engineers happy, we keep them on the moon, and we destroy Galt. That's the main point, Gregor. This fixes our Project Y problem."

Gregor shook his head. "So what you're telling me is that the fate of our social mission has come down to a hookup app."

Jennie and Roni nodded.

Although his expression hadn't shifted, Jennie could tell there was something underneath the feigned placidity. There was something dark in this man. Not that she cared.

"Fine," Gregor said.

"You mean you'll get us access to the data?"

"Yes."

Gregor stood and opened the door to his office. He kept his hand on the doorknob, as if worried they hadn't gotten the hint.

"And that's, like, legally okay?" asked Jennie, as she slowly backed out of the room. "I mean, all the user data, the pheromones?"

Gregor was trying to close the door on her.

"Anahata is a disruptive company," he said, slightly pushing the door against her toes. "If we don't upset people by doing something, they never get used to that thing, and then we can't do a new thing to upset them. It's the way technology moves forward."

The door closed.

Roni turned to Jennie and gave her a high-five.

ARSYEN

A rsyen was not as prepared as he had hoped. He had wanted to arm himself with a weapon of some sort, but Jennie was clearly so embarrassed by her earlier behavior that she hadn't even responded to any of his requests for help.

In fact, for all its mighty power, Anahata had proven surprisingly useless. From the airport, Arsyen filed a ticket in the company's internal system, asking for help with Pyrrhian corruption and security concerns. But it seemed the engineer who processed the request interpreted it as something having to do with Arsyen's hard drive and erased all of Arsyen's computer and account data. Now he was completely cut off.

To make matters worse, Arsyen had brought plenty of U.S. dollars with him but discovered they were of little use in Pyrrhia, where Korpeko had outlawed the existing currency ("the aimo") and replaced it with a barter system. In the border town of Kerfluff, Arsyen tried to obtain a mule by bartering one of Anahata's secret hardware products, but everyone in the town just tossed it aside like it was a cheap piece of plastic. As a result, it had taken him almost a week to hitchhike to Poodlekek.

And now here he was, traveling through the city his family had built over centuries of rule.

Little had changed since he had fled. Goats continued to huddle outside the stores, hoping for a handout, and the bison-drawn carriages still outpaced the rickety buses that his father had introduced to Pyrrhia. As far as Arsyen could tell, there had been no investment in public works and no attempt to improve the country's infrastructure beyond the miles and miles of icy curling lanes, which originated alongside the capital's main road and wound throughout the Pyrrhian countryside. The one nod to modernity were the internet cafés, which lined the streets like eager parade-goers, each competing with its neighbor via colorful signs and promises of free extra minutes. But they were all currently closed under Korpeko's strategy to cut off Poodlekek from the rest of the country.

They took the main road into the center, passing the statue of Jeeves, the great English sportsman flown to Poodlekek by Arsyen's grandfather in the 1960s to help install civilization and croquet fields across the country. Not far from him was the statute of Lascau, the French filmmaker summoned by Arsyen's father to produce Pyrrhia's first movies—documentaries and biopics exploring the great public works undertaken by the Aimo family. Jeeves and Lascau had both declared that Poodlekek would be the future capital of the world. And it would be, finally, once Arsyen reclaimed his throne. He would summon Bobby Bonilo, and together they would build a new Silicon Valley in Poodlekek—a Silicon Poodle, or maybe Poodlecon Valley. It would be full of young people, well educated, designing apps and websites that would save the world... and of course make Pyrrhia—and the royal family—loads of money.

But first he needed to confer with the Throne Reclamation Committee and ensure they were well-prepared for battle. Otherwise, Arsyen would happily grab Natia and go hang out in California until things were ready for him.

SVEN

If Sven weren't a man of science; if he didn't believe attraction was simply the intersection of timing and hormones; if he had ever, even just once, managed to kiss a woman, kiss her deeply, and know what that touch could do to a rational human brain—then he just might have considered the hypothesis that the woman before him, the one whom he had originally considered a harbinger of misery, was in fact destined to be his savior, reversing decades of frustration with one generous little act.

But instead Sven just stared at her image, dumb with lust but unable to entertain the greater cosmic possibilities. He assumed he wanted her simply because she might not want him. That had happened before.

His finger hovered above her picture, then flicked to a new photo, one of her with girlfriends, enjoying a night out. Then there was a photo of her with her computer. Another with her mom.

Sven sighed—they already had so much in common. He leaned back in the sleep capsule, wondering how he had gotten himself into such a state about her. He set his phone down.

She was irritating, he told himself, she dressed like a bag lady, and she wasn't very smart.

No, he countered, she had that California hippie chick vibe, and she was certainly smarter than him.

Ugh! He had to stop thinking about her.

Sven extended his legs, stretching himself along the bed of the sleep capsule. He stared up at the capsule's hard-shelled ceiling, supposedly designed to mimic a womb. He doubted an actual female womb was made of shiny white plastic, but the ceiling's curve and the cocooning effect it produced was certainly relaxing—as if you were in a different world. The curtained opening to the capsule ruined that effect somewhat, though it did make it easy to peer out into the hall. Sven adjusted the pillow, and a built-in speaker thanked him in a calming, therapeutic voice for his hard work that day. He wiggled his toes. A full recline was a luxury most standard beds and couches would never allow someone of his height.

Sven picked up his mobile phone. There was a message from Arsyen's personal account—a picture of him atop a mule, smiling, a broken-down bus and a line of scowling poor people behind him. He was asking whether Sven knew where to buy lasers in bulk. Such a funny guy. Was he building a startup? Something using lasers to solve poverty? He would have to find out more when his co-worker returned.

Sven ignored Arsyen's questions and sent him back a picture of his crooked second toe. That always made people laugh.

He returned to the picture of Jennie. She was as bossy and stubborn as Maria, his one almost-girlfriend. They could almost have been the same girl, though unlike Maria, Jennie seemed to bathe consistently, and her hippie dresses and occasional references to feminism and the environment seemed more like fashion accessories than a real belief system. Which pleased Sven, since only in America did there seem to be such a strong connection between poor hygiene and progressive politics.

Sven liked to hear Jennie talk about her grand plans for Mother Earth. She lectured Jonas on recycling Red Bull cans and told Sven that she would one day "really fix things." Sven thought it was cute that a nontechnical person thought she could change the world. It was ambitious, even if it was clearly delusional.

Sven considered the possibility that Jennie could be smarter than him, though he found that difficult to reconcile with the size of her breasts and her lack of an engineering degree. But she was definitely a good leader—probably the best he ever had at Anahata.

He yawned and rubbed his eyes. Since Roni and Jennie's score of the prized employee data, he and Jonas—aided by a handful of eager engineers—had been working nonstop on Social Me, making the application even smarter and more effective. They were almost ready to roll out the new version and had spent the day debugging the software and doing quality analysis.

Throughout the day, Sven had interacted with various women at the company using four fake profiles. Bob, Sam, Steve, and Logan all had different jobs, appearances, and interests. But to the credit of Social Me, all of them had experienced plenty of luck with the ladies that day.

In fact, all of Sven's twenty test interactions proved successful, the new version of the Social Me app generating such customized pickup lines and compelling conversation fillers that Sven's various profiles would certainly have had multiple coupling events in the offline world had he chosen to follow through. The new algorithm generated romantic French phrases for Steve after he chose Jamillah, who was registered in a company-sponsored French class. Bob had luck with Annie, convincing her that the best way to conquer her passive-aggressive behavior with her teammates was to engage in some role-play with him later that night. And Sam, armed with the knowledge of Camille's recent online purchase of a yoga mat, charmed her into doing a virtual downward dog with him.

Sven told himself it was his self-discipline and commitment to science that had kept him from following through with any meet-ups. But he knew the truth was more nuanced: Talking with girls on an app was one thing; actually meeting them—when he might fail to meet their expectations—was another entirely.

Just then, Sven's phone vibrated. It was a message for Logan from some girl who worked in marketing.

What would Jennie think of Logan? Of all Sven's fake profiles, Logan's was the one that came closest to the real Sven: tall, blond, and an engineer.

Masking himself as Logan, Sven clicked on Jennie's profile and read the information she had filled in. It was all stuff that he already knew from working with her, like how she liked dolphins and reading entrepreneur biographies. He wondered what else the app knew about her.

Sven hit the chat button floating above Jennie's picture, and a Social Me prompt popped up, offering to help kick-start the conversation. This was the same feature he had been testing all day, but now his pulse quickened. He pushed the button again, and a heart icon pulsed three times, preparing his first courtship line. She would never know it was him; Sven hit "send."

Hi, Jennie! I was just reading The Feminine Mystique *and thinking about how awesome it would be to discuss it with someone…*

Jennie responded immediately.

Your interpretation would be deeply colored by your phallus.

Sven reread the message. Was Jennie blowing Logan off? What was a colored phallus? He hit the Social Me suggestion button again.

Logan: *I am trying to transcend my phallus. I believe that history should be herstory.*

Jennie: *So what do you think of Sommers' gender feminist/equity feminist dichotomy?*

Logan: *I believe in deconstructing all binary oppositions and the hierarchies they imply.*

Sven had no idea what they were talking about. Plus, he was out of Red Bull. He selected the autopilot option so that Social Me could continue to generate lines on his behalf, then made his way to the micro-kitchen.

When he returned, the exchange seemed pretty intense.

Jennie: *But doesn't Sontag's model of Baudrillardist simulacra imply that sexual identity has significance, given that presemantic materialism is invalid?*

Logan: *The invalidity of presemantic materialism implies the negation of the intersectional immanence of the simulacra.*

Jennie: *That's an interesting point. Btw don't you think the layout of the Anahata cubicles is a hetero-masculine interpretation of an inherently feminine space?*

Logan: *Totally. Hey, check out this dolphin listicle!*

Sven did a double take. How did they go from phalluses to dolphins? Was Social Me as confused as he was, or was this how Jennie's brain worked?

Jennie: *I LOVE dolphins.*

Did Jennie not realize what was happening? Was the puppet master actually under the spell of her own puppet?

Logan: *I would like you to teach me about feminism.*

Jennie: *Shall we start with The Second Sex?*

Sven squealed in his sleep capsule. Jennie wanted to give him Second Sex!!! What *was* Second Sex?!? He stared at the empty text field, the cursor beating with promise. He had to stop this before Jennie found out who Logan really was. He tossed his phone to the back of the capsule. For minutes, he avoided it, face burning, listening to it vibrate with new messages from Jennie. He decided he would delete her messages without reading them, then come back into work the next day like nothing had ever happened. Jennie would never need to know. He could use Dogtown to ask her out in a few weeks.

Just then there was a knock on the outside of the capsule wall. Sven drew back the curtain and peered out, ready to yell at the encroaching passerby. He yelped as he saw Jennie standing there, dressed in a crocheted top and long, flowery skirt.

Panicking, Sven let the curtain fall back, dying for a refresh button. How had Jennie known that Logan's profile belonged to him?

But then it hit him: Of course Jennie would have known it was him. She had spent the day logging all the bugs reported by the various profiles; she could easily figure out which ones were coming from the different engineers on the team.

Sven sunk lower in his capsule.

"The Social Car location detection is really quite effective," came Jennie's voice from outside the capsule. "I told Jonas to turn it on only for women. That way, we women can find your exact location but won't worry about you men finding us. I think it's a good power balance, don't you? After all, when men stalk women, it's scary. But when women stalk men, it's kinda charming, right?"

Sven wasn't listening. Peering out from the half-inch space separating curtain and wall, Sven studied Jennie's face, gradually traveling down her neck, following the hemp necklace that hovered just above her breasts. He couldn't believe what he thought was happening, what was about to happen. He had no idea what to do, yet he knew the next step was up to him.

He grabbed his phone, turned off the autopilot feature, and typed a message to Jennie.

Do you really want to give me Second Sex?

Jennie's phone vibrated just a few feet away with the sound of his message.

She pulled back the curtain and stepped into the capsule.

And then the thought that was always in Sven's mind, from morning to night, for every day of his existence since puberty, now ran quickly, turned back on itself, ran again, and again, and life sped up and hope burst forth and

```
for girl in all_girls_in_world:
if girl.will_sleep_with_me():
girl.process()
```
And finally, he was at peace.

THE CAMPUS

Exactly thirty-five hours after Sven Svenson entered manhood, the Anahata campus shot into action. Sprinklers leaped from their subterranean sleep, twisting in unison to the left, then right, ensuring that not a single blade of Anahata grass went unwatered. The sophisticated irrigation system kept the company's imported Irish grass fertile and sparkling, impervious to California's perpetual drought.

The first Anahata jogger bounded across the sidewalk outside Building 2. Dressed in sleek black running gear, an orange HM emblazoned across the back of his jacket, the man reached Building 10 before even a minute had lapsed. In a few more leaps, he was off campus property, returning thirty minutes later, this time at a much reduced speed. He was now accompanied by five other runners, the newcomers all moving with considerable effort. The man lashed at their heels with a stick, spurring them forward as they jogshlumped past the corner at Building 20, gasping their way toward the campus lake.

The runners passed by a rickety gray shuttle just entering campus, a bulge in its center bouncing perilously close to the pavement. It had wobbled its way up the freeway from San Jose and now stopped in front of Building 2. Men and women slowly filed out of their oversized hearse, joking with each other in Spanish as they badged themselves into Fried Fred's to begin work.

A few hours after the gray shuttle chugged back to the freeway, the purple-and-green Anahata buses began to arrive on campus. Bus to Building 1. Bus to Building 8. Their black roofs moved between the white lines of the campus parking lots, slotting in and out like ever-shifting dominoes. Bus to Building 3. Bus to Building 20. Employees stumbled out. Bus to Building 14. Bus to Building 24. Moving to an unseen metronome, the young men and women of Anahata continued on to their buildings, made their coffees, grabbed breakfast, and headed to their desks.

One of the first meetings of the day was taking place in Building 4, where a girl with shiny black hair was more prepared for note-taking than decision-making. Her engineering team was waiting for her to make the final call on their highly technical problem, but the girl just shrugged. One of the engineers threw up his hands and left the room, pulling out his mobile phone and ignoring her feeble plea to return. He became so engrossed in his phone that he didn't notice the sleep capsule by the exit, which was shaking so vigorously that it seemed to be attempting liftoff. He exited the building, head down, mobile pointed in front of him. He cut across the lawn, trampled a flower bed, and left footprints in the newly raked volleyball court as he followed the blinking dot on his screen. A Galt recruiter jumped out of the bushes and dangled a set of Tesla keys before him, but the engineer's gaze was locked to his screen. He pushed past the recruiter, walked another ten paces, and came to a stop in front of a pair of red manicured toes. He looked up, blushed, and said, "Hello."

"Hello?" said a woman in Fried Fred's over the walkie-talkie, hitting the device a few times in hopes of a clearer transmission. "Do you all have bleach?" she asked. At the building next door, an older man in his sixties responded. He wiped his brow and reached below one of the counters, dragging out a large container. On his way to deliver the bleach to Fried Fred's, he called out across the kitchen to a female co-worker to see whether she had finished prepping the organic kale and quinoa salad. The salad selection changed daily, but his view of it did not: It didn't matter how many unpronounceable ingredients the meal contained—as a cafeteria worker, you still made less per hour than the cost of most of the dishes you made.

Fifteen minutes later, a tidal wave hit the walls of Fried Fred's as the cafeteria staff opened the doors and engineers rushed in with the fever of toddlers in a toy store. The bang of the wok, the tunnel sound of the soda dispenser, the sizzle of the fajita station—urgency and consumption mixed suddenly, newly, with light, feminine laughter, skipping past each pop and bang.

A man lined up five carts of catered lunch from Fried Fred's alongside the back entrance to Building 1. He knocked five times, the first three with the same speed, then a pause before the last two. The door opened, and a head slowly extended like a turtle from its shell. The head looked left, then right, then brought its entire body outside, revealing red Crocs and a faded T-shirt that said R-O-N-I. He pushed the carts into Building 1, taking care to secure the door behind him.

The operations employee in Building 22 postponed her lunch, crinkling her nose as she tried to make sense of the numbers before her. She had checked the data several times and was sure her figures were correct. According to her analysis, productivity rates at Anahata had inexplicably dropped ten percent over the previous week. While the deployment of the sales team to their new Horizontal Moves programs might have slowed sales employees' productivity, it made no sense that it would also slow the engineering teams. She assumed she had done something wrong and opened another spreadsheet to start over from scratch.

A few buildings away, the handful of Anahata sales executives who had been spared the Horizontal Moves program fidgeted in their seats, smoothing their black and navy blue suits with sweaty palms. Their heads turned in unison as Gregor Guntlag walked into the room. Without shutting the door behind him, and while continuing to thud his way across the room, he announced that all advertising services would be turned off in Africa to free up capacity for a special engineering project. Gregor rounded the far end of the table and now thudded his way in the direction of the door. Anyone unhappy with these changes, he said over his shoulder, was welcome to leave Anahata or join the Horizontal Moves program. The sole of his boots left a muddy trail as he exited the room.

Within minutes of Gregor's exit, a server at the edge of campus was pinged by an IP address in Nigeria. A split second later, a small business owner in Laos received a canned response from the Anahata customer service team.

Thanks for your email! We are sorry, but due to high email volumes, we are unable to provide a direct response. If you are an advertising partner in Africa, Liechtenstein, Luxembourg, or Andorra, we are no longer serving ads in your territories. This is part of a program to improve the Anahata experience for our users and ensure we remain focused on our mission to Improve Humankind. Given your account is in good standing, if you ever move your business to another country, we'd be happy to do business with you. Thanks!!

A man appeared just then on the roof of Building 1, cigarette in hand. He sat against the wall, head propped against its prickly stucco surface. He appeared malnourished and sickly, exhaustion gathering like puddles under his eyes. He closed his eyes to nap, a smile lingering on his face.

In the building below him, a TV ran in the background of an empty lounge. Images of burning storefronts and rioting youths crossed the screen, captioned with the words, "Pyrrhia upheaval."

But the employees in Building 1 were too busy to bother with TV. They had been alternating work on Project Y with hours of Social Me fun—investigations of moon rock composition with explorations of the differences in C and D bra cups. They were finding it difficult to concentrate on their main task, and they weren't the only ones.

A man and a woman on the Genie team sat side by side in their cubicle, using Social Me to flirt with each other. Eventually the man worked up the courage to ask the girl to visit the squid tank with him in the main building. For an hour, they stood before the squid as it bobbed among the kelp, the two of them moving closer and closer together until their hands touched.

Two buildings away, a man and woman who had been working together on the Internet Sombrero project made out in the second-floor stairwell, their Internet Sombrero headphones plugged into their ears, piping in songs that matched their moods—romantic saxophone sounds for her, *The Thong Song* for him.

The Thong Song was also playing in the marketing department, where Roni had unleashed a fresh pheromone dump and cut the air conditioning. Timed to the beat, the women peeled off their prim cardigans and blazers, swung their chairs to face their purses, and reached for their phones. Their well-manicured nails tapped on the engineers' Social Me profiles. They smiled. And tapped again. And again. Tap. Tap. Tap.

Down the hall from them, Jennie hummed a Grateful Dead song as she made her way to the smoothie bar. Sven had been her thirtieth Social Me convert—a mark of success not just in terms of her product usage metrics but also with regard to her draft manifesto (working title, "The Master's Tools *Will* Destroy the Master's House: Levels of Meta—Subverting the Patriarchy Through Sex with the Patriarchy").

ELSEWHERE

Two thousand miles away, a man awoke in Tapachula, Mexico, to the faint cries of a mariachi band. With a groan that came neither from pain nor alcohol but rather a long, uncomfortable sleep, he pushed himself up onto his elbows and surveyed his surroundings. He was in a dusty motel room with one small window above his bed.

He moved his hand to his head and ruffled his blond, uncombed hair, as though checking to see if it was still there. He touched his face and felt the slightest beginnings of a beard, his thin, slow-growing hairs jutting out like sharp grass across his chin and cheeks. He studied his hands, smooth and unharmed except for faint bracelet-like marks around his wrists. He was wearing a windbreaker that was covered in mud, partly obscuring an Anahata logo at the top right-hand corner. He glanced at his watch—it was a long time since he last remembered doing anything or being in any particular place.

The man peered out the window and saw a dry, unfamiliar landscape below him. He ran to his door and initially touched the knob with caution, as though afraid it might be electrified. But it opened without incident, and he slowly poked his head out into the hall. A squat woman wearing a simple dress was entering what appeared to be a communal bathroom, mop in hand. She nodded hello with disinterest. On the floor next to his door was an English-language newspaper. Written across the front page was a headline:

IS THIS THE END OF ANAHATA?

The word "Anahata" triggered something in him, and he suddenly remembered a basement and a bottle of wine. He scanned the rest of the article, but, like the headline, it was in English—a language he did not fully understand. His eyes studied the date: *May 15*. That must be *mayo*, he thought, scanning the article for other cognates. *Technology, Bobby Bonilo*—they were words that felt distantly familiar to him. But he could not make sense of the text.

The man returned to his cot, unsure of his next move. He suddenly became aware of the midday heat—a strong, dry heat that reminded him of the desert. Removing his windbreaker, he felt something lightly jabbing at him from an interior pocket. There he found a thousand pesetas, a Mexican passport, and a bank slip showing a transfer into a bank account for $15 million.

Just as in his previous existence, here again, money served as sufficient instruction.

ARSYEN

The Throne Reclamation Committee headquarters was little more than a dingy basement located below the home of the TRC treasurer. Mold was creeping up the stairs, and the basement smelled of rotten cheese.

The whole space struck Arsyen as entirely appropriate. After all, underground movements were by nature underground, and the TRC's thousands of members could hardly be expected to congregate in a public park, in plain view of Korpeko's men.

At the moment, however, there were only four supporters kneeling before him: the TRC secretary, treasurer, chief strategist, and the chief strategist's wife.

"You may stand," said Arsyen, infusing his voice with the beneficence of a king. He was still quite tired from the multiday journey to the capital, but already he was finding that being prince was much easier than being a product manager. Unlike at Anahata, people here actually obeyed his commands.

The group rose to their feet—not without some difficulty, as each member was well over seventy.

"Where's the rest of the TRC?" asked Arsyen, scanning the basement, expecting others to emerge from the shadows.

"Sssh!" The chief strategist's finger darted to his lips. "Someone may be listening. We do not call ourselves the TRC here." He leaned in toward Arsyen. "Here, we are known as the Legion of the Reckoning."

Arsyen smiled. This was a good sign.

Although his travel to Poodlekek had taken several days, his actual passage into Pyrrhia could not have been easier. No one at the border had even glanced twice at his fake passport. It made him worry that Korpeko no longer considered him a threat.

A secret code name for the TRC, while annoying, at least confirmed his relevance.

"So, where are my legions of the reckoning?" Arsyen asked.

"Oh… around," said the chief strategist, waving his hand in the air. "It's not so easy for them to move about."

"Of course," Arsyen nodded. "They must be careful."

"Soon, Your Highness, you will take back the country," the chief strategist said. "But first, please take a seat and recover from your long journey. Some of your greatest supporters have come to welcome you."

The strategist ushered Arsyen to a high armchair that required him to jump slightly in order to seat himself.

Arsyen leaned back in the stiff-backed chair, a poor-man's replica of his father's throne, tall and red and not particularly comfortable, with pearls of human molars studding the arms. Arsyen was certain the teeth were fake.

Arsyen gazed down at the TRC members.

"Bring my subjects to me," he said, with a snap of the fingers that was both dismissive and demanding.

He was pleased to see how easily the imperial gestures were returning to him.

Over the next hour, Arsyen was hand-fed prunes by the TRC secretary while the committee presented him to all the Aimo familiars they could round up—the ones who weren't dead or in exile, which meant about six. Without exception, they were all terribly old; at least two of them didn't seem to know where they were.

They all flashed some sign of wealth—an ivory knife, a shawl made of Embrian hair, or a bison's head cap—as though it were a special code, a signal to Arsyen that he too would have the good life once he retook what was rightfully his.

But now that Arsyen had lived in Silicon Valley, he knew what real wealth looked like. Real wealth had jet-like yachts and yacht-like jets and didn't bother with ivory knives or Embrian hair shawls unless they were part of an orgy with supermodels. Real wealth wouldn't be interested in a bison head cap unless it was a bison shot during an environmentally sustainable safari involving kite surfing and volunteerism with a local tribal community.

Watching the display of small-time wealth before him, Arsyen decided that when he was back in power he would make his country—or at least himself—Silicon Valley rich.

Nevertheless, Prince Arsyen smiled politely at his subjects' riches and stories and fabricated ones of his own in order to live up to the grandeur they imagined of his life in California. He spoke to them of pools and barbecues, of electric cars and Japanese toilets that cleaned one's bottom in a way that was at first invasive, then incredibly comforting.

"What are Americans like?" asked an old man who had come with his wife.

"There is food everywhere," Arsyen said, "and land for as far as the eye can see. The food rests atop the land, and the people gorge themselves upon it. Each home has a pool—not for swimming, but rather for cleaning. And the people are so rich they do not ever need to move—they just sit all day."

The man and his wife smiled in unison, their gold teeth lined ear to ear like rotted corn. Arsyen felt his stomach turn. Once he was in power, he would fix the teeth of his people... or at least the teeth of the richest, most beautiful women.

"Prince Arsyen," his chief strategist said, "may we present to you some of your most valiant soldiers: Novasglod, Trodol, and Pogol."

Arsyen leaned forward in his chair, straining his eyes to discern the warriors emerging from the shadows.

The first, Novasglod, was pruned and puckered. She leaned heavily on her cane and had difficulty recovering from her bow before the prince.

The second, Trodol, seemed even older. Trodol had fought Korpeko's men as they stormed the imperial palace. He was missing his right leg and left ear and wheezed with each breath.

Arsyen turned his attention to the third man. "And who are you?"

Although standing before Arsyen, the man's face was turned away from the prince.

"Pogol is a blind mute," the chief strategist whispered in Arsyen's ear. "He has been very involved with recruiting new followers."

Arsyen frowned. He hoped there would not be too many others like Pogol—a blind mute just wasn't the face of youthful vitality that he wanted to project to the masses.

After a minute of pleasantries, Arsyen had the three supporters escorted away. This took several minutes, as none were adept at climbing the basement stairs. Arsyen watched their slow progress with impatience. Having to wait on other people was such an annoyance.

"Enough!" he cried when the door finally shut behind them.

The TRC rushed forward in a crawling bow.

"We have much work to do, and it is time to discuss our attack. Tell me more about my army."

"Of course, Your Highness," the chief strategist said. "We have that all planned out. We'll just need to get them out of the trenches."

"And where are these trenches?"

The chief strategist took a step closer to Arsyen and lowered his voice, "The trenches are what we call the Poodlekek Convalescent Home. Everyone there is a member of the Legion of the Reckoning. We started with them, you see, because it was very easy to convince the elderly Pyrrhian population that things were better in the old days."

"But old people can barely move," Arsyen said.

"It is a valid concern," the chief strategist nodded. "But they have wisdom."

"What about strong young men who can fight?" Arsyen asked.

"Well, we don't have so many of those," the chief strategist said.

"None really," his wife said.

"But—"

"It was part of the plan," the chief strategist said, "but strong young men are fickle in their loyalties and would be expensive."

"But what about all the money I sent you?"

"New wheelchairs for fast travel," the chief strategist said.

"Canes for striking the enemy," his wife said.

"And don't forget the cows," the treasurer said.

"We planned on recruiting the strong young men in a few years, along with the purchase of the cavalry and the bomb. This has all happened a bit faster than expected."

"Then why did you tell me we were ready?" Arsyen said. He surveyed the four members before him. If he beheaded one of them, it would be an example to the others. But which one?

"Prince Arsyen, you have nothing to worry about. The entire country wants you back," the chief strategist said.

"Well, *almost* the entire country," his wife said.

"But how will we mobilize them?" Arsyen asked.

"You just need to tell them you have returned," the chief strategist said.

"Well," said his wife, with a nervous laugh, "you might have to do a bit more than that. Your family did kill quite a few people."

The chief strategist shot his wife a dirty look. "What she means is that *most* everyone is waiting for your return."

"But where are they?"

"They are everywhere, Prince Arsyen. Everywhere."

Arsyen threw up his hands. But then he had an idea.

"I know a revolutionary," he said.

"Revolutionaries? You don't want to fall in with them," the chief strategist said.

"Communists, likely," his wife said.

"Natia is the good type of revolutionary," Arsyen said. "I mean, she's a woman. Women get a bit bored and need something to talk about, and that's how they fall into these things. My father always said that female revolutionaries are only revolutionaries until they're pregnant. Anyway, I think I know where she is—at Sklartar's home."

"Impossible," said the treasurer. "Sklartar's home burned down during the coup. A police station is there now."

"We don't need revolutionaries," the chief strategist said. "We just need to rally your supporters. Our army at the convalescent home will help us spread the word. Just give us a moment to discuss the plan."

The chief strategist waved the committee members closer, forming a tight ball of gray, weathered faces.

"We could have our army go house to house," Arsyen heard the chief strategist say. "The wheelchairs can cover a lot of ground in a day."

"What about a subversive theater performance?" said another.

Arsyen shook his head. He had forgotten how useless old people were. Silicon Valley was right to ban them—youth and entrepreneurial daring were so much more important than experience.

He shifted in his uncomfortable throne and felt his mobile phone dig into his thigh. He thought of his GaltPage. How many followers had joined Justice for Poodlekek since he last checked? Probably millions.

His supporters were waiting for him. They were his people. Young people. Innovators and disruptors.

Arsyen slid off the chair and slipped up the stairs. He had to find Natia.

✳

Outside the Throne Reclamation Committee headquarters, Arsyen hailed a bison-drawn carriage and gave the driver Natia's home address. He wasn't sure she would be there, but Sklartar's old home was now a police station, and the police would surely arrest him on sight if he went there.

Natia's apartment was in a crumbling, 1970s-era building. Arsyen climbed three flights of stairs and could hear several voices coming from behind her door. He peered through a half-inch gap in the curtains of her front window. It was hard to make anything out, but it seemed there were several people, none of them in police uniform.

Arsyen knocked twice and within seconds Natia was there, staring back at him, as surprised by him as he was by the realness of her. He processed each bit of her separately—the flushed cheeks, the long nose, the green eyes, the mole on the chin, the sturdy neck. Natia cut off his inspection with a hug.

"I knew the email wasn't true! I knew you would come!"

Inside the cramped apartment were several other men. These were the strong, young Pyrrhian men he needed to retake his country.

"We're taking the city back!" Natia said to Arsyen, pushing him toward the center of the room, where everyone was gathered around a man with a map. Arsyen wondered if this was Niels_1973.

The man registered the arrival of the new visitor, his eyes flicking between Natia and Arsyen. The chance that Natia had perhaps been unfaithful crossed Arsyen's mind, but he pushed it away. What mattered was that he was there now, finally united with his beloved and ready to lead his people.

Natia gripped his arm and unloaded all of the government's latest atrocities—the cover-ups, the corruption, the "shackles of oppression." As Natia spoke, Arsyen surveyed the room. The men seemed to be poor students and artists. They were well into their twenties, but there was no gold in their mouths. Their sweaters had holes in them. By California standards—barring Berkeley, where a similar look was widely adopted by the citizenry—the men appeared homeless.

"You!" said the man with the map, suddenly rising to his feet and shaking his finger at Arsyen. "You are Prince Arsyen! As a boy I had to stare at your photo each morning in school. For years I had to hear about your croquet exploits."

"Comrade Vgad is right!" said another man, jumping to his feet. "He *is* an Aimo!"

"Arsyen... Aimo?" said Natia, turning to him wide-eyed. "You really don't look like..."

"Yes, well, I live in California now," said Arsyen, smiling, trying to pull Natia away from the group of dirty men. "I've gotten a bit tanner and in shape. You see, we have these great gyms at Anahata and—"

"You have no place here," shouted the man from across the room, taking a step toward Arsyen. "You are the very chains our people are trying to break."

"Chains?" said Arsyen, looking around the room. He turned. "Natia, I'm sorry. I should have told you. It's just that I didn't want it to change how you thought of me."

"You didn't want her to know because she would have hated you. Your country hates you," the man spat. "We all hate you, Bloodthirsty Aimo!"

Arsyen stiffened and turned toward the angry man. "I don't really agree with that assessment." He reminded himself to ask for the man's name—he wouldn't be long for the world once Arsyen was back in power.

"You have no business being here," said the man, grabbing a poker from the fireplace.

"Comrade Vgad—stop!" Natia said. "Arsyen built the Justice for Poodlekek page. He is on our side."

Arsyen's eyes scanned the hostile faces before him. Such disrespect made him look rather foolish in front of Natia. He would just have to win these dirty hippies to his side.

"She speaks the truth," said Arsyen, throwing out his chest and putting his hands on his hips, as his father used to do. "I am on your side. I have come back to lead you to victory."

Arsyen took a step forward and invoked all the silly poetry Natia had written him in her emails.

"We must join together to throw off the shackles of oppression," he said. "Throw the rich on their backs! Take back the means of production! Join me and my thousands of supporters and we will take back the city!"

"Thousands?" Vgad said. "Show me even a handful. King Aimo starved his supporters and beat his enemies. There is no one left who supports you."

"My father treated his enemies in a manner befitting of their treachery," answered Arsyen, puffing his chest out farther.

"Comrade," hissed a man to Vgad's left. "A prince's blood is still blood. We can put him in the front and he can shield the others. If he dies first, then he's saved one of us."

"Yeah, and the Aimos weren't *so* bad," another man said, "compared to, say, Stalin or Hitler."

"And still better than Korpeko," said another.

"That's the spirit!" Arsyen grinned. "You see, we can be revolutionaries together."

Arsyen felt the adrenaline moving through his veins. His father would have been proud. Arsyen had just converted the very people who wanted to destroy his family—and there were still thousands of his real supporters he could call on. He watched with satisfaction as Vgad put down his poker and turned to the other men.

"Come, we must finish our planning. We don't have time for these distractions." He beckoned the men to his map.

Arsyen turned to Natia and tried to speak, but his military bluster did not translate to suave courtship. If only he could have a few minutes alone with her before they started their revolution. She was speaking to him, but it sounded like his Justice for Poodlekek page. Injustice. Injustice. Blah. Blah. It mattered, of course, but he really wished she'd pay a bit more attention to his needs. Injustice would be there tomorrow and the next day—they could solve it then. Arsyen would eventually have to teach her that you can't really be a queen without allowing—even encouraging—a bit of injustice in your kingdom.

But Natia continued to speak, urging him, touching his shoulder. She blushed whenever their gaze crossed and would occasionally let her hand drift to touch his.

Vgad periodically looked over at the two of them, using each opportunity to glare at Arsyen, who likewise sized up his competition. Vgad seemed as poor as the rest of them, and his clothes were standard-issue Red Cross, but he had clear eyes and a thick beard—the trademark signs of Pyrrhian virility. Arsyen touched his own chin and felt the short stubble of two days without shaving. Vgad stood and addressed the group.

"We are ready to whistle."

"Whistle?" said Arsyen.

"It's how we protest," Natia whispered. "We walk through the streets whistling in peaceful protest."

Arsyen frowned. "But how does whistling—"

"Comrade Natia," Vgad called from across the room, "let's not waste any more time. We have a plan—with or without this pathetic prince. I for one have decided to whistle at the military barracks."

A tear fell from Natia's eye. "You are so brave, Comrade Vgad." She stepped toward him.

"The barracks are a very dangerous spot," said Vgad, his eyes meeting Arsyen's as he extended his hand to Natia. "It takes a brave man to whistle at the barracks."

Arsyen saw them then, Natia and Vgad, their lips pursed at the barracks, exchanging whistles, then caresses, and then final, gasping breaths as they dodged and were ultimately hit by Korpeko's bullets. They would die in each other's arms. He felt his insides begin to shake, as though Natia were being pulled from his very marrow.

"And I, Prince—I mean, Comrade Arsyen, will whistle at the imperial palace!" declared Arsyen, raising his fist.

The room went silent.

"Are you sure?" Natia rushed back to Arsyen's side. "We hadn't planned to whistle at the imperial palace just yet. There's a protest there tonight, but it will certainly be heavily guarded."

"The protest is the protest of my people. There must be justice for Poodlekek!" Arsyen cried.

Within minutes, Arsyen found himself equipped with a flag and a megaphone and was being pushed out the door by the group. He needed to find a moment to talk to Natia about his plans for them, but she kept pushing him forward as their group made its way down the stairs. She and twenty others would be accompanying him to the protest.

"My army," said Arsyen, sweeping his hand across the group when they were all on the street.

"We are the *people's* army," Vgad growled.

The sky had begun to fade into evening, and the streets were deserted. But as his eyes adjusted to the unlit streets, Arsyen began to spot shadowy figures darting between houses, moving in parallel to their group's own movements. They crept like thieves, jumping from one building to the next.

"Members of the resistance," Natia whispered.

Soon Arsyen could spot the imperial palace in the distance. Even from several blocks away, the architect's abuse of classical architecture was apparent, with row after row of Corinthian columns surrounding the palace like rotting teeth. Marble flowers and peacocks adorned the Greek capitals, but the passing of years had weathered their relief, and it now seemed the fruit was eating the birds, swallowing the plumage in their mighty petals. Arsyen would have to rebuild everything.

As they turned onto the imperial road, Arsyen gasped. Thousands of people were gathered in front of the palace. People carried signs bearing the words of Arsyen's new comrades.

"Give us our land!"

"Speak the truth!"

"Justice for Poodlekek! Justice for Pyrrhia!"

Arsyen made his way through the crowd. New faces huddled

around Natia and the other members of the group, pointing at Arsyen and pressing them with questions Arsyen couldn't hear. It was just as the TRC had told him. His people were there for him, urging him forward.

Arsyen and Natia pushed their way to the front. A group of women swarmed around them—mothers perhaps, their white handkerchiefs fluttering like anxious doves across their faces. "Help us!" they cried, grasping Arsyen's hands.

Natia pulled out a plastic recorder and played a few notes. All of the chatter ceased as people joined hands and began to whistle—a rapid blast of tweets, coupled with the occasional errant showtune. Arsyen joined in by whistling the tune to his favorite video games.

The whistling spread across the crowd, and now everyone was doing it, whistling and swaying, and then Arsyen felt himself pushed forward, the crowd moving up the steps in a wave. They moved forward again, and then he fell and was lifted up and suddenly was perched on one of the comrade's shoulders, carried higher and higher until he was on the top step, looking out onto the derelict landscape of his city, onto the faces of his people. They stared back at him, lips pursed like fish, and he heard Natia's voice in his ear. "Whistle, Arsyen, whistle! Let them hear the voice of the revolution!"

Arsyen ferociously pumped air through his lips as his girlfriend helped him off her ox-like shoulders. His eyes raced across the crowd, then over them, toward the city gates, looking for the Throne Reclamation Committee or someone who would tell him what to do next.

Someone emerged from the crowd with a megaphone and handed it to Natia. Natia held up her hand to silence the crowd. "This man speaks for our hearts," she said, pointing to Arsyen. "He is the one who will bring justice to Poodlekek!"

She surprised Arsyen with a kiss on the lips, a short but mighty kiss in which Arsyen saw fireworks explode across the sky, alighting his heart and the dreams of thousands of Pyrrhians. The crowd cheered. Then Natia pushed him forward and pressed the mega-phone into his hands. The crowd threw up their arms.

"Speak!" they shouted. "Speak!"

Arsyen looked into the sea of faces and saw himself, people who looked like less handsome versions of him.

Arsyen spoke. His lips were moving and a voice was speaking, but he was not there. It was not his voice, his mouth, or his brain that spoke. It was not his father's voice, or the voice of the TRC, or any voice Arsyen had ever imagined in any daydream of the throne. It was a stranger's voice, repeating what Arsyen had seen on his Justice for Poodlekek page—the same invectives, the same charges against the government. With each squeeze of Natia's hand, Arsyen's calls for revolt grew stronger, and the cheers likewise grew in intensity. His people loved him, and he would give them more of what they wanted to hear.

"It is time for a new social order," he said. "Let us rid our country of fancy palaces, of wealthy, corrupt landowners, and empty curling lanes. Pyrrhians unite! Comrades, we have nothing to lose but our chains!"

The crowd roared and then surged, rushing toward the entrance of the imperial palace. What a wonderful thing to be one with one's people, Arsyen thought. To be a comrade.

"Long live comrade-ism!" he cried.

They tried to climb the tall gates, rattling the cage that housed the acropolis, kicking at the guards as they thrust their bayonets through the rails. Arsyen felt a strong arm pull him away from Natia, their hands separating as she screamed. He felt a sharp pain in his side, and then something against his head, and then nothing at all for a long time.

When he awoke, Arsyen was in a dank cell lit by suspended torches. His supporters were nowhere in sight. He was completely alone.

Maybe this hadn't been such a good idea.

GREGOR

G regor studied Anahata's head of security as he briefed the
group, his gaze moving from one member of the management
team to the next, collecting their worried expressions with thinly
masked delight. But Gregor refused to join in. He would save his
concern and attention for when it mattered. None of this had any
consequence unless Bobby joined the conversation. And for that,
Bobby would need to wake up. Instead, every few minutes, a loud
snore, like someone suffocating a pig, came from his end of the table.

Gregor's mobile buzzed in his pocket with an update. It was yet
another story about Anahata's share price.

Anahata Shares Continue to Fall Over Moon
Colony Rumors

News Wire News, 9:43 a.m. EST, May 21—Anahata stock fell a
further 5 percent today, marking a week in which the Palo Alto–
based internet firm shaved more than $300 from its share price in
the wake of widespread investor belief that the company is losing
focus.

The problem began earlier this month after a former senior ex-
ecutive, Niels Smeardon, claimed on social broadcasting site Flitter
that the software giant was building a moon colony.

In a blog post issued in response, Anahata said Smeardon had
already left the company at the time of his fleet, suggesting that
the comments on Flitter were the work of a disgruntled employee.
This morning, Smeardon posted a retraction of his moon colony

comment on Flitter, stating he was sorry for any confusion. He said there was not any moon colony on Anahata and that his account had been hacked. Calls to Smeardon were not returned.

"There is no Anahata colony today on the moon," an Anahata spokeswoman said.

Analysts, however, were skeptical.

"Moon colonies just aren't a part of Anahata's core business," said Mark Roberts, an analyst with Sterling Platinum Capital. "The market wants to see more focus on Anahata's strongest products and advertising services—not money being thrown at 'pie-in-the-sky' projects. If Anahata can't explain what is happening, investors will quickly lose faith."

"Tech companies don't last forever. They get replaced by young upstarts at a remarkably fast rate," Vargrite Mestayer said. "Anahata's had a good ten years—that's a century in normal industry years. Maybe this is it for them."

Gregor flipped to the next article. Galt had just released an update to the productivity tool they had copied from Anahata. The company had only just released it, what, a month ago? And already it had an update. Gregor couldn't help but admire Galt's speed.

He glanced again at Bobby. The founder slept at the head of the table, head thrown back, mouth open. It reminded Gregor of the war movies he watched as a child with his father, rain collecting in the mouths of dead soldiers as the battle raged around them.

Gregor had never been interested in the company's financial affairs, but he had sat in enough management meetings over the years to have developed some sense of pecuniary trouble. He wondered what Fischer, Anahata's CFCAO, really thought about Anahata's share price. Bobby refused to discuss it and had told Fischer to keep his investor relations and PR teams from saying anything more about Niels or the moon to the outside world. The only thing he had approved was the retraction published that morning on Flitter by "Niels," courtesy of the Progressa team. But even that effort had been lost amid the cacophony of investor and journalist voices predicting the company's downfall.

"Like the tide ebbs and flows, the stock moves up and down," Bobby had said in response. "If it didn't move one way, it couldn't move the other, and then there'd be no point in having a stock market at all."

A *thud* suddenly sounded from the other end of the room. And then again.

The head of security dropped a small, weighted beanbag a third time on the table, this time with even more force.

"Blood! Guts! Swords! Chariots!" he yelled.

Bobby's eyes flew open, and for a brief second his arms flailed as though he were in a free fall. His head darted around the room.

"Where? Where?"

"I was just explaining the Pyrrhia situation," said the head of security, an old hand after working with the founder for six years. He quickly distributed enlarged photos, placing one directly in front of Bobby.

"This is where we believe he's being held—the imperial palace." He pointed to a high-resolution aerial shot of a brown, acropolis-like structure. It sat atop a small hill, a large hunk of columns chomping down on the land like angry jaws.

"How can we be certain he's there?" Bobby asked. "And who's 'he'?"

Old Al sighed audibly. The head of security began again without complaint.

"Arsyen Aimo, one of our product managers. He's been taken prisoner in his native Pyrrhia. We've traced his Anahata badge here," he said, pointing to the compound.

"It's very important that we ensure our employees' safety," said HR Paul. "I think it would send a very powerful message if—"

"Oh, shut up, Paul," Old Al barked. "We all get why it's important to save this guy. No one wants a dead employee."

"You know," Al continued, "none of this would have happened

if we hired only Americans. Practically every year we have to go save an employee from some despotic regime. In my day, we would have hired only Americans to work in America."

The head of security allowed a moment of silence out of respect for the wisdom of the aged, then restarted his briefing from the top. This time, Gregor listened.

According to the security head, Arsyen hadn't badged into anywhere on campus in more than a week, though his own team had never reported him missing. Security had been alerted by his former manager, a guy named Roni, whom Arsyen had contacted, asking for help buying horses.

"Horses?" asked Bobby. "One of our product managers asked for horses? That makes no sense. Horses don't get smarter as time goes on. They're useless. Horses don't scale. Horses die."

"Then you will be pleased to know that Roni didn't fulfill the request," the head of security said. "In any case, the day before he disappeared, Arsyen created a GaltPage—"

"A GaltPage? Really?!?" Fischer moaned. "We have the same product here—Blabber. It's just as good. Why don't our employees use that instead? Can't we force them to do that?"

"As I was saying," the head of security said, "Arsyen created a GaltPage that seems to have inspired an insurrection in the capital of his home country, Pyrrhia."

"Did he use his twenty percent free time to do this?" Old Al groaned. "We need to get rid of that perk—engineers shouldn't be starting revolutions on company time."

"At least not ones we're not supportive of," Fischer nodded.

"Also," the security head said, "it turns out Arsyen is the son of the deposed king."

"We hired a prince?" HR Paul asked. "Is that good for company culture?"

"It's neutral for the company but good for the world," Bobby said. "We have a lot we can teach world rulers about leadership."

"That said," the security head continued, "we can't find any significant history of political involvement. Arsyen's only connection there seems to be a young female revolutionary—"

"Women," chuckled Bobby, shaking his head. "They're harmless until suddenly they're not."

"We could send in Progressa to save Arsyen," Fischer suggested.

"We looked into that," the head of security said. "They're currently in the Philippines, helping rebuild a town that was devastated in a recent typhoon."

"So if we divert them to Poodlekek, that town in the Philippines dies," Bobby said.

"Well, it's more like that town doesn't get computers for its schools."

"That town *dies*," Bobby said. "So, the question is: Is an Anahata engineer's life worth more than thousands of Filipinos?"

The room was silent.

"It is," said Gregor, after a few seconds, lifting a piece of paper with some numbers scratched across it. "From a quick calculation, on average, an Anahata engineer will save 600,000 lives during his lifetime through the products he builds. If we lose Arsyen, we kill 600,000 people—and lose the benefit that his no doubt superior offspring could also produce for society."

"To be clear," the head of security said, "Arsyen Aimo is a product manager on the engineering team—not an engineer himself."

"Fine," said Gregor, making a few more scratches on the paper. "So he is worth a little less than that. But even a janitor at Anahata is worth several thousands of lives."

Bobby nodded and rose from his chair. "Our brave employee has taken it upon himself to fight tyranny in the darkest corner of the earth. He has taken the Anahata mission to heart and has set out to improve humankind. We should shut down the company until we can find him!"

The room was quiet.

"Or at least give him some massage credits," Bobby said. "I'm sure that whole revolution thing is exhausting."

HR Paul nodded and began to pull out some of the massage coupons he walked around campus dispensing each day from twelve to one p.m.

"As CFCAO, there's another consideration I feel I should raise," Fischer said. "If this guy Arsyen started a GaltPage and the government ends up being overthrown, then Galt will get all the credit for having spread a revolution and ushering in a new era of democracy. We've done a handful of revolutions now—that's *our* space. We can't let Galt take this by themselves."

"You're right!" exclaimed Bobby, leaping to his feet. "We can't let Galt own democracy. And… and… if we free Arsyen and Pyrrhia, then we free ourselves, too, from all this moon colony attention. All people will want to write about is our inspiring commitment to democracy."

Bobby paced the length of the room, then turned. "We must send him an army—an army of engineers. An army that will storm the city, turn it upside down, and show the world the truth of Anahata!"

His eyes blazed.

"Here!" he said, pointing to the photo showing the back entrance to the structure. "Here is where we enter! We put forty men here. And then fifty men at this door. And one hundred along the outer perimeter. How many men can the drawbridge hold?"

"Drawbridge?"

"Yes, the drawbridge, to cross the moat—here!" Bobby pointed at a dark path surrounding the compound.

"I think that's a road."

"No matter! Come bridge or pavement, our horses can cross it! What will we do if they throw scalding wax upon our heads? We must make sure that the armor fully covers our engineers' bodies. Regular Anahata T-shirts won't be enough. Fischer, talk to your marketing team. I want the special long-sleeved, fireproof shirts we discussed, the ones with the purple Anahata logo and the little trees sprouting out of the H. Remember that, because the other version you showed me has the tree coming out of the T, which I think looks too expected and undelightful."

Gregor could feel everyone's eyes on him, hoping he would reign Bobby in.

"Arsyen will likely be in the dungeon," Bobby continued. "We must make sure they don't try to ferret him away to another location. Let's have our men dig a hole from here, cutting across over there, and then coming up on the other side. We will take Poodlekek, and we will install a new government. A good government that is reasonable and believes in the internet. Because if you have the internet, you do not have revolutions. The internet *is* the revolution!

"Bobby," Gregor began.

"And," said Bobby, holding up a finger, "this won't just help solve the moon colony problem. If we can get a new world order going on over there, I'm sure we can sell the government all of our enterprise solutions. Pyrrhia will run on Anahata technology!"

Bobby paused to catch his breath.

"Bobby, this won't work," Gregor said.

Bobby looked at Gregor, then turned toward his head of security, who nodded in agreement.

"We can't do this on our own," Gregor said. "For one, we don't have an army."

"Gregor, didn't we discuss you building an army just a few weeks ago?"

"It will take some time," Gregor said. "And as I understood it, it was an army of engineering evangelists you were asking for, not an army of real soldiers."

"Clearly our army should be multipurpose," Bobby said. "In the meantime, what if we just made some fighting robots? How long would it take us to build some Terminators?"

Gregor had run those numbers a few weeks earlier and was annoyed to discover he couldn't remember them. He grabbed a Post-it and began to run the necessary calculations.

"Regardless," the security head said, "we'd need to work in collaboration with the U.S. government."

"Aw, c'mon," Bobby whined. "We've done it before. Besides, if Anahata were a country, we'd be the fourth wealthiest nation in the world. Doesn't that give us some kind of extra rights? Fischer, has your legal team looked into this?"

Fischer shook his head. "Don't you remember the warning the president gave us last time? If we're going to have anyone on the ground, we need to involve the State Department."

"Over my dead body," said Old Al, rising from his seat. "We have a strong libertarian contingent here. If the engineers find out we're working with the government, we'll have a mutiny on our hands."

Bobby's gaze wandered to the whiteboard. "I wonder..." He was silent for a minute as his eyes darted across the empty canvas. He turned back to the group.

"Your verdict tries to put me in chains, but I am a chain breaker. In fact, I now realize that I was overlooking our greatest strength. We *do* have an army. One that never needs to touch the ground, that the government never needs to know about. An army that never sleeps. It is..."

Bobby paused, looking around the room. "It is the internet!"

Fischer snorted, but Gregor leaned forward in his chair.

"We will point our weapons in one direction. Our search engine, Flitter fleets, F-Square check-ins—wait, never mind, no one uses F-Square anymore. But the rest of them, we will use and expose Poodlekek and free Arsyen through the internet! Gregor, go work up the plan."

✳

Anahata loved democracy. Democracy meant free speech. Democracy meant an open internet. Democracy meant a boundless sea of opportunity for online advertising.

But there was even more at stake in Pyrrhia. This wasn't just a battle to free an inconsequential country. If Anahata could succeed in overthrowing the government, Bobby was convinced the company would see a democracy uptick in its stock price.

Under Gregor's direction, Anahata's infrastructure engineers harnessed all their skills—IP prestidigitation, networked hot-air balloons, Wi-Fi-enabled squirrels—to work around the government's block and make the internet accessible again in Poodlekek.

The search engineers created a new ranking algorithm, designed to ensure that negative articles about the despotic government would appear in the topmost position of Pyrrhia's search results. Immolated monks, raped women, limbless elderly, and dead orphans would all be listed on the first page for any number of search queries, with graphic images and tales of atrocity immediately leaping to the eyes of anyone searching for even the most innocent information. Even if the government managed to keep the internet down in Poodlekek, Anahata would flood the rest of the country with the reranked results. If previous Anahata revolutions were any indication, the incendiary results would incite unrest elsewhere in the country, eventually leading to revolt and a total collapse of the government. A new, progressive leader would take over, Arsyen would be freed, and the world would celebrate the triumph of democracy and Anahata.

For eight hours, the Moodify team worked to build a new Pyrrhian search engine, going through thirty cans of Red Bull, twenty bags of Anahata's signature organic potato chips, and trying their best to ignore the beckoning Circean pings from their Social Me app.

Finally, in the darkest hours of morning, taurine and glucose dripping from their pores, they reached the last, dramatic step. The team typed in the final line of code. The cursor blinked back at them, pulsing like an explosive light. They turned to Gregor, who gave them the nod. The team lead put his index finger atop a single "enter" key, closed his eyes, and on the count of three, pushed.

ARSYEN

President Korpeko was not so much fat as oversized, each part of his body a comic exaggeration of what it was intended to be. His ears hung like drooping question marks. A flat, expansive nose dominated his face as though a manifestation of his own imperial ambitions. The bones of his fingers popped in and out of their joints as his pudgy hands moved across his desk, sometimes reaching for a paper, other times for his porcelain teacup.

The president leaned toward Arsyen, his pale, pockmarked face punctuated by bursts of red veins. Arsyen met his gaze and jutted out his chin but hardly felt so confident. He wiggled his hands behind his back, trying to loosen the ropes, but they seemed to grow tighter the more he squirmed.

It occurred to Arsyen that the president might kill him. He was the exiled prince, after all. And while he had no desire to die, any outcome less than that was slightly insulting to someone of Arsyen's standing.

But none of this was really his fault, and Arsyen hadn't truly intended to take back the throne just yet. It had just been an idea—a passing fancy brought about by the intoxicating influence of the internet. Perhaps Arsyen could offer up the Throne Reclamation Committee in his place. Korpeko could save face, do a nice Sunday execution jamboree of the committee leaders, and everyone could go on their merry way.

Arsyen's thoughts turned to Natia. Did she know where he was? Had she thought he was brave when she saw him dragged off by Korpeko's men? Perhaps he would never know.

An aide tiptoed toward President Korpeko. The president's head cocked like a teapot to receive the whispered briefing. This had been the routine for the past ten minutes: a thirty-second briefing from an aide, a long study of Arsyen's face, then the arrival of a new aide and his news. Finally, after several minutes, Korpeko addressed his prisoner.

"Well, Prince Arsyen?"

"Look," Arsyen said, "Pyrrhia doesn't interest me. The television here has only four channels. In America, we have ten thousand, and we watch all of them. Here the people sleep on blankets and hay. In America, they have this thing called 1-800-MATTRESS, and, I mean, you get a mattress like an hour after you call. And then—anyway, my point is it's the TRC you want. They are behind all of your problems. Them and a group of dirty revolutionaries led by a young man name Vgad. I will lead you to him."

The president laughed without smiling. "Yes, I must be mistaken. You didn't create the Justice for Poodlekek page. The impassioned speech you gave just now in front of that motley band of whistlers wasn't you. Anahata, the company you work for, isn't the company that my telecommunications minister now tells me is trying to hijack our Great Pyrrhian Wall of Fire."

An aide whispered in the president's ear.

"Our firewall, I mean. Our Great Pyrrhian Firewall. I am sure none of these silly political matters have anything to do with you. You are just a good Poodlekek boy who happens to be the son of the deposed leader and came to Pyrrhia for a little vacation."

Arsyen sighed. It was clear that Korpeko would not be won over easily.

Arsyen grimaced as he lowered himself from the chair to the ground to perform the traditional Pyrrhian bow—nose to the ground, fanny pointed skyward. It was a humiliating posture for a prince, and he knelt only long enough for Korpeko to register his submission. Then he sat back on his heels.

"Please let me go," said Arsyen, his head still bowed. "I promise you'll have no more trouble from me."

"Silence!" said Korpeko, throwing his teacup past Arsyen's head, shattering it against the opposite wall. From his belt he pulled a gleaming Pyrrhian lobate blade, slicing the air with a swish.

A guard materialized and yanked Arsyen to his feet, only to then knock his legs out from under him. Arsyen fell and landed squarely on his hip. He howled, but no one cared. The president already seemed to have turned his attention elsewhere. He was conferring with someone new, a man Arsyen recognized as Colonel Okonkwi, Korpeko's right hand. Colonel Okonkwi's face was red and he sputtered as he spoke. A storm moved across the president's face, his eyes flicking rapidly between the two men.

Colonel Okonkwi gestured at a black screen occupying most of the wall opposite the president's desk. An aide pushed a button, and the screen was suddenly illuminated in white. He typed something into a device, and an Anahata search box appeared, the purple-and-green logo bouncing gently on the page. He then typed "Pyrrhia" and hit the search button.

President Korpeko gasped. The first result accused the president of sleeping with dogs. The second charged his top advisers with corruption. The third was an unfortunate photo of him vomiting at a state dinner.

"Search for something else," ordered Korpeko.

The aide tried "government," then "elections," then "healthy recipes for weight loss." But no matter what the query, the results seemed to be skewed, designed to show the worst of President Korpeko and his officials. Arsyen watched as the rigged search results cascaded down the screen. One result in particular seemed to catch the president's attention. It first appeared as the tenth result, then, within seconds, as the aide performed subsequent searches, the result moved up the list, gaining in popularity as a nation of Pyrrhians clicked to read its damning evidence—a birth certificate suggesting that President Korpeko was not actually Pyrrhian but Embrian. In a manner of minutes, it was the top search result, no matter what the query.

The president's officials gazed at their leader and took a step back. Only Colonel Okonkwi, the president's longtime confidant, remained where he stood, his face hardening.

"This is *your* fault," said the colonel, turning to Arsyen. "You are a traitor to your country." He turned to Korpeko. "What shall we do with him?"

The president, his eyes fixed on the screen, didn't answer. The colonel leaned in and repeated the question.

"It doesn't matter," said Korpeko finally, his voice almost inaudible.

"To the gallows!" the colonel shouted.

The guard dragged Arsyen out the door, hauling him down a short corridor and then down four steep steps. The opulent tapestries and gold-plated furniture of the upper floor gave way to a dingier space sparsely populated with shabby chairs and cupboards.

"The dungeon's full today, so the old kitchen will have to do for now," the guard said.

Arsyen limped toward the room's sole chair, his hip throbbing after his fall.

The guard walked over to the far end of the kitchen and opened what appeared to be a freezer stuffed with ice packs. "You're lucky we have these," he said, tossing a few at Arsyen. "The president has repetitive strain injury from curling, so we keep them stockpiled here. Throw one on your hip—we don't want people thinking we tortured you before we killed you."

The guard shut the door and turned the key on the other side. Arsyen's eyes scanned the room. There were no windows and just a single door. The room was so dusty that he found himself sneezing.

The guard returned in a few minutes with a cold potato and some salt and sugar.

"Colonel Okonkwi wants to squeeze you into the noon executions. You're lucky, really—the waiting list is long and the dungeon tends to make people's limbs rot. Enjoy your last few hours."

Then the guard left, locking the door behind him.

Arsyen stared at the potato and pushed the plate away. Just a few days before, he had been in sunny California; now he was about to be executed for doing something that he only sort of intended to do, for a girl he barely knew, but for whom, even in this dark moment, he still pined.

Arsyen studied the kitchen—the chipped white cabinets and dusty floor, an old broom resting against the fridge. Of all the ironies—the prince turned janitor back in his palace, held prisoner in the filthiest spot.

So much dirt surrounded him. And without Arsyen, who would clean it up?

Arsyen had never loved being a janitor, but he recognized the importance of the job: Someone had to clean up the messes people made each day. All those men in the Valley went about building their riches and never looked back to see what filth they had left behind. They needed people like Arsyen to sweep things away.

And so it was, then, just hours from death, that Arsyen wondered why, with all the extraordinary brain power in Silicon Valley today, no engineer had ever tackled the fundamental human problem of dirt. Dirt affected everyone; dirt was democratic. Dirt scaled, dirt climbed, dirt 10x'd everything it could. And there was so very, very much that lay below the surface of things. Arsyen vowed that if he somehow made it out of the palace alive, he would take the problem straight to Bobby Bonilo.

Arsyen felt his stomach rumble. The rumble turned to a growl, and he reconsidered the potato the guard had left him.

Arsyen sprinkled the potato with salt and took a bite. He wrinkled his nose and spit it out—there was something wrong with that salt. He poured a bit into his hand and tasted it cautiously with his tongue. It looked like salt, but it wasn't salt. It was... saltpeter? Totally useless as a salt seasoning, but it had proven useful in a pinch during Arsyen's cleaning experiments.

Arsyen paused: Would God let him experiment with chemicals in heaven? Could he continue to work his Aimo Air Freshener there?

Would Arsyen be a janitor or a king in heaven? Could he be a king if there was God?

Arsyen pushed away the plate and salt shaker.

But a second later, they were back in front of him. Arsyen stared at the potato, then looked at the salt shaker, his mind spinning. Could it be?

His gaze moved across the table, from the saltpeter, over to the sugar, and finally to his ice pack. He smiled for the first time in hours. From his jeans pocket, he pulled out a small heart-shaped bottle—the Aimo Air Freshener he had planned to give Natia. And then he waited for the guard to return.

KORPEKO AND OKONKWI

In the lavish command room of the imperial palace, the extent of the damage to Pyrrhia's internet was quickly becoming clear to the president and his colonel.

News of unrest in the capital had quickly spread throughout the country. In the city of Kolkikek, a man searching for a chat room was directed to a blog post about the government's cover-up of the train crash. In Pokikek, a woman searching for information on curling techniques was taken to a list of the government's excessive expenditures on exotic birds. In Krakikek, a college student researching European history was redirected to a video of the demonstration outside the imperial palace. It wasn't long before Klokikek, Pokikek, and Krakikek—and a host of other Pyrrhian cities—were up in arms, plotting action against corrupt local and national officials.

And then Anahata played its ace, bringing citizens across Pyrrhia to their feet, pitchforks in hand, as their searches for online porn were greeted by a 404 error page and a message that the government had censored all inappropriate images.

The president dismissed all of his officials except Colonel Okonkwi. The two sat silently before their glasses of scotch, the president thinking back on his years of rule, the colonel contemplating the best military strategy to protect the country from revolt. As night fell, the crowds outside the palace grew louder, and the first gate, then the second, gave way to the angry masses. Colonel Okonkwi wondered how much time was left before his men began to abandon their posts.

Suddenly, a loud explosion from the floor below knocked

Colonel Okonkwi to his knees. He dashed into the hall and nearly collided with an aide. "It's Prince Arsyen. He's gone," the panicked aide said. "He blew up a wall in the first-floor kitchen!"

The colonel returned to the command room and locked the door behind him, preparing to summon his reserve army.

"My friend, sit," said President Korpeko, handing the colonel his glass.

The command room was dark save for the white screen. Its light cast a sickly pallor across the president's face. Just then, the search results on the screen began to melt together, dripping into a dark circle in the middle, then opening into a spiraling rainbow. The rainbow dissolved into the dancing face of Bobby Bonilo, chiseled and set against a blue sky. "Improve humankind!" said the talking head, floating through the clouds, blinking for just a few seconds before disappearing. And then the search results returned.

"Who was that man?" Colonel Okonkwi raged.

"Anahata," said the president quietly, but his mind had moved well beyond any thoughts of revenge.

President Korpeko had always known this day would come, but he had hoped to stave it off long enough to see his dreams to fruition. He now saw that his great hope—to ease hundreds of years of hatred between his native Embria and his adopted Pyrrhia through a mutual love of curling—would die with him. The curling high schools he had created would be restored to Aimo croquet preparatories. The lanes he had crafted alongside the main roads would be left to melt, the ice turning sooty, patches of weeds shooting up like a long-dormant plague. The statue of him in the central plaza, his body bent close to the ground, hand on the curling stone, eyes staring forward into the future, would be toppled by a gang of dirty, illiterate youths. In his place, the same statues, just with different faces and names, would be erected by Arsyen Aimo.

He shook his head and placed his hand on the shoulder of Colonel Okonkwi. "My friend, it is over. I will see you on the other side."

President Korpeko walked slowly through the adjoining door to his private quarters. There, after kissing a photo of his prized curling stone and donning both Pyrrhian and Embrian bison capes, he put a bullet in his head.

Colonel Okonkwi heard the shot from the other side of the door.

BOBBY

B obby was only three seconds into his pranayamic breathing when the suits cut him off.

"Bobby. Bobby. BOBBY!"

He lifted his head, glancing at the figures before him.

"We didn't come here to watch you do yoga," one suit said. "That's not what a board is for."

Bobby projected the positive energy from his stomach onto the suits. Poor suits, they didn't know how misguided they were. If only they would let him guide them to the light. He had been avoiding their calls for days in the hopes of teaching them the importance of patience, but instead they had stormed Anahata with their assistants and made those poor women go on a hunger strike until Bobby would agree to see them.

Bobby stood, adjusted his turquoise pajamas, then brought his hands together in namaste. He bowed to the six suited men standing before him.

"Board. Boardmen. Welcome."

The suits took their seats and wasted no time in launching their interrogation: Was there a moon colony? Who had come up with the idea? Why hadn't the board been told in advance? Did the FTC know? The FCC? The FEC? NASA? Were rocket ships involved? Had they found aliens?

They were such a tedious bunch. Bobby held up his hand to stop their babbling.

"You may call yourselves 'the board,' but let there be no pretense as to why you are here. I could heard your little feet approaching, scampering through the clouds of capitalism, sailing down on your golden carpets, landing on my verdant lawn. I *know* what you want."

"What we want," a suit hissed, "is to keep you from destroying one of the world's wealthiest companies."

"We exist to help keep Anahata on track," another suit added.

Bobby again held up his hand and closed his eyes.

He thought of the poet Rumi.

Then he thought of freezing some vials of his blood to keep him virile at eighty.

But then he again thought of Rumi.

"The truth was a mirror in the hands of God. It fell and broke into pieces. Everybody took a piece of it, and they looked at it and thought they had the truth."

The suits looked at him blankly.

Bobby shook his head.

"Rumi. That was the great poet Rumi. My point is you don't know the full picture yet. So please calm down."

He projected a serene, benevolent smile.

"To protect our company's future, it was clear we needed to start from scratch, to rebuild the rules and fundamentals of society. You see, I looked up one day and there was this fiery sun and—"

"Is there a moon colony or not?" said one of the suits, glancing at his watch.

Bobby sighed. Why was everyone so hung up about the moon? The important part was the society.

"Yes, it's on the moon. But don't pretend you care about the moon. I bet none of you even know your astrological sign. You just care about our rapidly tanking stock price, yes? Let's just put that out there and be clear with one another."

"I didn't think any of us were hiding it," said the suit. "This is *all* about the stock price and the fact that there are already indications that your shareholders may sue."

"We'll be fine," Bobby said. "The PR team put out a blog post refuting the whole moon thing."

"That was days ago, and in case you haven't noticed, it's had *zero* effect," said a different suit, a suit whose name Bobby could never remember but whom he recalled was the richest man in India. "Your PR team has managed to write a blog post where they say nothing at all."

"Well, yes, but that's the purpose of a PR team," Bobby said. "Like I said, we'll be fine. The stock moves up and the stock moves down. Things come and go. Yin and yang."

"Do you understand how serious this is? When people find out how much money you are wasting on a moon adventure—"

"Look," Bobby said, "on the advertising side, everything is great. We essentially automated the sales team, and our whole sales operation is more efficient and profitable than ever. And as for the rest, we just need a few weeks to get everything ready. Our earnings are going to be well above the street's forecasts. You'll see, all will be fine."

"All will *not* be fine if you have to wait a few weeks to be able to prove that Anahata isn't run by a nutjob looking to befriend aliens," the Indian suit said.

"Ah, but you have all forgotten about *this*, my trump card," said Bobby, pushing that day's newspaper toward the center of the table. He had asked his assistant to pick it up that morning—wherever it was these days that one could still buy a print newspaper.

The Indian suit read the headline aloud.

Pyrrhian Ruler Ousted by Anahata

Bobby beamed.

"You must not have seen the stock price this morning," said the Indian suit, tossing the paper on the table. "It's down another five percent. The street doesn't like revolutions. Philosophic ideals are rarely connected to the promotion of successful economic models."

"But the media is loving it," Bobby protested. "We ushered in democracy!"

"Human rights don't benefit anyone but humans. The market sees no upside."

"Hmm." Bobby paused, irritated by this wrinkle. How could people expect you to be a visionary if they were constantly fogging your glasses?

"I think Bobby should call the Fixer," the Indian suit said. "The Fixer can fix this."

"The Fixer's a great idea," another suit said. "He doesn't even really need to fix anything. People just need to think you've brought in some adult supervision."

"Wall Street likes adults," nodded the suit next to him. "The Fixer can action any action plan, synergize any synergies. Provided, of course, that you open the kimono and—"

Bobby looked down—he had not worn his kimono today. This suit spoke in riddles.

"The point is, the shareholders will sue if they feel you are destroying their company."

"*My* company," Bobby said. "It's *my* company. I own fifty-one percent."

"Bobby, take this seriously. You don't want to be sued," another suit said.

"Or be pressured to resign," said the Indian suit.

Bobby turned toward the suit closest to him. With his pale, wrinkly body, he looked just like the suit next to him, who looked just like the two men sitting next to him, who—well, didn't look anything like the Indian billionaire. But in spirit, at least, the suits were all the same. In Bobby's new society on the moon, there would be no suits. There would only be… progress.

Bobby crossed his arms and leaned back in his chair, throwing his feet up on the table. He contemplated whether falling into a sudden nap would send the capitalists away. He wanted more time to think about innovation… or breasts… or innovation.

"Look at it this way," said the Indian suit, cutting into his thoughts. "If you don't get the share price back up, you're not going to have any money left to reinvest in the moon project. And then the moon project will collapse."

"Or worse—Galt could beat you to it," another suit said.

Bobby's feet dropped to the floor. He hadn't considered that possibility—or any others, really, as he had forbidden Fischer to distract him with financials.

"If you want to save the moon colony, you have to save Anahata," the Indian suit said.

Bobby frowned. It did sound like he might have a problem.

"Fine, I'll call him. But you'll see that this will all blow over. The market shouldn't be so focused on the short term. You know, when we designed Anahata, we didn't want to be a normal company. We wanted—"

The Indian suit stood, signaling Bobby to stop. "Bobby, you'll have to excuse us. There are children dying in Africa—and, you know, other corporate issues—that we must attend to at our own companies. Let us know when you have the Fixer."

✳

For a man who seemed to be everywhere and on everyone's lips, the Fixer was an elusive figure. He popped up now and then at internet conferences and industry events, but even then he was more whisper than presence. He hid in green rooms and VIP suites, sipped his cocktails in the shadows of discreet Davos and Sun City condos. But only those as powerful as the Fixer could claim to have seen him.

Bobby liked to think he was equally elusive. In fact, his first thought after capitulating to the board's suggestion was that the Fixer should have to call *him*. But even Bobby could be practical and knew that telepathy had yet to be invented (though he had Gregor working on it). So he put his Progressa unit—just back from its operation in the Philippines—onto the task of tracking him down.

There was a reason Bobby trusted his most confidential and tricky tasks to Progressa, the Anahata team in charge of solving big problems like poverty, famine, drought, and hassle-free distributed computing. He had realized early on that the same skills needed to save the world were also those needed to make pesky executives disappear—or to quietly recruit slippery visionaries like the Fixer.

They tracked him down at a Hopi reservation near the Arizona border. The Fixer agreed to meet with Bobby, but in a place far away from the watchful eyes of technologists. And so, eighteen hours after the Anahata board meeting, Bobby hopped on his jet to the Santa Fe Holistic Wellness Center to find the Fixer alone in a meditation room containing only two burning candles, a miniature Japanese garden, and a freshly groomed goat.

The legendary tech healer briefly opened his eyes, acknowledging Bobby's trespass in his sacred space. At first glance, Bobby found the balding, middle-aged man unexceptional in appearance. But then the Fixer bent over in prayer. His belly pushed in and out of his caftan like a peach-colored pillow, in and out, in and out. Bobby found the rhythm of the breath soothing. He wondered if his own breath could also inspire such calm. He waited.

The Fixer inhaled and exhaled, inhaled and exhaled. With the persistence of the ocean tide, his caftan slowly inched its way up his lower back, soon revealing what Bobby had long heard to be true. Rising along the right of his spine were a series of hatchet marks, a tally of companies the Fixer had resurrected from the depths of bankruptcy, geopolitical nightmares, oil spills, and murdered mistresses.

Bobby knew that the Fixer would not speak to him right away—it was standard practice in the technology industry to use meditation as a negotiation tactic. Letting the room sit in silence was an effective way to instill calm as well as establish dominance. Bobby sat back on his heels and began his own meditation, closing his eyes and silently repeating his latest mantra.

Not my will but Thy will, not my will but Thy will, not my will but Thy will…

His mind was a blank canvas. It was a still lake. It was a round peach. It was a perfectly shaped breast.

Focus, Bobby!

Not my will but Thy will, not my will but Thy will...

Bobby could feel the goat gnawing at his shirt. It shouldn't have bothered him—it usually took just a few seconds of meditation to tune out life's little distractions. But now his mind kept flashing to the Fixer and the warnings from his board, his chant soon morphing to *Not my will but the Fixer's will*, then *Not me but the Fixer*, and finally, *Not my money but Thy money*. He was glad no one could read his thoughts.

Fifteen minutes later, the Fixer opened his eyes.

"Hello, Bobby," he said.

"Hello," said Bobby, meeting his gaze.

"You have caught me at a good time," the Fixer said. "Just returned from an ashram in Goa. Real cleansing, intense stuff. I would say it changed me, but then I often feel that I myself am change."

"Change is the poem that flows through me," Bobby responded.

"And me," the Fixer said.

In unison, the men breathed in and out. The goat bleated.

"Your breath is a gift back to the world," Bobby said.

"And yours," said the Fixer, his nose now touching the floor, then rising to lead his body into poodle pose.

"I've been told of your troubles," he said after a moment had passed. "I believe I can fix them."

"I have no troubles," said Bobby, hearing his own voice waiver. He stretched his arms out in front of him, also moving into poodle pose.

"I have seen the future, and it is not Anahata," the Fixer said.

Bobby felt his arms quiver, but he did not respond.

"The future," the Fixer said, "is something called GaltSpeak."

Bobby broke poodle pose, his head whipping in the direction of the Fixer. "What?!"

"Galt's universal translator, built by a few ex-Anahata engineers. It translates anyone's speech—even animals."

"Impossible."

"I saw it just last week. A demo where they translated a

Jessica Powell

conversation between a cat and his Korean owner in real time. And then, because they're Galt, they managed to reduce all the communication to just the most important bits."

"Wow," said Bobby, genuinely impressed—and impressed that he was impressed.

"They plan to launch it next year. They've even figured out how to monetize. Every few minutes, the animal or person whose speech is being translated will read a text advertisement, targeted to your conversation."

Bobby's head darted around the room. The goat. The candle. The bonsai tree. What could he build that was better than GaltSpeak?

"They say it will only take them one more year to extend the functionality to corpses," continued the Fixer, now turning to lock eyes with Bobby. "That's not just bleeding-edge innovation, that's an enormous monetization opportunity. After all, the dead on this planet far outnumber the living."

"The dead," Bobby said. His legs were shaking. He could feel a bead of sweat fall from his forehead.

"Galt is the next Anahata," the Fixer said. "In the future, everything will be reduced to almost nothing—our thoughts, emotions, pictures, feelings. That plays to Galt's strength, not yours. Anahata just expands. It's all you know how to do. You're so desperate that you gobble everything up, thinking size alone will secure your future. But listen to me when I tell you that you have no future in the future."

"No," said Bobby, collapsing to the floor and burrowing his head into the yoga mat. "No, no, no, no! I want to build the universal translator—and then shrink everything!"

The Fixer did not speak for a few minutes.

"I can help you," he said finally.

"Please!" yelped Bobby, his desperation bouncing off the walls, surprising even the goat.

Baaaaa.

Bobby coughed.

"Please tell me," he said with a level voice.

"We need to build something on Mars."

"Mars?!?"

In his fifteen years in the technology business, Bobby's intuition had never led him astray. And now his gut was telling him not to listen to this man. But maybe his gut was wrong. Maybe it had been wrong for a long time, like ever since he had stopped taking his probiotics. How else could Galt have outpaced Anahata? They had monetizable cats—even monetizable *dead* cats!

"Hold on," said Bobby, jumping to his feet.

He walked to the far corner and opened the door. Gregor's combat boots shuffle-thudded into the room. The goat bleated. The Fixer's forehead wrinkled for a split second as he broke his pose to look toward the door. He took in Gregor's meditation-inappropriate camouflage attire.

"This is Gregor, our SVP of engineering," Bobby said.

The Fixer pushed his hands together and gave a small bow. Gregor nodded and pitched forward only slightly, his eyes never leaving the Fixer's face.

Bobby turned toward Gregor. "He says we need to build something on Mars."

"Just something small," said the Fixer, smiling at Gregor. "Obviously, I don't know all the details about your moon colony—just what I have seen in the press. But then you wouldn't be here if it was all a lie, right?"

Gregor did not answer. The Fixer shrugged.

"I think it's great. Someone needs to think big like that. But it's a problem for your stock price—you need air cover. My idea is that we build something on Mars. It can be something meaningless but which we make seem significant. For example, what if I told you that I recently found evidence of microbial life on Mars? If you had that research in your pocket—and I can make that happen, you know—you could easily construct a little microbe breeding cave there. We could say it's a step toward understanding the beginnings of the universe—or that it will help us solve global warming. Something like that. Something so big and audacious that people are embarrassed to ask about the details.

"The point is it doesn't really matter what we do—we can blind everyone with data. This project will be public, relatively cheap, and we can confirm it immediately. Then we insinuate to the press that people confused our Mars project for a moon colony, and in the process correct the rumors that are swirling about right now."

Gregor grunted. Bobby looked over at him, desperate to read his reaction, but Gregor's face offered little insight into what he was thinking.

The Fixer used the small Japanese rock garden to illustrate his plan. Bobby was transfixed by the small rake and the smooth, unhindered path it took across the garden. With each pass of the rake, his Galt fears seemed to attenuate.

"If only we were all rakes," he whispered to Gregor.

The Fixer pointed out the key elements of his plan, using bonsai trees and small rocks to reconstruct his microbe breeding cave. Bobby felt his confidence building. He could already read the success of the Mars plan in the lines snaking across the sand.

"This seems very elaborate," said Gregor, breaking Bobby's train of thought.

"But this will get us to the moon," Bobby said. He turned toward the Fixer. "What do you need?"

"First, my fee. I want $20 million—$10 million in cash, and $10 million payable when the stock rises $200 more than its current value. I am certain it will surpass that, but I'm giving you a deal because I'm genuinely excited by your innovative thinking."

"Done."

"Second, the structure. In order to pull this off, we need to rearrange how all of Anahata works. Everyone must be moving as one fluid unit."

"Your vision is radical," Bobby said. "It should be accompanied by an equally radical new organizational structure."

"I will need to have engineering, product, sales, and strategy reporting into me."

"But—" said Gregor, his face suddenly collapsing as he looked to Bobby.

Engineering was Gregor's world, and Bobby knew there was nothing more important to him. But Bobby also knew none of that would matter if he couldn't get the company back on track. He would just have to find a way to make it up to Gregor later.

"Radical vision requires radical transformation," Bobby nodded.

"It's not simply that he's power hungry?" Gregor said.

"If I wanted control of everything," said the Fixer, "I would have also asked for your other departments. Like finance. Or HR."

"Everyone knows those departments don't do anything," Gregor said.

The Fixer shrugged and turned again toward Bobby. "Take it or leave it. And by the way, I also want his office," he said, pointing at Gregor.

"I'm sorry, Gregor," said Bobby, averting the engineer's gaze. "But I have no choice. Galt is monetizing corpses."

Gregor's mouth opened, but he did not speak. He turned and made a brisk exit, momentarily slowed by the goat, which tried to block the door. Bobby felt a moment of sadness but quickly recovered once the Fixer offered him the miniature rake to play with.

Dragging the rake through the rock garden, Bobby outlined his plans for the moon colony. He could tell the Fixer was excited by the idea, and the men agreed that speed was of the essence. The Fixer suggested they perform a sequence of sun salutations in lieu of a contract. "The word," he said, "is more sincere than paper."

They decided he would start the following Monday.

※

That Monday morning, even before rising from bed, Bobby did something he hadn't done in all of Anahata's ten-year history: He checked the company's share price. It was still falling—that was no surprise—but he wanted to peg it to an exact number before the Fixer's arrival reversed its downward spiral.

Things could only go up from here. Within 24 hours, the company's share price would be on the upswing; then, just a week later, Anahata would release its quarterly earnings report, recording an impressive 40 percent growth from the previous quarter. The world would be in order yet again.

Bobby jumped out of bed and skipped into his yoga room. Outside, the sky was a boundless blue. Somewhere up there was the Fixer, making his way toward Anahata in his golden fleet, the exhaust from his sky ship leaving a trail of diamonds in its wake.

He couldn't wait to share his moon colony vision with another great thinker. Gregor was great, but he was a doer. Sometimes you wanted to be with a be-er—someone who could just soak in the essence of genius. Once the Fixer was fully on board, maybe he and Bobby could meditate together or fund a solar-energy side project. The possibilities were endless when two great minds were united.

Bobby looked out the window, then inhaled and exhaled deeply. What a great day. Now was a good time to think about cold fusion. He hadn't thought about it in a while, and someone really needed to be doing that.

Bobby's phone buzzed.

"Damn it!"

It was the Fixer. Cold fusion would have to wait.

"Let's cut the pleasantries, Bobby. There's a problem. I'm not flying in today."

In the privacy of his yoga room, Bobby allowed a smug smile to settle on his face. For all his fanciness, it seemed the Fixer didn't own a backup jet. Bobby pictured him boarding a commercial flight, his body squirming awkwardly in a business-class seat where thousands of poorer rich people had sat their well-fed bottoms over the previous year.

"After I saw you, Galt came to me," the Fixer said. "You speaking to me made them want to speak to me. So my price has gone up since we last spoke."

Bobby rolled his eyes. Why was everyone so obsessed with money? Why couldn't they just follow their passions and go with the flow?

"So, how much do you want?" Bobby asked.

"Enough so that I can go back to Galt and get them to give me even more money."

"You mean you'll be working with Galt regardless?"

"GaltSpeak just seems more feasible than your moon colony thing," the Fixer said. "And monetizing the thoughts of the dead is a *huge* opportunity. Anyway, Galt probably thinks you're giving me a counteroffer right now. As we speak, my value is rising two-fold—no wait, threefold!"

"But we had a deal!" Bobby said. "We did sun salutations together!"

"Look, I do downward dog with a lot of people. I only count pigeon pose, with both of us facing each other, inhaling and exhaling five times, as a true deal. If your team had done proper due diligence, you would have known that. But no hard feelings, right? Let's grab a beer at Davos."

The Fixer hung up.

Galt!

Despite his board's fears, Bobby himself wasn't worried about Wall Street. They only had one more week of this to go. Once Anahata posted its stunning quarterly results, no one would even care if Anahata said it was building a colony on the sun.

But Galt... Galt!

The Fixer would tell them everything about Anahata's moon colony, and then they would start to build their own version. They were so fast and scrappy, maybe they could even beat Anahata to the moon.

His engineers would want to live on Galt's moon colony, eat Galt's moon food, and sleep with Galt's moon girls. Within five years

Anahata would be nothing more than a relic of the early twenty-first century, and Bobby would be reduced to little more than a passing caption in a computer science museum.

"Noooo!" Bobby screamed. He jumped on his five-wheeled dragon bike and pedaled furiously to Anahata, his panic carrying him straight to Gregor's office in Building 1.

But his trusty engineer wasn't there. Nor was his stuff.

"Gregor!" he yelled, running down the hall. The welders, architects, moon horticulturists, and rocket scientists looked up from their Social Me app to see their barefooted founder searching for Gregor inside space capsules and under tables. He circled the building four times, ran up and down its stairs three times (though once was just for fitness), before finally coming to a stop once again outside Gregor's empty office, throwing his body against the door and pounding his fists.

"Gregor!!!"

A familiar crew cut appeared in a doorway a few feet away. Bobby rushed forward, but Gregor took a step back into the room.

"Oh, Gregor! Where have you been?"

"You kicked me out of my office, remember?" said Gregor, keeping his distance.

"The Fixer's not coming," said Bobby, throwing his hands up.

Gregor shrugged and turned toward his desk.

"Gregor, he's going to go work for Galt. He'll tell them everything!"

Gregor did an about-face, and Bobby saw his eyes widen. And then his face hardened.

"We can't let them beat us," Gregor said.

"How soon can we launch Project Y? Galt's probably building a rocket as we speak!"

"We're just working on the coupling issue, which is tied to the Social Me expansion," Gregor said. "We've rolled it out to thirty percent of the campus engineering and female population."

"Expand to one hundred percent. Expand it to all of my engineers!"

"We might want to be a bit more cautious. I think we can still beat Galt if we—"

"Tomorrow. I want all of my engineers on Social Me by tomorrow. And the moment you see that it's working, I want to launch Y."

Gregor opened his mouth, but Bobby held up his hand. He couldn't stay any longer. He was worried the Fixer would tell Galt about the new cafeteria menus Bobby was working on. Bobby had mentioned it while they were in eagle pose, and the Fixer had complimented him on his innovative plans for chia and hemp seeds. If Galt knew he was plotting a menu revamp, they might try to beat him to the punch. He had to speak to Anahata's head chef so they could rework the menus immediately. He had an idea that involved goji berries...

As Bobby raced across the lawn toward Fried Fred's, a fleeting sense of guilt descended upon him—Gregor was clearly still upset about the whole business with the Fixer. Bobby needed to find a way to make it up to him, but he also knew he didn't have the time right now to give Gregor the attention he wanted. Bobby had a company to save.

THE CAMPUS

Not much was getting done at Anahata.

The sprinkler system went down, and the engineer who had designed the company's elaborate watering system was nowhere to be found. The lawn's signature green (#008000) had quickly given way to a more authentic, Californian brown, and the janitors arrived on campus each morning to find bedsheets and beanbags strewn across the lawn like slaughtered ghosts.

But none of the employees seemed to notice or care. They all had their heads pointed down at their phones, their bright heels and plastic Crocs clicking along an invisible course of pulsing lights. One spotted them coupled in stairwells, bushes, and sleep capsules; sometimes the glimpse of a foot or bare leg would emerge from the kale beds in the compost garden.

The shyer ones flocked to Roni's "user experience sessions," where the scent of vanilla candles and the gentle notes of bossa nova wafted through the room as engineers and female employees stood at opposite ends, like at a middle school dance, speaking to each other through the Social Me app.

Meanwhile, the more outgoing ones ended up at Roni's Island Paradise—formerly the volleyball court—each evening ablaze with orange tiki lights between the palm trees. Robot butlers rolled across the grass, offering a vodka Jell-O shot to any woman who had the Social Me application on her phone.

To the right of the Island Paradise, just past the main entrance, employees locked lips in beanbags below the dinosaur and rocket ship that charged across the building's skylight. To their right, a TV was on mute, flashing with the day's news. At the tenth minute of the broadcast, Anahata employee Arsyen Aimo briefly appeared on the screen, first shown raising the Pyrrhian flag above his head, then atop a podium in front of a large brown building, his fist raised in triumph. Below him, shattered in large chunks, were the remains of a statue of the deposed leader, President Korpeko.

No one saw the news, and no one saw what was happening across the hall, either, where the Anahata squid moved across his tank, tentacles pumping vigorously through the water as if desperate to attract someone's attention.

On a positive note, not a single Anahata employee had defected to Galt in more than two weeks.

GREGOR

G regor charged into Building 1 and marched down the hall toward his office. Rounding the corner, he saw Roni hovering in the shadows, the outline of a female form hidden behind him, her blond hair half-obscured by a potted ficus. Gregor growled, and the woman scampered. Glaring at Roni, Gregor grabbed the ficus and dragged it down the hall, unsure of his aim with that particular ficus, but certain that the fewer hiding places Anahata provided, the sooner he could unearth his burrowing engineers.

He hauled the tree into his office and set it next to his desk. He would confiscate every last ficus tree if necessary. And not just ficus trees—he'd also collect all the bushes, stairwells, and sleep capsules, lock them all up in a data center, and get his engineers back on course.

Of course, the easier solution would just have been to shut down Social Me. But Gregor knew that wasn't an option: Doing so would provoke a mutiny among his engineers, and then there would be no hope at all for launching Project Y.

No, he needed a more discreet route—something that would limit the impact of the app without destroying it. Gregor considered restricting the hours the app was available or cordoning off the female staff. Perhaps he could replace the female employees with robots, or he could ask the Building 1 chemistry team to use its pheromone technology to turn the women into lesbians during working hours. *If*, that is, he could find his Building 1 chemistry team. They were missing along with everyone else.

"Agggh!" Gregor hit his fist against the desk.

He closed his eyes and tried to force calm, rational thought. How would Gregor Guntlag solve this problem?

He thought.

And he thought.

The answer was obvious.

Gregor Guntlag wouldn't know what to do. He would ask Bobby.

But Bobby, of course, would offer no guidance. Nor would he ever recognize that this was all his fault.

If Bobby had simply fired Niels, Gregor wouldn't have had to go to such extremes to get rid of him. Then Niels never would have fleeted anything about the moon, the stock price wouldn't have sunk, the Fixer would never have entered—then exited—their lives, the engineers would still be engineering, and the moon colony would still be a secret.

Instead, Bobby and Fischer were now off carousing with online sales girls; HR Paul was hiding from all of the company policy violations bumping, humping, and smacking their way across the campus; and Old Al was busy getting a colonoscopy. Only Gregor understood what was happening: Social Me, that tangential, ridiculous project, was destroying his masterpiece.

Gregor stared at his mobile.

Although Social Me had been deployed to his phone at the same time as the rest of the company's engineering population, Gregor had yet to open it.

He tapped the cloying pink S&M logo, and a dashboard vaguely similar to Social Car materialized before him.

Gregor hit a button that said "match me." Profile photos of various female employees spun before his eyes like a slot machine, a kaleidoscope of blondes, brunettes, and the occasional redhead. Gregor felt his eyes blur. He slammed his index finger into the phone, blindly choosing from the flickering profiles.

Ding! Ding! Ding! went the Social Me slot machine. He wondered just what he had won.

When he opened his eyes, Gregor saw a photo of an attractive woman, probably in her late twenties, staring up at him from his screen. He clicked on the profile to see what would happen next.

Her name was Kerstin. She worked in HR and was a Capricorn. She liked swimming and was looking for "not Mr. Right—just Mr. Right Now."

Just then, the Social Me message icon beeped and his phone vibrated. Kerstin was messaging him.

> hi. ur checkin out my profile. like what u c? ;-)

Gregor felt his heart quicken. He looked to the door, hoping someone would enter just then, looking for advice or a product review. Anyone, any problem, would have served as a welcome interruption. But no one appeared. It was early evening and most of the employees had left—or were hiding away somewhere on campus.

He tapped his fingers on the desk, then stood and walked to the other side of the office. He didn't like the idea of interacting with someone on the app. He just wanted to understand how it worked.

Gregor looked out the window. Two pairs of legs extended from a bush along the opposite building; by the volleyball court, bodies of a man and woman were smashed together in a never-ending embrace.

Beyond them, far in the distance, Gregor spotted a robot butler abandoned in the field, its arms open in supplication. It was supposed to rain that week. Given the state of things, the robot would surely rust and no one would notice.

Gregor could feel his throat constrict, the anger rising inside him. He tried to push it away. This was not a productive way to respond to a problem. He breathed deeply until he felt it recede.

Now, what would I normally do if there was something wrong with one of our products?

I would do a thorough feature-by-feature review.

Gregor sat down again and typed a message to Kerstin.

> Gregor: I am here
> Kerstin: what r u in the mood 4?
> Gregor: I want to try the app.

Kerstin: *u want 2 try anything else?*
Gregor: *What do you mean?*
Kerstin: *ur silly. u know what im saying.*
Gregor: *No I do not.*
Kerstin: *ur older than me (hot) and run something in engineering (hot)*

Gregor grimaced as much at Kerstin's spelling as at her flirtatiousness. He ignored Social Me's prompts to help him with his conversation, putting the phone aside for a moment so he could note some feedback for the Social Me team.

He started with the design—all pink and dizzying with its many profile pictures. It was miles away from Anahata's design aesthetic, which, as Bobby always reminded his employees, was "purple and green and magical like a fairy but practical like a gnome."

He then turned to the notification feature. It was smart but a bit too persistent. It would be better with —

His phone buzzed again.

Why don't you want to talk to me? I've always wanted to talk to the big brain that runs Anahata.

Gregor's eyes lingered on the screen, surprised to discover that Kerstin was suddenly capable of forming complete sentences.

I've heard that nothing happens at this company without you. That all the good ideas are yours.

Gregor reread her message a second and then a third time. How did she know him so well?

He studied her heart-shaped face and bright-green eyes. *Kerstin.* His babysitter's name had been Kerstin.

You're the big genius.

Gregor blushed and decided he should respond. It was the best way to understand this coupling thing Jennie and Roni had been talking about.

I enjoy working at Anahata.

Kerstin responded immediately—she must have been a fast typist.

It can be hard when it feels like people don't appreciate your talent. That was one of the reasons I left Europe.

Gregor inhaled sharply. Kerstin was European, too! She knew what it meant to toil in the shadows, to have people eschew progress and innovation in favor of philosophical debates and endless films in which people did nothing but talk and stare into clouds of cigarette smoke.

It meant... she knew failure.

Gregor stood and shut the door to his office, then returned to his desk and typed:

It is good to meet a fellow European.

gregor, i want us to be friends.

Kerstin seemed to have tired again of capital letters.

turn on the video button. let me see ur face

Without a moment's hesitation, Gregor pushed the video-chat icon within the Social Me app. Kerstin appeared on the screen, looking even prettier than her profile photo had suggested.

"Hi there," said Kerstin, smiling. She had no trace of a European accent.

Gregor blushed and tried to smile.

Without saying a word, Kerstin began to take off her top. She was smiling at the camera, biting her lip. Gregor felt the stirrings of an erection.

"Gregor likey?" she asked.

She was the kind of woman who would normally ignore someone like him, and yet she was moving her bra strap off her shoulder, watching him watch her as it fell down her arm.

"Gregor," she said, leaning into the camera, "you've gotta give to take. This can't be a one-way interaction. So, if you want me to continue, I need you to do one little thing for me."

Gregor nodded and started to undo his belt buckle, surprised at the ease with which he had handed all control over to this mysterious woman. He had gotten his pants to his knees when Kerstin spoke again.

"Now click on the blue button to the right of the video."

Gregor did as he was told, watching as Kerstin undid the clasp of her bra.

He smiled at Kerstin.

She smiled back at him.

Then a payment screen popped up. Kerstin was charging him $49.95 for a ten-minute session.

Gregor shrieked and threw down his phone.

Gregor sat at his desk, unable to move. What had Anahata come to that one of its HR employees was running a porn business on the side?

But more than that, he was disgusted with himself. He was an engineer; only idiots clicked unknown links in emails and chat messages.

The computer on his desk began to beep. Gregor glanced at the screen. It was a video call from Bobby—a welcome distraction from his thoughts.

Gregor scanned the room: the recycling bin, the poverty poster, the ficus tree. All was normal. The only thing out of place was Gregor. He quickly buckled his pants and answered the call.

Bobby's face took over his screen. He was wearing a Hawaiian shirt, unbuttoned at the top, his hairy chest on display. He was sitting next to a plastic palm tree. Cardboard waves moved behind him like a cheap set from a high school prom.

"Hey!" cheered Bobby, lifting a fruity, umbrellaed cocktail. "Come join us at the Polynesian barbecue. Roni's gotten more than 500 Anahatis to come. Actually, Kerstin—hey, Kerstin," said Bobby, turning away from the camera, "Come on over. I'm talking to Gregor."

The temptress from Gregor's Social Me adventure bounced onto Bobby's lap.

"Kerstin's a rather entrepreneurial HR employee. She was telling me about her little side business this morning. It made me think that with video chats and Social Me, we could really empower a whole generation of women to become small business owners."

Gregor felt himself sinking in his chair.

"So I thought, hey, what better way to make it up to Gregor after that whole Fixer thing than by giving you the first test drive of Kerstin's product?"

Kerstin giggled and batted her eyes at Bobby, then turned her attention toward Gregor, pouting her glossy peach lips.

"What did you think about the UI of that payment screen? Watching you two, I was thinking it might be better if we put the payment button across her chest. You know, stretched from nipple to nipple."

Gregor opened his mouth but could not speak.

"By the way, how are we on Y? How soon can we launch? It seems like Social Me is working great and so—"

"You!" Gregor screamed, ripping the computer from the desk and hurling it to the ground, raising his boot over and over again.

He knew it meant nothing. He could destroy as many machines as he wanted, but he could never destroy the information itself. His shame was forever recorded on Anahata's servers, forever stored in Bobby's memory.

Gregor crumbled, his knife-straight posture folding in defeat. He felt himself move toward the door, shards of computer crunching below his feet. A plan began to form, something beyond him, beyond logic, the only chance to escape.

Twenty minutes later, Gregor found himself at home, grabbing his backpack and a knife. As he stomped through his kitchen, he stopped and descended to the basement. It had only been a few weeks and yet that day with Niels seemed very long ago. He grabbed a bottle from the rack closest to the stairs, not bothering to check the drink-by date. Then he was upstairs, back in his car, speeding out of Atherton and toward the freeway.

As he headed south out of the Valley, his ancient Jeep swerving from one lane to another on an empty freeway, Gregor found himself crying for the first time since he had left his parents' home in Liechtenstein at the age of seventeen.

ARSYEN

"You're late," boomed Arsyen, knowing full well that the man kneeling before him in the Grand Hall was not late in the slightest.

Arsyen's father had kept his advisers on their toes by falsely accusing them of minor acts of treachery. Although he was only two days into his reign, Arsyen had embraced the technique with enthusiasm.

The adviser made the sign of the red-breasted woodpecker, darting his head to the left and right six times. "I am sorry, Your Highness."

"Had you arrived on time, you would have already updated me on Project Tabletop," Arsyen said. "Instead, the progress of my kingdom has been delayed five minutes."

"Tabletop?" whispered Natia, squirming next to Arsyen.

He wondered whether her discomfort was owed to her Embrian scalp dress or the human-toothed throne upon which she sat. As a commoner, she was not used to such luxuries.

"Tabletop is the code name for our plan to clean up the country," Arsyen explained.

Natia clapped her hands.

"Oh, that is wonderful news! The people have suffered so much at the hands of Korpeko and, well, excuse me, and your father. You must start completely from scratch."

"Exactly. I want it all cleaned up," he said, kissing Natia's hand before turning back to the adviser, who produced a chart for his review. Arsyen briefly studied it.

"There's nothing about brooms in here. I want more brooms for Pyrrhia."

"Yes, Your Highness. What shall we do with them?"

Arsyen sighed loudly, lamenting for the fifth time that day that his intelligence was too great for his advisers to grasp.

"Do not bother me with small questions. I only think big thoughts. Now, how many supply closets are there? And are we stocking them with the yellow sponges with the rough green backings?"

The adviser looked to the floor. "I am sorry, but I—"

"How can you not know this?"

Arsyen felt a tap on his shoulder. It was Natia. Again.

"I'm sorry, my love, but how will more brooms help our people? They are starving and sick and—"

"My dear Natia, I am cleaning up the country. This is key infrastructure."

"But—"

Arsyen patted her head. "Let the king be a king, my little lamb."

Natia shook her head. "You keep using that word—'king.'"

"Do you not like how it sounds? I think it has a certain panache, but perhaps it could be more modern. What do you prefer? Almighty Ruler? CEO of Country?"

"What about a government of the people?"

Arsyen chuckled. Natia's jokes about democracy were a cute little phase. Eventually she would move on to a more feminine hobby like watercolors or the piano.

"These are symbols of Pyrrhia's bloody and corrupt past," said Natia, sweeping her arm past the gold doors and hanging tapestries. "You are different. You are Arsyen, the Great Reformer!"

"The Great Reformer," Arsyen repeated. "I like that."

"You should start with this, the palace. Rid yourself of all its trappings."

"I completely agree."

He snapped his fingers, and an adviser materialized. "Where are we on the palace revamp?"

"We have cleaned it top to bottom, Your Highness."

"Then why do I not smell my cotton-candy air freshener? It should waft through these hallowed halls." Arsyen paused and felt genius descend upon him yet again. "In fact, I want the Aimo Air Freshener distributed throughout the country. Everywhere the people go, they will smell cotton candy. A populace that is thinking of sugar is a happy and complacent populace."

He turned toward Natia and gripped her hand.

"Imagine, when our youth walk into their schools each morning, they will smell cotton candy. When we hunt bison or peasants in the countryside, we will smell cotton candy."

The adviser coughed. "Apologies, Your Highness, but it may be difficult to make the whole countryside smell like cotton candy."

"Enough with your small thinking!" shouted Arsyen, rising to stand. Being a king was like being the father of many, many stupid children.

"Let me tell you something I learned in Silicon Valley," he said. "It is only by dreaming the impossible that you can make significant progress. And it is only by failure that we learn about ourselves."

Arsyen paused.

"But, of course, only losers fail. So don't do that."

"Your Highness may recall that the royal coffers are empty."

"The monetization of our nation will figure itself out," said Arsyen, waving the adviser away and motioning another one forward. He returned to his bison-toothed throne.

"Your Highness. I am here about Project Stain."

Arsyen felt Natia tap his hand. He wondered whether he could limit the number of questions she could ask each day. He turned to explain the project to her.

"We are improving everyone's quality of life by moving some peasants to a nice new neighborhood in the swamplands and installing a modern industrial park and supermarket atop what used to be their land."

Natia frowned, but Arsyen waved at his adviser to continue.

"They don't want to move," the adviser said. "They ask that the king consider a different plan—one that would preserve their land and their livelihood."

"Did you explain to them that such a move is good for them? That we are disrupting the real estate market?"

"They do not seem to want to have their lives disrupted."

Natia gripped Arsyen's arm.

"Please," she said, "we should put our people first."

"Yes, and they will love it by the swamplands. There's so much water there!"

He turned back to the adviser.

"Install a whiteboard in the center of the swamplands so the people can brainstorm new livelihoods. And one dry-erase pen for each household—if they want more, they will have to pay for it. I don't want to create an entitled populace."

The adviser nodded and made a note.

"Now, about that palace revamp. I don't like the carpet color Korpeko chose. Such a funny shade of lavender. I want a red shade—a masculine one, but one that also inspires hope. It must be a beautiful and delightful experience for anyone who walks upon it, meaning me, mainly, and occasionally her." He pointed at Natia.

"Arsyen, what are you saying?" Natia cried. "This palace, the throne—this is your father's legacy, not yours!"

"That's why I've been spending so much time thinking about the decorative doorknob on the east gate," Arsyen said. "It's a lion—that was my father's symbol. Which do you think is more *me*: a panther or a shark?"

"What has happened to you?!?"

Arsyen leaned toward Natia. "You know I find these antics of yours very sexy," he whispered, "but this is not really the time or place."

"You pig!" she hissed, rising to her feet and stomping out of the room.

Arsyen chuckled.

"Don't mind her," he said, turning to his group of advisers. "If she was actually serious about influencing my policies, she would have already slept with me."

BOBBY

Bobby pinched the fat around his midriff and moved it a bit to the left before letting it jiggle its way back into place. Then he jiggled the bit over his love handles—same thing.

Fat always knew where to go. It needed no instruction.

Why couldn't people be more like fat?

Bobby tossed the thought around in his head for a few seconds before deciding he was quite pleased with it. Maybe he could include it in his next book, *Becoming the Me, Again*. A whole chapter on what people could learn from fat—about being more autonomous, more stubborn, having growth ambitions. Perhaps his editor would be more amenable to that idea than she had been about his proposed chapter on what people could learn from breasts (plentiful, variable, flexible, responsive—like agile coding).

Bobby exited the bathroom into the management meeting room on the adjoining side.

Everyone else was already there. Old Al had taken a seat opposite the door, and Fischer, as usual, had strategically placed himself near HR Paul, braving his colleague's flatulence just to ensure that his updates looked good in comparison to Paul's whiny complaints and touchy-feely reports on employee well-being. Across from Fischer was the chair Gregor usually claimed. Although the seat was empty, Bobby quickly averted his gaze. He never should have set Gregor up with Kerstin—Gregor hated pop-up advertisements. He was probably furious with Bobby.

Bobby caught Fischer fiddling with something on his phone and made a hissing sound. His CFCAO looked up and quickly placed his phone facedown on the table. "Sorry," he mouthed, knowing Bobby's dislike of the use of devices during management meetings.

Bobby took a seat.

"Okay, who's up first?"

"I am," said HR Paul. He bent over his computer to project some slides, and his oversized glasses fell toward his nose, forcing him to push them up every few seconds with his pudgy index finger. Bobby tapped his fingers on the table. If HR Paul was involved, a task always took double the time. There were so many people to consider, issues to debate, laws to follow, and, in this case, a button to find and then press.

Paul mumbled something about the presentation not loading properly—as if it was the engineers' fault and not his own error. Bobby felt his lip curl. He wondered whether a punch to Paul's face would alter his ever-placid, cow-like expression.

Bobby touched the meditation beads on his wrist, trying to pull his thoughts back from the Dark Place. He closed his eyes, just as his yogi had taught him, and took a deep breath. When he emerged, he found himself gazing at his grumpy but lovable engineer, Old Al, Bobby's living piece of history. Bobby felt peace settle within him and leaned back in his chair.

"Well, let me start with the good news," HR Paul said. "We haven't had a single defection to Galt in two weeks. That's the first time that's happened in a *really* long time. I think it's because I told our HR staff to give free hugs to anyone who wants them. With their consent, of course, and only when observed by an employment lawyer."

Old Al snorted. "In my day, no one hugged anyone and we all got a lot more work done."

"Well, that's the bad news," said Paul, clicking on to his first slide. "These are the latest productivity figures. The bottom line is that there's been a sixty percent drop in productivity over the past two weeks."

"Sixty percent?" Fischer stood and approached the screen.

"Right, it's not good," said Paul. He took off his glasses and rubbed his face. "Ever since we stopped the sales team from doing sales, productivity has just tanked. You can see the decline begin around that time, and then it's accelerated week on week. But here's the weird thing—the less productive the sales team is, the happier they become. We're now seeing very high sales team satisfaction."

"That's not surprising," Old Al said. "We're paying them to do pushups."

Bobby stared at the numbers on the screen and thought of his own productivity over the previous week. Between Social Me and yoga class, he really hadn't gotten much done.

"What do you think, Al?" Bobby asked. Old Al was all-knowing—when he was awake.

"I don't think it's just the HM program," Old Al said. "Everything's moving slower here. The work, the food… people's brains." His hand was shaking in HR Paul's direction. Paul frowned, but Bobby merely laughed. Al probably just had early onset Parkinson's.

The group stared at the slide until finally Bobby spoke up.

"You are what observes, not what you observe," he said, his gaze moving slowly from one team member to the next. He had spent an hour working on that thought the previous day and was eager to see their reaction.

But Fischer seemed to be smelling his armpit, and Old Al was just tinkering with his hearing aid. HR Paul was listening, but Bobby didn't really care what he thought.

"You are what observes, not what you observe," Bobby tried again. His eyes took another pass around the room. No response.

Where was Gregor? He would've understood.

"Ignore sales and look at the rest of the company," said Bobby, pointing at the right side of the graph. "Notice that productivity for operations, online support, legal, and other support staff is only slightly down. The big drop—and it's a huge drop—is in engineering, PR, marketing, and HR."

Bobby looked at HR Paul, who looked back at him dumbly. His eyes moved to Old Al, who was cleaning wax from his ears, and then on to Fischer, who was fiddling again with his phone.

"SOCIAL ME!" screamed Bobby. "How many of you have been messing around with it—like you, Fisher, put your phone down!"

Fisher's phone flew out of his hands, landing faceup next to Bobby. Susie, 23, an Aquarius from HR, flashed him a rosy smile.

"But why would the productivity rates of HR, marketing, and PR fall if it's a tool designed for engineers?" HR Paul said.

"They're all women in those departments," Bobby said. "They are the Yokos sleeping with our Johns, the ones pulling them away from their work."

"Ohhh. It all makes sense now," said Paul, hitting his forehead with his palm. "On Monday, Roni Herman's hackathon turned into an orgy. I saw it myself. One minute they were all coding. Next minute there were all these women from the PR department. There was," he winced, "flesh... everywhere."

Bobby grinned, remembering what a wonderful night that had been.

"But... why would we launch an app that would turn our engineers into lovesick idiots?" HR Paul asked.

"Think about it," Bobby said. "Think about the juicers and the massages and the volleyball courts."

"But we do that because Anahata is more a lifestyle than a job," Paul said. "You come here in the morning, and you stay till late at night, and all throughout the day we are here to nurture you—"

"Cut the crap," Old Al said. "We feed you, and in turn you work more."

"*And* as a byproduct of all that, you spend time with other employees," Bobby said. "But historically our female employees spent more time with the sales team than our engineering team."

"Well, sure," HR Paul said. "The sales team are, sorry, no offense, but, you know, socially better adjusted, generally more attractive, have better hygiene, and—"

"Now you understand why we had to get rid of sales," Bobby said.

"What? B-b-but you didn't tell us," said HR Paul, his voice rising.

Bobby's eyes locked onto his HR head, the sole member of the management team who had been kept in the dark. He smiled and rose a bit in his seat. Next time he'd exclude Fischer from his plans. He had to keep people guessing!

Paul wiped at his eyes with his sleeve. "Well," he said, avoiding Bobby's gaze, "I for one never bought the line you fed us about greater profits through more automated sales."

"Automation is generally only good for the person doing the automating," Bobby shrugged. "Besides, if you had known the truth, you would have raised all sorts of HR problems that would have slowed us down. The point is, we got rid of the competition and then gave the engineers an app to help act as the social lubrication."

"Lubrication is right," Fischer smirked.

"So the answer seems to be that we should kill Social Me," HR Paul said.

"Easy for you to say," Fischer said. "You don't need Social Me. You live with a bunch of cats."

"We can't kill Social Me," Bobby said. "The engineers aren't productive, but they are *very* happy, and that's crucial to the success of Project Y. You yourself told us the other day that the latest happiness survey indicates ninety-eight percent satisfaction among the engineers. That's why no one's going to Galt."

"So we need to keep Social Me, but temper it somehow," Fischer said.

"We should just lock all these kids in their rooms until they get their work done," Old Al said. "Back when I was at CERN, we used to make any physicist who was under thirty clean the floors with a toothbrush. It taught discipline."

Bobby held up his hand. "If our engineers are happy, they will stay at Anahata and we will continue to have the best people and the greatest innovation. Therefore, engineers' happiness is just as important as technological advancement. We need technological advancement to make money, and we need money to survive as a company. So…," Bobby closed his eyes.

My will not Thy will. Thy will not my will. Thy will not my money. My money not thy will. What do I do with my will? What do I do with my money? Where is thy will? Where is thy money?

"Bobby…?" said Fischer, thirty seconds later.

Bobby opened his eyes.

"Where's Gregor?"

"I haven't seen him since Monday," Old Al said. "He seemed to be in a bad mood."

"He hasn't responded to my messages for two days," Bobby said.

Everyone around the table shook their heads.

"Gregor has no life outside Anahata," said Bobby, his brow furrowing. "Therefore Gregor must be missing."

GREGOR

G regor poked at the clump of brown mushrooms in his hand, examining their caps and gills. If the forest just had a decent internet connection, he would know in a second whether these would satisfy his grumbling stomach… or kill him on the spot.

Gregor sighed. He had spent years preparing for nuclear fallout or a foreign invasion, building a bomb shelter in his backyard, arming himself to the teeth, and securing power and food supplies to last for at least two years. And yet at no point had he ever contemplated an event in which he would find himself relying on the natural environment for his survival.

What did it matter if the mushrooms were toxic, anyway? It would serve Bobby right. He imagined the founder confronted with his corpse, his face flooding with tears, body raging at the unjust universe that took his right-hand man away from him.

Gregor shut his eyes and threw the mushrooms into his mouth, downing them with the remaining dregs of his wine.

"My death is on your hands, Bobby Bonilo!" he shouted, shaking his fists at the sky.

Gregor lay back against a log and waited to die.

Though, really, he knew he wasn't going anywhere. Gregor had seen a squirrel picking at those mushrooms earlier, with no ill effect.

Well, fine, he might be too cowardly to kill himself, but no matter what, he would not talk to Bobby ever again. He was done with Bobby, done with the internet, done with innovation and disruption and iteration and… everything.

He knew Bobby would try to win him back—they had been

through this before. Bobby would call Gregor and apologize in his roundabout way, never actually saying he had done anything wrong, but instead talking about a Great Historical Wrong—how horrible it was that Nikolai Tesla had died in obscurity, or that people were still using answering machines in the twenty-first century. The subtext somehow being that it would be a much, much worse fate if Gregor were to stop helping Bobby bring magic to the world. And then Gregor always gave in.

But not this time.

A deer and her fawn appeared in the clearing, not more than ten feet away. The fawn rubbed up against its mother, and she turned to brush her head against the fawn's neck. Gregor felt a tear on his cheek.

"It's just rain," he said to no one in particular, quickly brushing away the tear with the sleeve of his windbreaker.

He looked up at the sky, so blue and full of possibility. As the minutes passed, Gregor filled its canvas with people flying in self-powered vehicles, pedestrians strolling in a tube-like bridge above the ocean. He imagined drones spiriting medicine to rural medical clinics and delivering fast food to city dwellers. Slowly, the figures began to grow into giants. They wore Victorian costumes and all looked like his mother. They lectured him about physics in German.

Something was licking his hand. Gregor looked down and saw Bobby perched on his leg, his red, bushy tail brushing over Gregor's knee, his small hands wrapped around an acorn.

"Don't you think you're blowing this out of proportion?" the squirrel asked.

"You make me do everything," Gregor said. "I clean up all your messes, and you never even say thank you."

"Is that what you want?" the squirrel asked. "For me to say thank you?"

"Yes, I think so."

"Thank you. Now do you feel better?"

"Not really."

"What do you really want then?"

"You were too nice to Niels!" blurted Gregor, the sharpness of his voice surprising even him. "You were going to let the Fixer run the company. And you gave away my office. I was in that office for almost ten years."

"Let us observe your anger together," the squirrel said, "and then let us let it pass through us."

Gregor shook his head.

"Don't you realize I'm human, too?" the squirrel said. "I mean, I'm a squirrel right now, but I'm also a human. A human with my own problems and defects. If you put me on a pedestal, I'm always going to disappoint you. "

"It doesn't matter anymore," Gregor said. "I'm done."

"Nothing is ever done. Life continues to move. Hey, can you crack this acorn for me?"

"Y is a joke," Gregor said. "The engineers are too busy with the women to get anything done. They've failed me, and I've failed them."

"No one's failed at anything. Look, this is our chance to iterate on the human race. You and me, we will build this together, our own imperfections a testament to our great achievement."

The squirrel jumped onto Gregor's chest and began to whirl around, its bushy tail hitting Gregor in the nose every few seconds. Its arms waved in the air, pushing the clouds to the edges of the sky, filling it with purple and green swirls that unfolded into the Anahata logo.

Gregor lifted his palms into the sky and pushed it all away.

"You ruined Social Me," said Gregor, shaking his finger at the squirrel. "We never should have turned it on for the whole campus. We should have figured out how to dole it out."

"So dole it out," said the squirrel, whirling around on Gregor's knee. "Dole it out, man, dole it out."

The squirrel suddenly stopped and fetched two acorns from the ground. He pressed them against his chest like two perky cones.

"Let's pretend I'm a lady squirrel and you are a dude squirrel, and all you can think about are touching my acorns. You'll do *anything* to get at my luscious acorns. Are you following me?"

Gregor grunted.

"You're suggesting we sell our female employees to the men in exchange for code submissions?"

"Funny you say that—I had Fischer look into it. Turns out prostitution is too complicated legally, not to mention that the pool of prostitutes with PhDs is actually pretty small. But then I came up with a better idea after I ran into one of the girls you brought on board—the lead of the Social Me team. Janie something? Anyway, she said something about women not being the tools of the oppressors. And it made me think, well, *shouldn't* they be?"

"Make them tools," nodded Gregor. "Dole it out."

He felt his stomach grumble again.

"We need you. *I* need you," the squirrel said. "We are a team, the sun and moon in the sky. We rise and set and orbit together."

The squirrel nestled against Gregor's chest and rubbed its cheek against his windbreaker.

"Did you like that thought, Gregor? I came up with it a few days ago but had been saving it just for you."

"Yes, Bobby."

The squirrel smiled, then shimmied off Gregor's chest and crawled onto his backpack. It tried to move the zipper, but its hands and mouth were too small to make any progress on its own.

Gregor leaned over and unzipped his front pack. The squirrel scurried inside and emerged a moment later with Gregor's mobile. He dialed Bobby's number and handed the phone to Gregor.

"Gregor!" Bobby cheered on the other end. "I'd been hoping you'd call."

"I'm coming home," Gregor said, "and I have a plan."

BOBBY

With the exception of an IPO, no other ritual in the Valley provoked such bloodlust as the quarterly Anahata earnings call. The analysts, shareholders, and Suits of Nefarious Intent all crouched around their phones, asking cynical, doubtful questions, their hearts bleeding with greed. None of them could grasp Bobby's vision. They were always hoping to catch him out on a false step or slip of the tongue, looking to glean insight helpful to their various capitalist machinations.

Bobby found the whole thing repulsive, a bit like being forced to speak to people who were just above-average.

He took comfort in knowing he would be rid of them soon, leaving behind Fischer, his chief financial and corporate affairs officer, to deal with the terrestrial bankers.

He would go out with a bang. Rather than hold an actual phone conference, as was now common practice in the industry, Bobby instead ordered Fischer to "radicalize" the event and invite all the relevant financial analysts out to Palo Alto, with the promise that Bobby would answer each and every one of their questions in person. In preparation, he had Shanley Field cleared of any errant robots and asked the marketing team to construct a suitable space where he could host the visiting analysts for the afternoon.

The marketing team, which up until that point had only ever orchestrated events for bloggers and engineers, decided to rent a circus tent. They set about making sure it was the most connected, Wi-Fi'd tent in the world, ensuring that any analyst could livestream, live blog, and live eat from the comfort of a beanbag. One wall of the tent was covered in Red Bull cans, and another was lined with potato chips and beer. Masseuses were on hand to relieve any fiscal stress. A spiral staircase was installed in the tent's center, leading from the ground to the very tip of the tent. While it served no purpose, it pleased Bobby. "Staircases are aspirational," he told Gregor and Fischer as they entered.

The three executives walked to the back of the tent, where they took their seats at a long table. There were twenty black-suited analysts before them, flown in that morning from New York and now squirming in their beanbag chairs, computers and notepads balanced on their knees.

Bobby's assistant flashed him the signal that everything was ready to go. Bobby pulled out his special gavel and began to knock: *one, two, three, pause.* He giggled and did it again. *One, two, three, pause.* It was like he was a musician! *One, two* —

Fischer's hand came down on his and pried the gavel from Bobby's fingers. Then the CFCAO cleared his throat and began to read from the disclaimer prepared by the legal team.

"Welcome to Anahata's first-quarter earnings call. During this call, representatives of the company will make certain statements within the meaning of the U.S. Securities Act and the Securities and Exchange Act. Anahata undertakes no obligation to publicly update any forward or backward-looking statements, whether as a result of new information, future events, historical revisionism, or otherwise, and at no point should any statement be considered binding or reflective of the full truth. Please refer to the risk factors described in our Annual Report on Form 20-F for discussion of some of the important factors that could affect future results or change the course of history."

With the legal mumbo jumbo out of the way, Fischer began his presentation: a glorious, one hundred–slide affair in which the most important piece of news—Anahata's staggering 40 percent rise in quarterly profits—would be revealed at the three-minute mark, after which would follow twenty-seven minutes of detail in which the analysts would only feign interest, but which, out of a need to justify their jobs, would constitute the majority of their resulting analyses.

Bobby tuned out Fischer the moment the CFCAO began to speak, and instead studied the group of suits before him. On the whole, they seemed younger than the suits of his board. This irritated Bobby—young people were supposed to love technology. Instead, these men had chosen the old-man institution of banking; they were little more than well-dressed gamblers. All they wanted to talk about was how he could make them more money. They cared nothing for Anahata's Progressa program or its charitable endeavors. Bobby wondered whether his next project should aim to destroy banking altogether.

Or maybe he would just draw. Fischer had given him some crayons and paper before the start of the meeting, and Bobby now made use of them. He doodled on the corner of the quarterly report, sketching an idea he had for an enormous flying worm that would carry people through congested cities. Then he made a list of his ten favorite meditation retreats. When he tired of that, he worked on a few ab-tightening breathing exercises his personal trainer had taught him. He was just getting ready to do his neck rolls when he heard Fischer open the meeting to questions. It was the only part of the meeting Bobby ever found interesting; the only time the hunter capitalists had a chance to prick him with their judgments, questions, and irrelevant musings.

A German-accented analyst spoke first. "There are rumors that Galt is working on a drone so small it can enter people's ears and study their biomes and thoughts by analyzing their earwax. I'm wondering what Anahata is planning to do in order to compete."

Bobby winced. It didn't matter how much Anahata profits rose each quarter, the analysts were always fixated on Galt.

"We focus on our own innovation," Bobby said. "We don't pay any attention to the competition."

The next question was about differences in mobile versus desktop revenue—the same question the analysts had asked the previous quarter, and the same one they would ask the next quarter. Bobby didn't bother to listen to Fischer's response. He knew his reliable CFCAO would give the same answer he always gave, which was essentially to say nothing at all.

Bobby craned his neck to catch a glimpse of the plastic clock attached with twisty ties to the spiral staircase. There was still a half-hour to go. His nerves tingled as he thought about what was to come. Once the questions were done and the tasteful, tree-shaped Anahata keychains had been dispensed to the analysts, Bobby would lead the crowd out onto the field, where he would unveil Project Y—the biggest idea in the history of ideas.

The next analyst struggled to climb out of his beanbag chair, his acrobatics leaving one pant leg tucked halfway into the top of a purple-and-green-striped stock. Those were Anahata colors, Bobby observed with a smile. He wondered whether he should buy similar socks for his employees. Cotton or a cotton/polyester blend—which one screamed "hot young startup"?

The analyst at the mic was droning on.

"Eighty-four billion dollars not accounted over the past year... moved between projects... outputs not correlating with inputs..."

Bobby felt a nudge in his side.

"The moon," Gregor whispered. "He's asking you about the moon."

"I have here the proof that you took company funds and diverted them into a secret project—"

The analyst's mouth continued to move, but the remainder of his sentence was drowned out by a sudden commotion at the front of the tent.

THE ZOMBIE AND THE ARK

All eyes were now on the bedraggled figure who had just entered the tent. The man's pants were torn, and he wore a grime-blackened windbreaker, the trace of an Anahata logo still visible along the pocket. A pair of blue eyes peered out from dirty skin and mud-chunked hair. *"La luna!"* gasped the man, his finger shaking as he pointed toward the front of the tent where the Anahata executives were sitting. *"Van a la luna. Van a la luna!"*

The analysts all shifted in their beanbags, keen to put a few inches between the man's filth and their expensive suits.

"It's Niels!" Fischer whispered to Bobby and Gregor.

The man jerked forward like a zombie escaped from the grave, his left leg dragging behind him, arms guiding him forward. Bobby's assistant tried to speak to him, suggesting in a low voice that the man was lost, but he did not seem to understand English.

"Les van a decir que no hay ninguna colonia, pero es mentira," the man wheezed, lurching toward a cluster of analysts. They recoiled as his arms reached out to them.

"Is this the entertainment portion of the earnings meeting?" one of the analysts asked.

"Hmm. Doesn't he look a bit familiar to you?" said another.

"Galt had its execs jump out of a plane last week. Maybe this is just Anahata trying to outdo them."

The zombie reached the middle of the room, where the analyst at the mic was still trying to ask Bobby his moon colony question. He placed a hand on the analyst's shoulder and leaned in, spreading his hot, putrid breath across the man's face. *"La luna!"* he hissed, his finger pointing at the back of the tent, where Bobby, Gregor, and Fischer were sitting.

"*Están locos! La luna! Tenemos que pararlos!*"

"You need to wait. It's *my* turn to ask a question right now," huffed the analyst, pushing the zombie back and sending him tumbling to the ground.

"Gregor! Get security!" Bobby yelled.

Gregor nodded and dashed toward the tent's back flap, where an opening revealed a sliver of the sky.

The zombie rose to his feet and shuffle-lurched his way forward. "*Te voy a matar, te voy a matar,*" he repeated.

He heaved one step, then another, his hands strangling the air as he made his way toward Bobby, who now backed into the folds of the tent.

"Gregor! Come back!" screamed Bobby, hiding himself behind Fischer and closing his eyes.

"I recognize him!" said one of the analysts, pointing at the zombie. "It's their old head of sales, Niels Smeardon. The one who fleeted about—"

"The moon!" yelled the analyst at the mic, waving his documents in the air, furious that this circus was distracting from the issue at hand. "Listen, everyone! I have proof that they are going to the moon! We're talking about billions of dollars the company is wasting on—"

"*La luna!*"

The security team rushed in through the front entrance. Within seconds, the zombie was toppled in a hail of purple and green beanbags.

The head of the security team rushed Bobby and Fischer out through the back flap, where Gregor was already waiting.

"Go! Run!" the head of security urged.

The three men began a slow, unpracticed gallop toward the other end of the field, leaving their head of security to play defense.

Back inside, the tent filled with conjecture and heated words, outrage soon propelling the analysts to their feet.

A senior analyst put his fingers in his mouth and whistled loudly. The room went silent. "Where'd they go?" he yelled, pointing at the table where the executives had been sitting.

"Out the back!" shouted another.

The analysts scrambled over each other, visions of a Wall Street–style massacre filling their heads as they jumped over the beanbag-covered zombie and headed out the back flap of the tent. On the other side, they were met by the security team, which managed to tackle seven of them, reducing the army of analysts to thirteen.

Onward those thirteen pushed, their treadmill-trained legs carrying them at a much faster speed than the Anahata execs, whom they could now spot in the distance, awkwardly loping toward an enormous structure situated at the edge of the field, covered top to bottom in a red-and-white fumigation tent.

The two groups raced forward, with the analysts quickly gaining ground. But just as soon as the Anahata execs seemed within their grasp, they disappeared into the tent.

"We'll surround it!" one of the analysts yelled. "The fumes will eventually drive them out!"

"The market needs answers!" screamed another, carrying a beanbag above his head, already relishing the moment when he would watch it crash atop Bobby's head, forcing him to answer the product roadmap question he had dodged on the last two earnings calls.

The zombie was also in the race. He had climbed out from under the beanbag dog pile and followed the analysts out of the tent, staggering behind them initially, but quickly catching up after discovering a Segway lying next to the tent's exit. He motored ahead with practiced skill and soon was leading the pack. "*Vámanos! Vámanos!*" he screamed, his two-wheeled chariot blowing dust in the face of his troops.

Just then, the analysts began to feel the ground rumble below their feet. A loud noise, as if someone had opened the exit door on a plane, suddenly invaded their ears. They pressed on toward the fumigation tent, but the shaking intensified, making it difficult to move. The men halted as the tent before them began to sway and heave, its outline violently transforming as though a wild animal were tearing at it from the inside. A crack appeared in the dirt, and then another, and another. Amid the shaking, the zombie was tossed from the Segway, landing on his face.

The zombie spit out a mouthful of dirt and at first thought he might be suffering from a concussion, for what he saw before him seemed like a hallucination. The fumigation tent was rising, first a foot, now two, now five, then ten feet in the air, some sort of engine underneath it blowing the field's red dirt into the men's eyes, transforming the frozen analysts into rusted statues. It rose another few feet, and then the tent itself began to rip, coming apart in four sections like a banana peel, its skin gently floating to the ground, revealing an enormous boat-like structure rising ever farther into the sky. There were endless rows of windows, each portico occupied by a smiling face or, occasionally, the terrified stare of an animal. At the front of it all, framed in a wide window running the length of the bow, were Anahata's leaders. Gregor peered down at the zombie, a smile stretched wide across his face. To his left, Bobby beamed, pointing down at the analysts and even doing a little jig as the boat floated upward. Behind them, the tentacles of the Anahata squid waved frantically within its tank.

"Nooo!" screamed the analysts.

"Nooo!" screamed the zombie.

For a moment, as if it had heard their cry, the boat stopped, gently bobbing in the sky. But it did not rise farther or move beyond its spot above the field. Seconds passed, and the light bobbing became a strong jerking, soon accompanied by the sound of an engine sputtering. The boat fell ten feet, then rose again, fell, and rose.

From below, the analysts could hear the screams of its passengers. A chunk of metal fell from the vessel's side, crashing to the field and puncturing the tent where they had all sat just minutes before. Another chunk fell from portside, rushing to the ground in a multicolored comet.

"*Que lástima!*" the zombie wailed. "*Que lástima!*" His ears filled with a rumbling he would never forget.

THE MOONGINEER

One man had taken his suitcase. Another offered him a pink cocktail and a warm towelette. Even the squid waved hello. And now he was standing here, in a long, white arrival hallway, a bit cold, a bit uneven on his feet, but excited to explore his new home.

He had waited two years for this, had added his name to the sign-up list just as soon as it appeared. Sure, the philosophy thing was cool—a new community crafted on visionary, healthy principles of living and a high-quality population—but really, he just wanted to live on the moon, without gravity and monthly internet bills.

And now he was here.

But where to start? There was so much to see on the new moon campus that he wasn't sure where he should direct his attention. There was the squid, waving its arms in an endless tank that stretched from the space elevator landing dock all the way to the colony's first building. There was his new company badge, fluorescent and sparkling, occasionally lighting up as though it were communicating with his new environment. And then there was the girl, the tour guide named Jennie, dressed all in white, just like the rest of them, standing before the group with a wide smile.

The group followed Jennie through the hallway, past two large doors that led to the outside, emitting small gasps as they discovered their new home—a gray, rocky landscape, groomed to make way for pathways and a gentle river that wound its way around the campus. A series of white two-story buildings sat within a smattering of shallow craters. At the center of it all was the volleyball court, sand freshly combed like a Zen garden, waiting under the dark sky for a new set of players to arrive. Behind the court, a neon cactus with arrows sprouting from its trunk pointed in various directions—to the apartments, the mines, the gym, and other destinations. But instead, Jennie led them to the river—a narrow, canal-like body filled with a thick, turquoise liquid that Jennie said was resistant to evaporation.

One of the gondola cafeterias was there waiting for them. Everyone climbed aboard and began to pile around the different food stations as the gondola floated through campus. A muscular, good-looking gondolier made his way down the boat, taking drink orders and offering up the chef's special moon cookie. For a moment, the man reflected that he had never seen a waiter so well-suited for his job. The smooth gestures, his discreet, attentive style—it was like the man had been born to do this.

But it was a passing thought that interested him little, and the man waved the gondolier away as he approached. The man was really only interested in speaking to Jennie. He had seen her somewhere before but couldn't manage to place her. He watched as she fingered her hair, then removed her white moonjacket. Underneath was a white T-shirt. There was something painted across her chest—a moon and a sun, each encircling her breasts. Below them, in black block lettering:

Ask me about interplanetary feminism.

That did it—this girl was the hot hippie receptionist who used to work in Building 7!

"I think we've met before on Earth," he said, as she passed by him on the gondola's noodle stand. "You're a campus tour guide, right?"

"I *was* a campus tour guide," Jennie said. "I'm now a moon orientation manager."

"So, uh, like giving tours of the moon?"

"Totally different," she said. "My job's to ensure that you all have a holistic perspective of the moon. First, because we're building a totally new society here and trying to reverse centuries of patriarchal constructs. And second, because you might get lost if I don't show you around."

The man was confused and didn't know how to answer.

He shuffled back to where the rest of his group was sitting.

"You know," said one of the other recruits, who had just seen him with Jennie, "we have Social Me up here. You can talk to her that way."

The man was well aware. As a member of the Genie team, he had been part of Social Me's terrestrial testing pool two years earlier. Unfortunately, the testing period had been short. Once Anahata went to the moon, they had disabled the service on Earth, claiming it had encountered a technical glitch that could only be overcome in a thinner atmosphere. No one believed the excuse, but almost everyone immediately applied for a spot on the moon colony.

The gondola floated past the collection of Svevonius plants—an Anahata creation, still in beta, that dispensed shots of pure oxygen from purple and green stamens—and halted outside a large door marked "Anahata 1."

The group disembarked and entered a huge atrium filled with light. On a white table were twenty devices—one for each moongineer. Jennie stood in front of the table and turned toward her group.

"The Anahata Space Project is about building a new world of wonderful people doing wonderful things. So, part of your role, like mine, is to help Anahata understand just what that looks like and how it should evolve. But the other part is less experimental. You are also here to work on top-secret projects. We have no worries of corporate espionage or snooping journalists here!"

"Now, Anahata wants to give you *everything* on the moon—but in a way that ensures we don't go the way of the Roman empire. We believe that all good things—chocolate, kombucha, and all the hot girls on Social Me—are best used in moderation."

"Social Me?" asked the lone female engineer in the group. The man didn't like her—she had hogged the armrest during the entire ride in the space elevator.

"I heard that women are only here on the moon to be the supply for Social Me... like, only here to meet the men's needs," she said, crossing her arms.

Jennie laughed. "Of course not. We have women doing all kinds of things here, like human resources and marketing and legal stuff and teaching and—"

"You mean like you?" the female engineer said. "But weren't you on the Social Me team? Now you're just a guide."

The smile left Jennie's face. She opened her mouth to speak but was interrupted by something like a camera flash. The man's company badge pulsed with purple light, and an image of white text wrote itself across the pitch-black sky.

Thanks for asking your important question about diversity on the moon. The Anahata Space Project is a pure meritocracy. If there's a disparity between the numbers of men and women among our engineering workforce, it's because women don't excel in science and engineering fields and there's not a large pipeline for us to hire from. That's why we've contributed to nonprofits that work to help women understand science better from a very young age. We are also speaking out publicly about how important it is that society fix this problem. In the meantime, we have hired many women to work in areas where they can achieve great things.

"Well, that's your answer," Jennie said flatly.

"Tell us more about Social Me!" a male voice called out.

"We love Social Me!" shouted another.

That seemed to perk her up.

"Oh, you're going to love Social Me," Jennie grinned. "I actually invented it. I mean, I'm, like, the founder of Social Me."

Jennie began to clap for herself but was cut short by a tall man in the front, waving his hand.

"Where's the bathroom?"

A frown settled on Jennie's face for a split second before

vanishing. She pointed the tall man down the hall, then turned to the group.

"Now let's talk about the devices you see behind me. They're moon mobiles, and they have something very special on them. We call it the Manager. It's essentially a task management application, but integrated into all aspects of your life."

Jennie grabbed one of the devices from the table and floated it before the crowd like a game-show hostess. As the device passed before the man, his badge vibrated and pulsated again with a purple light. A second later, he was surrounded by images of himself wearing white moon clothes, engaged in everyday activities like eating, sleeping, coding, and composting. No matter what the task, he appeared quite happy and content.

"The Manager is always running as you go about your day," Jennie said. "When you have breakfast in the morning, it logs that you had breakfast. You will get points for that activity, as our own research demonstrates that engineers who eat breakfast are more likely to come up with a revolutionary idea.

"Next, you go to work and complete a task. Based on what the task was, you earn more points. For example, a product launch or patent filing earns more points than a small code submission. These points are then redeemed against certain premium activities, which you can request and cash in via the Manager—like playing *World of Warcraft* for an entire weekday or meeting up with a girl on Social Me."

"I hear it takes one thousand points to get a date with Jennie," the man's friend whispered. "This guy I know, Sven, he's filed like forty patents since arriving here, and he spends it all on her."

The man looked at Jennie. She caught his eye and grinned just for him. He couldn't wait to get his hands on her app.

"So all that stuff we get at Anahata on Earth for free is now suddenly to be earned and paid for?" the female engineer harumphed.

"Everything you had on Earth for free is still free here. Like food, massages, and personal trainers, just to name a few. But on the moon we also offer 'extraordinary experiences'—things that all of us would like to do but, if not done in moderation, could be really dangerous for the individual and the project as a whole. It's like we're giving you legal heroin—but making sure you can't have it all the time. After all, no one wants you to become a drug addict, end up in a lunar gutter, and force all of us to do a really awkward intervention."

The female harumpher kept harumphing. The man hoped she wouldn't be assigned to the same team as him.

"Now, of course, different people want different things," Jennie said. " While you may want to spend all of your points on Social Me, someone else may want to never have to lift their arm when they eat cereal in the morning. So that person will want to spend all their points on a personal feeder. Or maybe someone wants to have a go at playing on the moon crane for an hour. Not a problem—just submit twenty moon points to the Manager.

"Using the Manager, you can trade services or ask for a task to be performed for you—at the price you're willing to offer. You can outsource what you hate and earn extra points by doing what you love. We've gotten rid of money and liberated people in the process. It's a revolutionary economic approach."

"But you said the app is constantly logging what we do. Doesn't that mean Anahata is essentially following us all the time?" the female engineer asked.

"It's entirely your choice whether you opt in to use the tool," Jennie said. "Do you really think we'd get away with designing an app for engineers that *wasn't* opt-in?

The crowd laughed.

"Of course, it does mean you won't be earning points," Jennie winked.

"Also, if, like me, you think a mobile app is *so* last century, you can choose to have the Manager installed in your body via a small, elegant incision." Jennie turned her palm and pointed at an invisible spot above her wrist. "Right here."

"It all sounds like a sci-fi dystopia," the female engineer grumbled.

Jennie smiled.

"That's an excellent point," she said. "We're trying to get the balance right between community management and dystopia. We think you'll find this all works really well, but definitely give us feedback via the online form. After all, this is Anahata, and what do we do?"

"We solutionize and iterate!" shouted the new moongineers.

✳

EPILOGUE

From behind the observation glass, Gregor watched the new recruits as they floated past his office.

"It's pretty amazing, isn't it?" said a voice behind him.

Gregor turned briefly to acknowledge Bobby. Although it was already late afternoon, Bobby was still wearing his white pajamas. Atop his head, as on Gregor's, sat a white beret—the latest improvement on Anahata's internet sombrero.

Gregor's gaze moved to the full-length screen on the opposite wall. He silently commanded his beret to flip past live camera footage of the cafeteria and a moonball game, then paused on one of the child prodigies sitting in his moon apartment. The boy was playing a video game, his hand reaching up now and then to pick at the pimples scattered across his cheeks.

Bobby took a step closer.

"Which one's that—Jonas? He looks a bit different to me. New haircut?"

"No haircut, but we've made improvements to him and the others over the past few weeks."

Gregor ran his fingers along the rim of his beret as if he was playing the piano. Jonas paused his video game, stood, and crossed the room to his small kitchen, where he removed some apples from the bowl.

"You've convinced the engineers to eat fruit?" Bobby asked.

Just then, the apples went flying into the air, orbiting the space above Jonas like a collection of small planets. One by one, they fell into his hands, touching his fingers for a split second before shooting up again.

"You've taught him to juggle!" Bobby clapped. "Was it nontrivial to execute?"

"Not really. Teaching them to juggle was harder than getting their faces to host preteen acne, but much, much easier than creating their souls and an illusion of free will."

"Yeah, I bet that was tough."

"We also built in fighting capabilities, just as you asked." Gregor tapped his beret again, setting Jonas off in a series of lethal kicks to the air.

Bobby clapped again.

"Think of the things we can do," he said. "Destroy dictators! Tear down capitalism! Infiltrate the corrupt stunt double industry!"

Gregor nodded and tapped again. Jonas removed his shirt and unscrewed the metal plate embedded in his chest. He extracted a series of purple and green bolts and chips from inside his chest cavity and began to polish them with a nearby cloth.

"Gregor, this may well be your finest work. You've thought of everything. Our child prodigy even repairs himself!"

"Some challenges remain," said Gregor, holding up his hand to pause Bobby's enthusiasm. "For example, we've made our prodigies technically and physically capable of almost anything, but emotionally, we can't seem to push them into adulthood."

He gestured at Jonas. "This one has an IQ of 184 but the emotional intelligence of a fourteen-year-old. It seems the smarter we make them, the more they regress emotionally."

Bobby shrugged. "I wouldn't worry about it. For now, sentience is simply a means to an end. What we need is an army."

"Yes, the army. You'll be pleased to know that over the past month we've managed to embed five of our child prodigies in Galt's engineering team."

"And no one's caught on?"

"Not as far as we can tell. Once we created the cover—that the young geniuses were recruited from poor foreign countries—then we could hide all sorts of shortcomings, like their lack of school records, or the occasional failing of our English translation tool. It was all much easier than we expected. We signed their names to some open source projects and waited for the Galt recruiters to come after them."

"Galt!" Bobby laughed. "They seemed like such a threat once."

"They *were* a legitimate threat," Gregor nodded. "But they went too far when they tried to reduce all communication on Flitter to just three syllables."

"Reduction will one day be *so* last century," Bobby said. "In the future, all people will want to do is expand—to find more ways to talk about themselves, to be and become themselves. More words, more sounds, more pictures. Less thinking, but more of everything. In the future, we will all be very, very large. Galt will be so tiny, no one will even see them."

A gong chimed the hour, and Gregor switched to a camera trained on the colony's entrance. It was time for the squid's evening feeding, a special moment Gregor and Bobby shared each day.

Gregor zoomed in, and the squid's body filled the screen, its heaving mass seemingly threatening to break the glass. The men watched as its horny beak tore apart two fish at once. It seemed much happier now that it had a larger space to roam.

"I've been thinking about Project Y expansion," Bobby said.

"It's an obvious next step," Gregor nodded. "But there will be some resistance. We'll have to convince people that our way is the right way."

Bobby sighed. "I know the world needs stupid people, but sometimes I wish we could just get rid of them."

"We don't need to get rid of them. We just have to convince them," Gregor said. "What if we open-sourced the project and made it freely available so that everyone can benefit? People like things that aren't controlled by corporations."

"But if it's free, people won't believe it's any good," Bobby said. "And if we open-source it, then that means people can do what they want with it. And you and I both know that the best society is the one that Anahata controls—not the one that it simply inspires."

"We could go to other planets," Gregor suggested. "Neptune or Mars could be doable."

Bobby brightened and started to answer but was distracted by a blinking message on the screen.

"Oh, it's Arsyen," he said. "You remember him—the product manager who took over Pyrrhia. I've added him to my World Leaders Mentorship Program."

Bobby tapped his beret, and Arsyen's image filled the screen.

"Hello," said Bobby, waving at the screen. "What's new?"

Arsyen shook his head. "People complain, always complaining. And there is crazy woman, my ex-girlfriend. She say I am capitalist-pig king who destroy country. She and her dirty students want to kill me."

"You will not be recognized as a great leader until you are assassinated," Bobby said. "That is the price of freedom."

Arsyen frowned. "I give no freedom. Why would I do that?"

"That's a good question," Bobby said. "Let's cover it in our next session. Anything else I can help you with?"

"Yes, I have idea—big idea," said Arsyen, grinning. "I want you to make new Anahata here in Poodlekek. Clean place, with volleyball and croquet courts. Juice bar. Pretty online sales girls. Together we make Silicon Poodle."

"Silicon Poodle," Bobby repeated.

"I make deal with you. You give me new palace and video games, I give you Silicon Poodle."

"You mean you outsource the country to us?" asked Gregor, exchanging a glance with Bobby.

"Outsource?"

"It means to improve something by giving it to someone else to take care of it for you," Bobby said. "You outsource Pyrrhia to us, and we'll improve it."

"Yes, yes," said Arsyen, waving his hand. "You do what you want. Just make me big palace and get rid of dirty students."

"We will need to think about it," said Gregor, glancing at Bobby.

"Yes, of course," Bobby said, "but there is no reward without risk. No chalice of hope without a well of—"

"We'll be in touch," Gregor said. He touched his beret, and Arsyen's face disappeared from the screen.

Bobby and Gregor sat in silence. The squid wiggled before them on the opposite wall.

"Gregor, I want you to think of a drop of water as it flings itself over the waterfall... Are you thinking of it?"

"Yes, Bobby."

"By itself, that drop of water is just a drop of water. But when it joins with other drops, it becomes a river, then eventually becomes an ocean. One drop leads to two drops leads to an ocean. No one can live without the ocean."

Gregor was silent for a moment, then spoke.

"You mean we start with Pyrrhia, and then expand Project Y to the rest of the world."

"Exactly," Bobby said.

"But... if Arsyen outsources Pyrrhia to us, then we just govern his ignorant masses instead. How is that a good thing? Our moon colony works precisely because it *doesn't* cater to the masses."

"Watch," said Bobby, walking over to the whiteboard, where he drew a collection of circles.

He wrote "P" in the middle of the center circle and tapped his pen.

"We get Pyrrhia, we kick everyone out, and then we start from scratch just like we did with Project Y. Only the best and brightest of Pyrrhia will be part of the new society, which will be built on the same principles as Y."

"And the rejects—the ones who don't make it into the Pyrrhian utopia?"

"We push them into Embria—right here, next to Pyrrhia, you see? They are poor and won't be able to put up a fight. And when they protest, which of course they will, since normal people never recognize enlightenment, we will offer them the same deal: Let us run your country and make it perfect. Then we push their rejects into the next country, which will weaken that country and make them easier to… help. One by one, the Earth's countries will begin to fall. They will all become terrestrial versions of our Space Project."

"Eventually we'll run into a border that won't accept the rejects from all of our perfect societies," Gregor said.

"Yes, but we leave those countries to the end, at which point our model will be obvious and desirable even to them. And if not, well, we have our army of child prodigies we can deploy to… pacify them."

"And the masses of rejects?" said Gregor, pointing at the collection of frowning stick figures that Bobby had drawn outside his circles.

"We'll give them the chance to improve themselves by providing STEM schooling in the reject refugee camps that we'll establish in Siberia. And those who never improve themselves will be kept in Siberia, or maybe stored in a country that we could just purchase outright for this purpose—maybe Canada. You can work that part out later. Anyway, the best part is that the more people we reject, the more parents will emphasize the importance of an engineering and science education. So, you see, this is good for humanity on multiple fronts."

"But what if other countries come to Pyrrhia's defense?"

"We won't *invade* anything. These countries will *want* our new world order," Bobby said. "They'll invite us in—you know, like you do with vampires."

Gregor nodded slowly, working through the numbers in his head.

"This all seems very doable," he said. "Though my team will need considerably more servers if we're going to tackle world domination."

"Jeez, Gregor, I'm not talking about taking over the world," Bobby said.

Gregor's stiff, bushy eyebrows lifted slightly.

Bobby laughed. "Okay, I guess I *am* talking about world domination. So, let's see… we'll need more marketing schwag, more in-country cafeterias and masseuses. This is going to get expensive. It's not very fair—I mean, we're practically a nonprofit. Good work on behalf of society should be free."

"So a country would pay us to invade them?"

"Not invading, Gregor, *empowering*. Once we have a handful of Anahata-run countries, world domination will fund itself. But we do need to figure out an extra revenue stream to fund the initial rollout."

"How about we just automate everything and install a robot race?"

"Ugh, think of all the social unrest we'd have to wade through once the humans aren't really necessary anymore. And it'll just be too economically efficient—there will be no one but robots left to buy our stuff."

"But we won't need money because robots don't need money," Gregor said. "In utopian societies, money becomes—"

"Look, I don't want a robot society until our life-extension project is fully functional. After all, this is all pretty pointless if a robot can just kill me."

Bobby turned to face the whiteboard and made a quick sketch of what appeared to be a lima bean.

"The brain," said Bobby, tapping at the bean with his pen. "That's the answer. One day we will pay for everything with our thoughts."

"An integration with the brain chip?"

"Oh, Gregor." Bobby smiled, shaking his head. "I admire your ability to live in the present. I must confess it can get awfully lonely in the future…"

Bobby's voice trailed. Gregor followed his gaze toward the observation glass, where a group of men and women strolled past. A blond girl tossed her head and laughed. The sound of her shrill voice scratched like long, pink fingernails at Gregor's ears, but the engineer next to her was beaming. With them were a group of men, casually engaged in moonball as they made their way to work. Following a few steps behind them was a Horizontal Moves employee—a Jack or Greg or Bif or Stu, his arms packed with useful muscles. He was balancing a mop and a load of fresh laundry as he followed the larger group toward the engineers' apartments. Everyone had their place.

Gregor turned to the founder.

Bobby caught his eye and smiled.

"You know who could figure out how to monetize all of this? Niels. Let's bring him back."

"But—"

Swiiiiiish. A dark-purple curtain moved across the sky, replacing the previous blackness and signaling the start of evening. Inside the moon's core, the axle slowly turned, the ground rumbling almost imperceptibly as the moon began its daily, five-minute move across the galaxy.

A bumping sound drew their attention to the screen. The squid's body was thumping against the tank, its arms grabbing one, then another stalk of kelp, using them like poles to propel its incredible mass forward. Two arms, then four, then six, and eight, the arms grasped at whatever they could reach, kicking up sea dust as the squid's mouth dropped open, chomping at the water, its horny beak spearing any aquatic traveler as it swam through the water.

"Lower the tank," Bobby commanded his beret.

Panels slid out from the under the tank, and the structure began to drop below the ground.

With a faint click, the tank disappeared below the surface, and the panels slid shut. Lunar rock and vines quickly scattered across the surface that sheltered Anahata's prized mascot.

A person arriving just a minute later would never guess there was an enormous squid hiding below, expanding gently and nearly imperceptibly with each passing second, just beneath their feet.

AFTERWORD

The following essay was originally published on Medium alongside *The Big Disruption* in October 2018.

Why I Left My Big Fancy Tech Job and Wrote a Book

Several years ago, I was sitting in the audience at a big tech conference, learning about a startup that made it easy for people to rent rooms in other people's houses for short stays. In a world where people can now travel to any part of the world and share someone else's home, could we hope, the CEO asked, for greater cross-cultural understanding? "Would nations have less war if the residents lived together?"

I closed my eyes, breathed deeply, and felt an immense sense of peace and hope for humanity wash over me.

Then I opened my eyes and thought, "Isn't this basically a hotel in someone's house—a cool, convenient, unregulated hotel?"

When it was my turn to take the stage, I too had a grandiose proclamation: Our startup, I declared, was helping people make meaningful connections in the real world.

What I really should have said was: We help people hook up.

On the plane ride home, I began to write what would eventually become The Big Disruption, a satirical novel based on my experience working at both a startup and one of the biggest tech companies in the world. I had no goal at the time other than to provide a bit of cathartic escape from the tech industry, where, on the surface, things seemed really important and exciting.

We were doing big things!

Bringing the internet to the developing world!

Singing songs to orphans!

But also, on some level, it all felt a bit off.

So, where to begin?

Should I start with the early stage companies? Like the time I was at a startup and the founder I was working for—a guy who owned a hundred shirts in the same color and quoted Steve Jobs on a daily basis—asked me whether we should hand out dildos as company swag or consider converting our social media platform into an anonymous sex club. (We even whiteboarded it.)

Or maybe I could start with the money—all the absurd valuations with seemingly little basis in reality. Or the time a partner at a VC "jokingly" offered up my female friend, his employee, as an enticement for a founder to work with his firm.

Or maybe I should start with the tech workers. The employees at my most recent job—running PR at a huge tech company—were some of the smartest, most passionate people I've ever worked with. They worked through the night to help people in a natural disaster. They gave money and vacation time to help the sick family members of other employees. They ran marathons on the weekend to raise money for clean water in Africa.

They also spent the weekday complaining on company message boards about the brand of water stocked in the micro-kitchens.

Then there are the amazing products. The progressive politics. The mighty ethical stands against evil. These are the things that, in my twenties, pulled me to tech in the first place and made me think I was embarking on something truly different.

To be sure, Silicon Valley has built some great products that have truly changed our lives for the better. And I do think that in many, many ways, it has taken noble stands during difficult times and helped redefine what people expect from companies, well beyond just the tech industry. It has also led me to some of my best friends and greatest opportunities, for which I am very grateful. There is so much I really do love about this world.

But there is also what drove me to leave the big tech company last fall and take a break. The issues that I got tired of defending at parties. The endless use of "scale" as an excuse for being unable to solve problems in a human way. The faux earnestness, the self-righteousness. All those cheery product ads set to ukulele music.

I wrote this book for two reasons. First, I wanted to explore what drives the insatiable expansion of the big tech companies. Despite how the industry is sometimes portrayed in the media, I don't really think the management teams at Facebook, Google, Apple, Uber, or Amazon wake up each morning thinking about how to steal more user data or drive us all out of our jobs. Those are real consequences, but not the root cause. Rather, it's the desperation to stay on top and avoid being relegated to a dusty corner of the Computer History Museum that pushes these companies into further and further reaches of our lives.

Second, I wrote this book because we should be able to love and celebrate the products that we build—but without ignoring the hard questions they raise. We need to end the self-delusion and either fess up to the reality we are creating or live up to the vision we market to the world. Because if you're going to tell people you're their savior, you better be ready to be held to a higher standard. This book is my small way of trying to push us all to be better.

Meaning...

You can't tell your advertisers that you can target users down to the tiniest pixel but then throw your hands up before the politicians and say your machines can't figure out if bad actors are using your platform.

You can't buy up a big bookstore and then a big diaper store and a big pet supply store and, finally, a big grocery store, national newspaper, and rocket ship and then act surprised when people start wondering if maybe you're a bit too powerful.

And you can't really claim that you're building for everyone in the world when your own workforce doesn't remotely resemble the outside world.

When I wrote this novel, I eliminated almost all women and people of color from the story to make a point. It's an exaggeration—the book is satire, remember—but it's also true that the Valley has a diversity problem.

Would Uber have had such a toxic internal culture, rife with sexual harassment, if there had been more women on the management team helping to drive the company's culture? Would the Google Photos app have labeled the image of an African-American woman an "ape" had there been greater representation of African-Americans on the engineering, product, or quality assurance teams—someone who might have questioned whether the data pool feeding into the algorithm was sufficiently diverse? Would we see more funding for technology tackling problems affecting lower-income communities if venture capitalists were not graduating from just a handful of elite institutions?

That's also why I ultimately decided to publish this novel under my name. I was very tempted to publish it anonymously. I didn't really want the attention for myself, and I didn't want people to interpret the book as a specific take on one company. (For the record, I wrote it when I was between jobs.) Nor did I want readers to sit diagramming the characters, trying to figure out which character corresponded to a famous tech exec. (Hint: None of them do, except the one likable character. Clearly, that's me...just kidding. No one's likable in this book.) But at a time when tech is under scrutiny for a number of issues, it's important that those of us who can speak up publicly do so without the comfortable cloak of anonymity.

Writing satire feels a bit like trimming a bonsai tree with a machete. But it felt like the right approach for an industry that takes itself far too seriously and its own responsibility not seriously enough. Because sometimes you're not saving the world; you're just building an anonymous sex club. And that's fine—I'm sure there are plenty of people who like anonymous sex clubs—but let's just be honest about it.

Stop trying to convince us—and yourselves—that your dildos are diamonds.

ACKNOWLEDGMENTS

I'd like to thank Sarah Begley, Sandee Roston, Ryan Hubbard, Siobhan O'Connor, Ev Williams, and the entire Medium crew for their support and belief in this work. I had long given up on it when it landed in their hands in the summer of 2018. Just weeks later, we had a book with a beautiful cover and more readers than I could ever imagine. That manuscript would never have reached Medium had it not been for Lucas Wittmann, editor extraordinaire, and Molly Barton.

I am indebted to the readings, suggestions, guidance and general cheerleading over the years from Tope Folarin (my first reader!), Amanda Garcia, Kate Mason (a.k.a. Kate Morgan), Lorraine Babb, Jon Steinback, Jen DiZio, Robin Moroney, Peter Lattman, Kara Swisher, Felicia Eth, Claudia Ballard, Jamie Carr, Iska Saric, William Monteith, and Britt, Deborah, and Thomas Powell. And to Luke Miner, my loving and long-suffering reader, editor and code reviewer.

Finally, I'd like to thank the many wonderful people I've met working in the tech industry. I hope you laugh and cringe and continue to push your companies to do what is right.

ABOUT THE AUTHOR

Jessica Powell is the author of *The Big Disruption: A Totally Fictional but Essentially True Silicon Valley Story*. The first novel ever published by the digital platform Medium, *The Big Disruption* surpassed 100,000 readers in its first two weeks alone and was described by Farhad Manjoo *The New York Times* as "a zany satire [whose] diagnosis of Silicon Valley's cultural stagnancy is so spot on that it's barely contestable."

Until recently, Jessica was Google's Vice President of Communications and served on the company's management team. She is the author of *Literary Paris,* and her fiction and nonfiction has been published in *The Guardian, the New York Times, Time, WIRED,* and Medium magazine. She is also the co-founder and CEO of a startup that builds software for musicians.